Reading Comprehension

New Directions for Classroom Practice

Third Edition

John D. McNeil

University of California, Los Angeles

HarperCollins*Publishers*

Executive Editor: Christopher Jennison
Development Editor: Anita Portugal
Full-Service Manager: Michael Weinstein
Production Coordinator: Cindy Funkhouser
Cover Design: Darrin Drda, Publicaton Services, Inc.
Cover Illustration/Photo: Darrin Drda, Publication Services, Inc.
Production Manager: Priscilla Taguer
Compositor: Publication Services, Inc.
Printer and Binder: R. R. Donnelley & Sons
Cover Printer: The Lehigh Press, Inc.

Reading Comprehension: New Directions for Classroom Practice,
Third Edition

Library of Congress Cataloging-in-Publication Data

McNeil, John D.
    Reading comprehension / John D. McNeil. – 3rd ed.
        p.   cm.
    Includes index.
    ISBN 0-673-46425-3
1. Reading comprehension.   I. Title.
    LB1050.45.M38   1991
    428.4'3–dc20   91 –33617
                                              CIP

92 93 94 9 8 7 6 5 4 3 2

Acknowledgments

(p. 32) From "The effectiveness of a direct instruction paradigm for teaching main idea comprehension" by James F. Baumann, *Reading Research Quarterly*, 20, no. 1, pp. 93-115. Reprinted with permission of James Baumann and the International Reading Association.

(p. 41) From "Active Comprehension: Problem-solving schema with question generation for comprehension of complex short stories," Harry Singer and Dan Donlan, *Reading Research Quarterly*, 17, no. 2, p. 173. Reprinted with permission of Dan Donlan and the International Reading Association.

(p. 49) From "Using the experience-text-relationship method with minority children" by Kathryn H. Au, *The Reading Teacher*, March 1979, p. 678. Reprinted with permission of Kathryn H. Au and the International Reading Association.

(p. 61) From *Teaching Reading Comprehension* by P. David Pearson and Dale D. Johnson. Copyright © 1978. Reprinted by permission of Holt, Rinehart and Winston.

(p. 93) From *Hunger of Memory: The Education of Richard Rodriguez* by Richard Rodriguez. Copyright © 1981 by Richard Rodriguez. Reprinted by permission of David R. Godine, Publisher, Boston.

(p. 97) From "Alternative Frameworks: Conceptual Conflict and Accommodation: Toward a Principled Teaching Strategy" by J. Nussbaum and S. Novick in *Instructional Science*, Vol. 11, 1982. Reprinted by permission of Elsevier Science Publishers.

(p. 120) From *A Review of Trends in Vocabuylary Research and the Effects of Prior Knowledge on Instructional Strategies for Vocabulary Acquisition* by Dale D. Johnson, Susan Toms-Bronowski, and Susan D. Pittelman. Wisconsin Center for Education Research, University of Wisconsin, November 1981. Reprinted by permission of Dale D. Johnson.

(p. 127) From "The Acquisition of Word Meaning as a Cognitive Learning Process" by M. Van Daalen-Kapteijns and M. Elshout-Mohr in *Journal of Verbal Learning and Verbal Behavior*, Vol. 20, 1981, pp. 386-399. Reprinted by permission of Academic Press and M. Elshout-Mohr.

(p. 128) From "Investigating techniques for teaching word meanings" by J. P. Gipe, *Reading Research Quarterly*, Vol. 14, 1978-1979. Reprinted with permission of J. P. Gripe and the International Reading Association.

(p. 155) "The Lion and the Mouse" reprinted by permission of Scholastic Inc. from *Aesop's Fables* retold by Ann McGovern. Copyright © 1963 by Scholatic Inc.

(p. 167) From *Prose Analysis: Purposes, Procedures, and Problems* by Bonnie Meyer. Research Report No. 1 (Tempe, AZ: Department of Educational Psychology, College of Education, Arizona State University, June 1982). Reprinted by permission of Bonnie Meyer.

(p. 194) From "The Biggest Thing I Learned But It Didn't Have to Do with Science" by Denise Stavis Levin, *Lanuage Arts* 62, No. 2 (January 1985); pp. 43-47. Reprinted by permission of the National Council of Teachers of English.

(p. 195) From "Madness and Cure" by Robert Langs and "Weird Stuff in the Circumambient Numberosity" by Anatol Broyard, *The New York Times*, November 1985. Copyright © 1985 by The New York Times Company. Reprinted by permission.

(p. 197) Based on "Interpretive Communities and Variable Literacies: The Function of Romance Reading" by Janice Radway; by permission of *Daedalus*, Journal of the American Academy of Arts and Sciences, Summer 1984, pp. 49-73, Cambridge, MA.

(p. 210) From *Mind's Eye*, Escondido School District, Escondido, CA, Board of Education, 1979. Reprinted by permission.

(p. 212) From "Assessing Comprehension in a School Setting" by Thomas Dieterich, Cecilia Freeman, and Peg Griffin, *Linguistics and Reading Series: 3*, pp. 99-100, 1977. Reprinted by permission of the Center for Applied Linguistics.

Contents

Preface

This book attempts to throw light on two questions: (1) what should be taught in the name of reading comprehension and (2) how should instruction be delivered? Answers to these questions reflect the major shifts in thinking about reading comprehension—from *traditional* views, which emphasize the importance of gaining the author's meaning and acquiring the meaning that resides in text, to *interactive* views, which assume that the knowledge readers bring to text serves as a filter for interpreting and constructing the meaning of a given text, to *transactional* views, which regard reading as a generative act by which the reader's emotions, cognitive activity, purposes, and situation determine how the text is to be transformed and a new mental text constructed in the interest of self-actualization or a particular interpretive community.

This new edition synthesizes research on comprehension and its teaching, including an introductory chapter treating the historical development of conceptions of reading comprehension.

As in prior editions, cognitive studies of reading comprehension that underlie the interactive view of reading are given much attention. Teaching and learning strategies associated with this view are those for monitoring comprehension and changing reading strategies when comprehension breaks down (metacognitive strategies), generating questions, drawing inferences, summarizing information, and activating relevant background information, including knowledge of text structure. The strategies are differentiated as contributing to comprehension of (a) author/text-based knowledge or (b) reader-based knowledge. Both teaching and learning strategies are featured. For example, "cognitive mapping" is a *teaching strategy* that greatly enhances the comprehension of a given topic or text, whereas "reciprocal teaching" promotes a *learning strategy* that the reader can use independently to comprehend future texts.

This new edition moves beyond cognitive theory as the basis for understanding and defining reading comprehension and introduces literary critical
theory as an interdependent source for theory and practice of reading comprehension. This source is especially useful in suggesting ways to realize
personal and social goals for readers. Sections treating reader response to
literature, critical reading, and the formation of communities of discourse
are cases in point.

An added chapter on evaluation of reading comprehension is consistent
with both interactive and transactional views. Methods for assessing ability
to read for multiple purposes with different kinds of texts, such as reading
for literary experience, reading to be informed, and reading to perform a
task, are described in some detail.

This book is intended for use in undergraduate and graduate courses in
reading and literacy. In-service teachers will also find it valuable in their
work with learners. Various strategies are offered in each chapter to balance
the concerns of teachers of different age groups, types of readers, and different subject matters. Scholars concerned with the reading process will find
the book useful for the way it demonstrates how both theory and empirical
findings can inform practice.

Each chapter includes a background and rationale for the practices described, model lessons suggesting how to implement the strategies, and ways
for teachers to test the major hypotheses and the potential of the teaching
and learning strategies. Chapter activities offer opportunities to validate the
strategies with colleagues in a study group or in one's own classroom.

I wish to acknowledge my debt to Mary Ellen McNeil for her intellectual
and editorial support during the preparation of the manuscript. Also, I appreciate helpful suggestions made by the reviewers: Sam Sebesta, University
of Washington; Victoria Chou Hare, University of Illinois–Chicago; Karen
Kutiper, Southwest Texas State University; and Donna Ogle, National-Louis
University.

Finally, I wish to thank Christopher Jennison of HarperCollins Publishers, whose vision, guidance, and encouragement made the book possible.

Reading Comprehension

Changing Conceptions of Reading Comprehension

Transmission—the cultivation of reading memory, discovery of author's intent and oral expression in reading
Translation—skills for deriving meanings from texts
Interaction—relating background knowledge in comprehending text. Cognitive theories applied to the teaching of reading comprehension
  Schema
  Active Learning
  Metacognition
Transaction—the indeterminate meanings of text. Reader response and post-structural approaches to reading
  Reader-Response Theory
  Whole-Language Instruction
  Post-structure Theory
  Discourse Approach
Summary

OVERVIEW

As an introduction to topics that will be treated extensively throughout this book, Chapter 1 sketches a brief history of the changes in perspectives on reading comprehension, and it identifies the major ideas that drive current research and theoretical activity in the field. Noteworthy in this history is the shift away from the idea that reading comprehension is finding determinant meanings (author's intent and implicit meaning of text) and toward the notion that reading comprehension (a) requires recognition that text has indeterminate meanings and (b) empowers readers to create meaning.

The theory, research, and teaching of reading reflect in a general way how reading comprehension has been conceived. Four conceptions have been identified (Bogdan and Straw 1990; Fitzgerald 1990). The *transmission* view of reading comprehension was dominant until the late nineteenth century, the *translation* view had great influence throughout the 1900s, the *interactive* view has gained importance since 1970, and the *transactional* conception is on the growing edge of theory and practice. These conceptions differ in many ways, but particularly with respect to the origin of meanings to be comprehended, the purposes for reading, and the ways to teach reading comprehension. Bear in mind that, despite the predominance of one view-point over the others at any given time, each perspective retains the power to influence different individuals in different contexts.

TRANSMISSION

In the transmission view of reading, the author is the source and focus of meaning. In early America, an emphasis was placed on recitation of mostly moral and religious material as a way to capture the voice and message of the author. The ability to recite the written text, especially from memory, indicated that the reader had captured the meaning of the author.

The canon of authors appropriate for study increased greatly after 1826 to include secular works—poetry, biography, stories, history, and science—through which students would learn their civic responsibilities and acquire their cultural heritage. Accordingly, the task of reading comprehension went beyond memorization to include understanding or discovery of the author's intent. Meaning continued to remain with the author, and the role of the reader was to deduce this intent. To this end, the reader might be taught the moral stance and other information about the author, as well as the history of the period in which the text was written. Increasingly, teaching broadened to include three foci: *mechanical,* improving the student's vocal modulation, articulation, pronunciation, and emphasis; *intellectual,* helping students understand what they read; and *rhetorical,* attending to the author's phrases and figures of speech in an effort to promote emotional responses to literature and to capture the spirit and feelings of the author.

The transmission view is alive among traditionalists today, who value public display of familiarity with works chosen for their contributions to a national literary heritage and their promise to reveal moral truths and values, such as justice and compassion. E. D. Hirsch's *Cultural Literacy* is an example (Hirsch 1987). Hirsch rationalizes that, without some familiarity with the selections included in his collection, one is at a disadvantage when participating in the national community because of an inability to understand frequent allusions to these works.

The idea of an author's presence in text is alive among some literary critics. Robert Bly, for instance, laments that, in some modern poetry, poets erase any semblance of the self from their work. He believes that the great poets of this century—Neruda, Vallejo, Jimenez, Machado, Rilke—are not independent of the poem. Indeed the poem is "an extension of the man, no different from his skin or his hand" (Bly 1990).

TRANSLATION

Near the end of the nineteenth century, the conceptualization of reading comprehension as translation developed. Instead of discovering the author's voice, the reader sought to determine (translate) the meanings implicit in text; the location of meaning shifted from author to text. Accordingly, the teaching of reading comprehension focused on skills for translating text into meaning. Both word recognition skills and comprehension skills (e.g., selecting the main idea in a passage, paraphrasing the text, and recognizing literary devices) became common classroom activities. In the secondary school, close reading of literary selections was undertaken to show how *unity* (aspects of a work), *coherence* (parts fitting into a whole), and *emphasis* (unity and coherence highlighting particular meanings) reveal the true meaning of the literary text.

The belief that effective comprehension depends upon basic skills led to exercises centered on identifying main ideas, interpreting sequences, determining cause-and-effect relations, and drawing conclusions. Outlining, summarizing, and precis writing were thought to be helpful in comprehending (remembering) text. In most instances, students were asked to perform the exercises and tasks but were not taught how.

The translation conception continues to influence practice. In a study of elementary school teaching, Dolores Durkin found practically no comprehension instruction (Durkin 1979). There was only comprehension assessment and concern about whether children's answers were right or wrong. Reading was viewed as a recitation of what others have said. Assignments categorized as comprehension consisted chiefly of answering questions, matching partial sentences on one side of a workbook page with partial sentences listed on the other side, arranging sentences in sequential order, matching items, and explaining meanings of idiomatic expressions. The assumption is that students learn the skills as they are exposed to enough instances of the task.

A recent study among secondary school teachers of English found that teachers emphasized the importance of selecting interesting literature in building good comprehension (Gee and Rakow 1990). These teachers assumed that if readers enjoy what they read and perceive a connection between what they read and their own lives, then interest in the literature is high and comprehension of the literature is likely to be good. Prereading instruction, direct teaching of comprehension skills, and student discussions where students retell the plot, evaluate ideas, and justify interpretations are highly valued. In their teaching of isolated skills, these teachers apply the translation conception. Their emphasis on learner interest, however, portends interactive and transactive reading, which assume that meaning rests on experience and that the ultimate use of reading is for enriching the activities of life. The primacy of this assumption was maintained by those opposed to the skills approach in the mid-twentieth century; their teaching practice featured the use of guiding questions, preorganization of text, and relating the life experiences of students to what they were reading (Durrell 1949).

INTERACTION

In the late 1970s, the interactive view of reading comprehension gained influence among reading researchers and practitioners. In contrast to comprehending the author's meaning and learning the skills to unlock the meaning in text, the interaction conception regarded meaning as a product of the information encoded in text and the knowledge and experience of the reader. It was acknowledged that the reader's background influenced the perception of the text and the meanings generated. The closer the match between what the learner already knew and the content and structure of the text, the greater the comprehension. It was assumed that meaning ultimately resided in the text, however.

Teaching reading comprehension from the interactive perspective consists of developing learning strategies for relating previously acquired knowledge to words and concepts of a text, monitoring one's comprehension of text, and learning how to reorganize old knowledge with the new knowledge in the text. Comprehending is learning.

Chief among the cognitive theories underlying the interactive view are *schema, active learning,* and *metacognition.*

Schema

Schema theory attempts to specify how the reader's prior knowledge influences the information on a page, how this knowledge must be organized to support the interaction, and how readers' schemata (mental structures— knowledge as it exists in the heads of readers) affect the processing of textual information. As will be seen in Chapters 2 and 3, although schema theory supports the old practices of building background knowledge before reading and relating new information to what the readers already know, it suggests other practices related to the activation of relevant prior knowledge—the drawing of inferences, retention and organization of knowledge, and the transformation of prior knowledge that interferes with learning the content of text. Among these practices are the use of advance organizers, anticipation guides, semantic mapping, graphic organizers, study guides (schema activation and organization), mental imaging, inference training, questioning (elaboration), and dialectical models (restructuring of schemata).

Active Learning

Active learning theory holds that for students to be independent learners they must learn to set their own purposes for reading and to adopt their reading strategies accordingly. Merl Wittrock's generative model of reading comprehension, for example, is based on the idea of learners being the source of plans, intentions, memories, strategies, and emotions necessary for constructing meaning (Wittrock 1990). To comprehend what is read, readers must organize the information in a way that makes sense to them and accept responsibility for constructing meaning. Among the active processes involved are (1) selective attention—selecting relevant information from text; (2) memory—transferring selected information to long-term memory; (3) construction—making internal connections among ideas learned from the text; and (4) integration—building connections between existing knowledge and ideas acquired in reading.

Reading strategies used to carry out the foregoing processes include (1) underlining key words or phrases to help in selecting relevant information; (2) composing headings, generating main ideas, writing summaries, outlining, and organizing the information into patterns to make internal connections to text; and (3) drawing inferences, giving examples, finding applications, critiquing the information, and offering alternative explanations to integrate or tie new knowledge to one's existing knowledge and life.

Self-questioning is the most important aspect of active processing theory. In her review of self-questioning research, Bernice Wong proposes that the practice of helping learners generate questions to focus and guide their thinking in reading might be differentiated to meet individual needs. A child with poor selective attention, for example, might be taught to generate self-questions that focus on key words and ideas in the text. One with an integration problem might be taught to ask and answer "So what?" questions (Wong 1985).

Metacognition

Metacognition theory refers to awareness of one's own cognitive processes and self-regulation. The theory emphasizes the importance of three mental activities in facilitating reading comprehension: (1) awareness of when one is *not* comprehending text and awareness of possible sources for the difficulty, such as insufficient background information or, textual inaccuracies and dissonance; (2) regulation in reading, using compensatory strategies—backward and forward searches, self-questioning, and clarifying—to redirect and bolster faltering comprehension; and (3) monitoring, letting the purpose for reading guide comprehension, making predictions, and checking comprehension of text by posing questions; and (4) attempting to paraphrase and summarize.

Consistent with the interactive conception of reading is the belief that in reading literature, meaning is not only a private experience but a product of a shared system of communication between author and reader. Hence students are taught to generate meanings from text by identifying the structure and conventions of the text and the interpretations to which they point. The literary theory of structuralism assumes that literature requires interaction between the author as encoded in text and the reader. The meanings generated by the reader depend on how well the reader interprets the language conventions used by the writer. In his concern for how it is possible for different readers to converge on meaning, Jonathan Culler (1975) suggests that understanding particular literary forms tells what to look for in reading. Culler gives the illustration of how one can understand a poem by applying (1) the "rules of significance," the view that a poem expresses a significant attribute of some problem concerning man and his relation to the universe; (2) the convention of "metaphorical coherence," which causes one to look at consistency in the metaphors offered; and (3) the convention of "thematic unity," which leads one to seek meaningful connections among the events and situations in the work.

According to structuralists, readers are expected to create meaning from texts by understanding how the author expects them to use their imaginations and by filling in the author's gaps and his/her analogies. Indeed, some modern writers invite the reader to construct the work by confusing plot and characters and by upsetting conventional reader expectations and frustrating the habitual processes of sense making.

One instructional implication from structuralism is that teachers should help readers acquire literary conventions. Another is that in the reader-writer connection, readers should concern themselves with both what the author is trying to get them to think and be aware of how they ought to process the information.

TRANSACTION

The transaction conception of reading comprehension gives the reader major responsibility for creating meaning in response to text. Two theories underlie this conception. Reader-response theory holds that meaning of text is indeterminate because each reader brings a different background to the act of reading. Post-structural literary theory also assumes that texts are always open to new interpretations in light of different perspectives and contexts. Practitioners following reader-response theory encourage readers to recreate texts for their own purposes; those following post-structural theory value reading from different perspectives and critical analyses of text.

efferent
aesthetic

Reader-Response Theory

This theory assumes that meanings are reader-based—social, personal, and idiosyncratic. Accordingly, there are a variety of possible meanings to any text, and multiple responses (affective, personal, intepretive, descriptive) are present in reading. In her transactional model of literary reading, Louise Rosenblatt makes the distinction between "efferent" reading (where the reader focuses on what will remain *after* the reading—information and concepts to be retained, actions to be carried out) and "aesthetic" reading (where the reader is concerned with what happens during the reading event, the experience of relating with text) (Rosenblatt 1978).

Practitioners of the reader-response theory emphasize the value of readers using reading and literature to actualize their own purposes. Gordon Wells has suggested five such purposes, each with a different way of comprehending (Wells 1990): the *performance* mode, when one focuses on understanding the code to help determine the author's meanings; the *functional* mode, by which readers treat text as a means for carrying out a task in daily living (reading a time table, following a recipe); the *informational* mode, where text is consulted for the purpose of finding information without regard for the validity of the information; the *recreational* mode, when the reader captures a sense of engagement with the text and enjoys the pleasure of constructing and exploring a world through both text and one's own imagination; and the *epistemic* mode, when a critical reader tries to understand what a text can mean by considering alternative interpretations, rewriting the text, and drawing new connections, feelings, and understandings. The latter two modes are closest to transactional conceptions of reading insofar as they involve a transaction between the symbolic representations on the page and the mental representations in the reader's head that results in intellectual, moral, or affective change. The questions in Activity 1.1 will help students identify the five modes.

Whole-Language Instruction

This approach to teaching reading features authentic literature rather than texts contrived to illuminate language patterns, and it focuses on the meaningfulness of language and the interrelatedness of reading, writing, speaking, and listening. Whole-language instruction acknowledges the reader as a composer of meaning and views reading as analogous to construction in writing. According to Kenneth Goodman, reading is the mental composing of a parallel text (Goodman 1985). Also, writing is viewed as a powerful way to capture the insights and connections perceived while reading so the reader can examine them more carefully. Writing can physically represent the text created in the reader's mind. Both reading and writing are undertaken for practical and personal purposes. Actualization rather than communication constitutes comprehension.

Activity 1.1   Students' Purposes and Modes of Reading
_____

Ask your student(s) the following questions to clarify their purposes for reading
and their familiarity with reading modes.

1. Think of a story, poem, or book you have read. What did the author want to
   say? What was the author trying to get you to feel or believe? (performance
   mode)
2. What are some of the things you must read outside of school to help you do
   something? Examples may include bus schedules, recipes, and menus. (functional mode)
3. What do you read when you want information? Examples may include ency-
   clopedias, newspapers, directories. (information mode)
4. What do you read for pleasure? (recreational mode)
5. What have you read that has changed your way of thinking or feeling about
   something, someone, or yourself? (epistemic mode)

   Analysis of responses to these questions may suggest modes of reading that
should be encouraged. Consider what should be taught for students to have success in each mode.
_____

In typical elementary, whole-language classrooms, there are opportunities (excursions, resource persons, demonstrations, plays) to stimulate oral
and written expression and to create purposes for reading and writing. Children's problems and their search for texts that will help them understand
events in their lives directs the selection of reading and writing activity. The
range of reading material is considerable. Materials commonly associated
with schools (individual and classroom writing, reference and school subject matter texts, notices) and literature from the larger world (menus, signs,
commercial and informative publications) are included.

Similarly, reader-response–based teaching of literature in secondary
schools assumes that the individual reader is the source of meaning and
that the potential richness of the literary work will serve to initiate emotional and intellectual responses. The text provides material and experience
from which the reader formulates something new. Instruction takes the form
of (a) introducing a literary text that is likely to provoke responses significant
to the reader, and (b) accepting different responses by classroom members to
a text and using these different perceptions as points of entry into the literary
world. Learning to read means reflecting on perceptions of a work to see
what they reveal about readers and about the text. In contrast, traditional
teachers tend not to accept personal perceptions and associations as sufficient. Whether they are afraid of charges of anti-intellectualism and solip-
sism in interpreting and creating meanings, many teachers usually maintain
some conservative practices. Robert Probst, for instance, argues that teachers should ensure that students read accurately and be faithful to the text

as they form interpretations (Probst 1988). Their personal perceptions and feelings should be related to the text. Probst differentiates between stating a feeling or opinion and stating an inference. The first requires no proof or defense, only honesty. The second must be supported by textual evidence, since it is an inference about an author or character. The reader's exchange with the text, however, is expected to culminate in a sharpened, heightened sense of self.

Classroom practices that mitigate idiosyncratic meanings include the preparation of response papers that require careful reading, dramatizations of scenes from the text revealing thoughts and emotions of the characters, and discussions with others in negotiating a consensus about the most defensible meaning of a text.

Post-Structural Theory

One post-structural assumption is that meaning is a cultural process rather than the solitary invention of the individual. This belief is supported by the work of Lev Vygotsky who argued that, since our language and knowledge are the result of social interaction, the meanings we construct are mediated by our social experience (Vygotsky 1978). Also, in his new shift to learning as a "communal activity," Jerome Bruner recognizes culture as a forum for negotiating and renegotiating meaning (Bruner 1990). An example of a literary program that aims at community interpretation of text is found in Pablo Freire's work. It involves participants discovering (seeing anew) the realities (inequalities) of their local community, and then using their reading of text to transform that world (Freire and Donaldo 1986). A second example is Project Keep, which has successfully developed comprehension among Hawaiian children by introducing culturally sensitive activities, including co-narration, in comprehension activities (Tharp 1982). The creation of meaning and interpretation of texts by particular communities (social and intellectual) is everywhere. Consider the divisions among those in the legal field (strict versus contextual readers of legal documents) and those in religious groups (literal and nonliteral biblical readers). Workplace literacy, with its emphasis upon reading for special purposes, as well as reading in the prestigious academic fields requires engagement and acceptance of the conventions and assumptions about knowledge held by the respective communities.

The idea that the meanings generated from reading depend on historical and institutional extratextual frameworks is central to post-structural views of reading comprehension. The meanings generated by readers with particular political and social orientations, such as feminists and Marxists, reflect community interests. Post-structural critical reading aims at revealing new meanings that are hidden in text by (a) discerning the historical antecedents to the idea presented in the text; (b) recognizing the author's unstated assumptions about knowledge, learning, and the like; (c) identifying what the text does *not* say; (d) noting whose interests are and whose interests are *not* served by the propositions; and (e) evaluating the solutions to a purported problem (logical consistency and empirical support).

Discourse Approach *(now called) Socio Cognitive Construction of Meaning*

The late Michel Foucault's "concept of discourse" is giving rise to the discourse approach to reading. Briefly, Foucault held that the meanings of words, actions, and facts acquire their meanings from their relations in a social system apart from the text itself. Institutions control literacy through discourse that prescribes the role of the reader, what will count as knowledge, the partitioning of material and world views, and the interaction between reader and text (Foucault 1981).

In the discourse approach, the text is viewed in relation to a societal discourse regarding a social and ideological issue. The text and the ways students are taught to read it articulate a given stance with respect to the issue or discourse. By way of example, Ian Hunter has documented how the issue of moral character was institutionally treated through the practice of reading in the late nineteenth century (Hunter 1982). At that time reading became part of a discursive system centered on the study and appreciation of character. Students were expected to employ a definite set of techniques to construct a character's point of view. Reading materials represented the implementation of a state educational policy promoting character as an element in plans for moral training of a new urban, industrial middle class.

The issues of what literature will be acceptable, appropriate, and legitimate, and what methods will be used to teach it are answered by discourse systems. *The Heath Anthology of American Literature* for example, is influential in determining what students in about 400 colleges should read (Lauter 1990). This controversial anthology grew out of an institute at Yale University that formed an editorial board and asked professors for names of writers to include. What makes the anthology different is that it included writers who have been excluded from previous anthologies on the basis of gender, race, political perspective, or lack of fame. The works were chosen with a firm idea of pedagogy, that is, "intertextuality"—the placing of writings in juxtaposition to others on the basis of theme so that each work comments upon the other. While the authors hold that the expanded canon will help students become empowered as critics by confronting the diversity of views regarding what represents cultural literacy, others believe that the original structure of the anthology itself limits the pedagogy by placing writers in "their little slots." On the one hand, the editors are criticized "for giving short shrift to popular genres and minority groups such as science fiction, detective fiction, Harlequin Romances or writings by the elderly, teenagers, or rednecks" (McMillen 1991); and, on the other hand, it is argued that their broadening the canon reflected political consideration for approved victim groups rather than adherence to aesthetic criteria.

In his study of reading as discourse practice, Robert Morgan shows how the teaching of reading is crisscrossed by opposing traditions and competing interest groups, each attempting to define official reading policy (Morgan 1990). Through state handbooks, adoption of particular texts, teachers' manuals, staff development, testing of teacher knowledge of reading, and testing of student comprehension, institutions try to maintain a political reading discourse in answer to a social discourse or issue. Yet what counts as reading and reading comprehension always shifts with new institutional arrangements and the dominant social discourse issue of a period. Consider the political slants and interests represented in recent discourse reading systems such as competency-based literacy, literature-based programs, basal readers, whole language, and Reading-Recovery.

The discourse approach to reading would let students in on understanding how experience is produced, sustained, and rewarded in schools and in other contexts so they can take more control over text and meaning. Students are taught what counts in reading within different institutions and situations. John Willinsky argues that students should be taught how language operates to define them and how print acts on an informative and regulating medium in structuring society (Willinsky 1990). His literary program integrates reading, writing, and literature in the study of literature as a historical, political, and economic phenomenon. By way of illustration, in grades 4 through 9, students publish their poetry in half a dozen historical and contemporary techniques—humor and the oral tradition, the early days of drama, the scriptorium of the medieval monk, the movable type and the printing press, and the "small magazine." Students' works are delivered to school and community as a form of public expression; writing is seen as a production process that is not realized until the work is shared. Students learn how reading takes on the contours of its culture, how the market operates and regulates, and how the production of discourse is managed.

Activity 1.2 offers an opportunity to identify the prevailing conception of reading found in a familiar text.

SUMMARY

There is shifting thinking about what constitutes reading comprehension. Although the pursuit of meaning is common to all perspectives, there are wide differences as to where meaning lies (with author, text, individual reader, or community of discourse) and whether meaning is to be found or created. Each view of reading comprehension is associated with particular pedagogical practices.

Activity 1.2 Conception of Reading Comprehension in School
Discourse

Select a reading material or teacher's guide for a classroom and identify its underlying conception.
   The following indicators may be helpful.

Transmission: Text (a) calls for memorization and recall of content and reading
   with expression (b) features works by important authors and biographical
   information about them.
Translation: Text (a) calls for skill development and practice (e.g., selecting main
   ideas), (b) offers supplementary drills or worksheets (c) features dictionary
   vocabulary study, study skills, and close-reading practices.
Interaction: Text (a) calls for relating background of reader to text (e.g., analogies), (b) offers opportunities for students to generate topic sentences and to
   paraphrase text in own words (c) features mapping and organizing of information (e.g., graphic tables), and (d) presents strategies for self-monitoring of
   comprehension.
Transaction: Text (a) calls for students to make individual choices about what
   to read and the purposes for reading (b) requires parlaying of initial responses into discussion of own ideas and those of others (c) requires individual choices about what to read and the purposes for reading (d) uses reading as a way to understand the social world (e) challenges reading selections
   by identifying unstated assumptions and logical inconsistencies of reading
   from different perspectives, and (e) determines "what counts" as reading in
   different contexts.

Reading as transmission features recitation, reading memory, and familiarity with the author; content reflects a dominant culture. The translation
view of reading seeks wide transfer and applicability of discrete skills in
comprehending and learning from text and the unlocking of meaning in literature by close-reading practices. Followers of the interaction view teach
readers how to use their own knowledge and experience (schemata) to recall
and make meaningful inferences about text. Similarly, in the reading of literature, teachers with an interaction point of view stress acquisition of literary
conventions for learning how to comprehend what is written. Teachers with
the transaction conception encourage subjective and individual responses
to literature and reading in pursuit of one's own needs and purposes (self-
actualization). However, this individual orientation is tempered by attention
to the social context that influences understanding and interpretation. The
ability to rewrite text from different perspectives and to illuminate unstated
assumptions, inconsistencies, and hidden meanings is transactional.
   Finally, we are reminded how the materials and methods of reading
found in schools are part of a particular discourse system to promote meanings consistent with a given ideology.

REFERENCES

Bly, Robert. *American Poetry: Wildness and Domesticity.* New York: Harper, 1990.

Bogdan, Deanne, and Straw, Stanley B., editors. *Beyond Communication: Reading Comprehension and Criticism.* Portsmouth, NH: Boynton/Cook Publishers, 1990.

Bruner, Jerome. *Calling Psychology Home: Acts of Meaning.* Cambridge: Harvard University Press, 1990.

Culler, Jonathan. *Structuralist Poetics: Structuralism, Linguistics, and the Study of Literature.* Ithaca, NY: Cornell University Press, 1975.

Durkin, Dolores. "What Classroom Observations Reveal About Reading Comprehension Instruction." *Reading Research Quarterly* 14 (1979): 481–533.

Durrell, Donald. "Development of Comprehension and Interpretation." In *Reading in the Elementary School,* N. B. Henry, editor. 48th Yearbook, NSSE, Part 1. Chicago: University of Chicago Press, 1949, pp. 193–204.

Fitzgerald, Jill, editor. *Reading Comprehension Instruction, 1783–1987: A Review of Trends and Research.* Newark, DE: International Reading Association, 1990.

Foucault, Michel. "The Order of Discourse." In *Untying the Text,* R. Young, editor. London: Routledge and Kegan Paul, 1981.

Freire, Paulo, and Donaldo, Macedo M. *Literacy: Reading the Word and the World.* South Hadley, MA: Bergin and Garvey, 1986.

Gee, Thomas C., and Rakow, Steven J. "Guiding Comprehension: Techniques English Teachers Value." *The Clearing House* 63, no. 4 (1990): 341–344.

Goodman, Kenneth. "Units in Reading." In *Theoretical Models and Processes of Reading,* 3rd edition, Harry Singer and Robert Ruddell, editors. Newark, DE: International Reading Association, 1985, pp. 813–814.

Hirsch, E. D., Jr. *Culture Literacy: What Every American Needs to Know.* Boston: Houghton Mifflin, 1987.

Hunter, I. "The Concept of Context and the Problem of Reading." *Southern Review* 15, no. 1 (1982): 80–91.

Lauter, Paul, editor. *Heath Anthology of American Literature.* New York: D. C. Heath, 1990.

McMillen, Liz. "Controversial Anthology of American Literature: Ground-Breaking Contribution or a 'Travesty'?" *The Chronicle of Higher Education* 37, no. 18 (Jan. 16, 1991): A15–20.

Morgan, Robert. "Reading as Discursive Practice: The Politics and History of Reading." In *Beyond Communication: Reading Comprehension and Criticism,* Deanne Bogdan and Stanley B. Straw, editors. Portsmouth, NH: Boynton/Cook Publishers, 1990, pp. 319–337.

Probst, Robert E. *Response and Analysis: Teaching Literature in Junior and Senior High School*. Portsmouth, NH: Heinemann, 1988.

Rosenblatt, Louise M. *The Reader, the Text, The Poem: Transactional Theory of the Written Word*. Carbondale, IL: Southern Illinois University Press, 1978.

Tharp, R. G. "The Effective Instruction of Comprehension: Results and Description of the Kamehameha, Early Childhood Program." *Reading Research Quarterly* 17, no. 4 (1982): 503–527.

Vygotsky, Lev. *Mind in Society*. Cambridge, MA: Harvard University Press, 1978.

Wells, Gordon. "Talk About Text: Where Literacy is Learned and Taught." *Curriculum Inquiry* 20, no. 4 (1990): 369–403.

Willinsky, John. *The New Literacy: Redefining Reading and Writing in the Schools*. New York: Routledge, 1990.

Wittrock, Merlin C. "Generative Processes of Comprehension." *Educational Psychologist* 24, no. 4 (1990): 345–376.

Wong, Bernice Y. L. "Self-Questioning Instructional Research: A Review." *Review of Educational Research* 55, no. 2 (Summer 1985): 227–268.

Useful Readings

Bogdan, Deanne, and Straw, Stanley B., editors. *Beyond Communication: Reading Comprehension and Criticism*. Portsmouth, NH: Boynton/Cook Publisher, 1990.

Fitzgerald, Jill, editor. *Reading Comprehension Instruction 1783–1987: A Review of Trends and Research*. Newark, DE: International Reading Association, 1990.

Probst, Robert E. *Response and Analysis: Teaching Literature in Junior and Senior High School*. Portsmouth, NH: Boynton/Cook Publisher, 1988.

Willinsky, John. *The New Literacy: Redefining Reading and Writing in the Schools*. New York: Routledge, 1990.

Reading Comprehension as a Cognitive Process

OVERVIEW

This chapter looks at reading comprehension as an interaction between reader and text; however, it focuses on ways this interaction can be shaped by the teacher so that particular meanings from text are likely to be generated. It describes factors that are important in the reading process and introduces schema theory, a key to newer interpretations of reading comprehension. What is schema theory? What does it have to do with teaching? How can a teacher determine a child's schema for reading? How do different schemata for reading affect comprehension? How can schema theory be applied to enhance reading comprehension? These questions are answered in Chapter 2.

COMPREHENSION AS PROCESS

Comprehension is making sense out of text. From an interaction perspective, reading comprehension is acquiring information from context and combining disparate elements into a new whole. It is the process of using one's existing knowledge (schemata) to interpret text in order to construe meaning. Although writers structure texts for their given purposes, readers must interpret what they read and must arrive at their own construction of what the text means. Comprehension includes understanding the information in the text as well as changing the knowledge one used to understand the text in the first place.

Accordingly, reading comprehension is *not* memorization by rote, as illustrated by John Dewey's visit to a class that had read how the earth was probably formed. Mr. Dewey asked the students whether, if they could arrive at the center of the earth, they would find it hot or cold. No child answered. The teacher then told Mr. Dewey that he had asked the wrong question. She turned to the children and asked, "What is the condition at the center of the earth?" All responded in unison: "In a state of igneous fusion."

In contrast with the older emphasis on teaching reading comprehension as a *product* by asking students to answer questions about their reading, interactive approaches stress teaching reading comprehension as a *process*. Accordingly, students are taught techniques for processing text—making inferences, activating appropriate concepts, relating new information to old, creating picture images, and reducing the information in a text to a main idea.

Four assumptions underlying the process approach are as follows:

1. *What students already know affects what they will learn from reading*. The reader's prior knowledge interacts with text to create psychological meaning. Background knowledge determines the interpretations made from text. Researchers refer to prior knowledge as knowledge structure, scripts, frames, or *schemata* (plural for *schema*). Schemata are frameworks for interrelating different elements of information about a topic. Comprehending a message involves constructing a correspondence between an existing schema and the elements in the message. That is, the schema is a framework of expectations. It allows the reader to take what is directly perceivable and to make inferences about its unseen features. By way of example, try to comprehend the following sentence suggested by Bransford and McCarrell without using schema:

The notes were sour because the seams split.

Although the syntax is simple and the individual words are easy, the sentence does not make sense to most people. However, it does become meaningful as soon as one hears the word *bagpipe* which fits into a schema containing slots for associated objects (pipes, pipers), actions (playing a musical instrument, marching), and qualities (musical) (Bransford and McCarrell 1974).

Teachers will regard the researcher's emphasis upon the role of background knowledge as consistent with their traditional practices of preteaching vocabulary and providing requisite background experiences. Other, newer techniques for activating background knowledge—semantic mapping and student-generated questions—are also relevant, however.

2. *Both concept-driven and data-driven processes are necessary in comprehending text.* A concept-driven process calls for activating schemata and applying them when setting expectations for reading, and it calls for filling gaps in one's schemata with information read in the text. A concept-driven process is a "top-down" strategy in which the reader's goals and expectations determine what is read. Schemata guide one's search for what is important in the text. In contrast, data-driven processing occurs when the reader attends to the text and then searches for structures (schemata) in which to fit the incoming information. The reader monitors information from the bottom up, replacing initial expectations with new ones triggered by the text. Different words and sentences suggest new expectations.

Good readers approach texts with top-down strategy, using selected schemata to integrate the text, but then they apply the "bottom up," text-driven process of discarding schemata that are inappropriate and finding more suitable ones. Less able readers tend to overrely on either a top-down strategy or a text-driven process, which has a deleterious effect on comprehension. An overemphasis on top-down processing results in inferences that are not warranted by the text, while an overemphasis on bottom-up processing (staying close to print) results in word calling.

3. *The deeper a person processes text, the more he or she will remember and understand it.* The deep-processing thesis rests on two strategies for understanding text—elaboration and the use of the author's organizational framework. Elaboration is an embellishment of text; readers accomplish it by drawing on their prior knowledge, making inferences, paraphrasing the text in their own language, and relating it to their own purposes.

As an example of elaboration and its effects, consider a study in which less successful fifth-grade students received training in how to produce precise elaborations and, as a result, showed a large increase in retention of what they read (Stein, et al. 1982). Students were first made aware of sentences that were difficult to remember or difficult to learn. Next, they learned to differentiate precise elaborations from imprecise ones. Precise elaboration clarifies the significance or relevance of a stated fact. Thus for the sentence *The hungry man got into his car,* the elaboration *to go to the restaurant* would be precise (relevant); while the elaboration *and drove away* would not be. Students were prompted to activate knowledge that would make the relationships between a statement and its elaboration less arbitrary and to spontaneously ask themselves how their elaborations related to the statements. Elaboration is treated more fully in Chapter 5.

Deep processing using the author's framework requires that the reader identify the patterns by which the text is organized—narratives, for example,

are most often organized by general structures such as setting, characterization, theme, key episode, and resolution of a problem that motivated the
character to take action. Expository texts are usually organized by use of
certain patterns for ordering statements—presenting facts and details in relation to more general and important statements, for example. To process
more deeply when reading narratives, the reader relates specific events and
details to the general structure. Similarly, when reading expository selections, readers achieve deeper processing as they find the connections among
supporting details, examples, main ideas, and high-level abstractions. The
relevance of organizational patterns of text is developed in Chapter 9.

   4. *The context in which reading occurs influences what will be recalled.*
Important text elements are more likely to be learned and remembered than
less important ones. The reading context, including the reader's purpose
and perspective, affects the reader's judgment about the importance of text
elements as they are encountered. Anderson and Pichert demonstrated that
students interpreted passages differently when given different perspectives—
specifically, those of a home buyer and a burglar (Anderson and Pichert
1978). The "home buyers" learned and remembered information relevant to
the problems of living in a home. The "burglars" learned and remembered
information related to security, such as the location of doors, lights, and
windows. Apparently, the perspective activated particular schemata.

   Prior knowledge and attitude constitute major contexts for comprehending. Wrestlers' and music majors' recall after reading the same text, for
example, was found to evidence the selectivity patterns of each group's
prior knowledge and interest (Anderson, Reynolds, Schallert, and Goetz
1977). Individuals with a strong stand on a particular issue (ego-involved
individuals) will interpret statements about that issue differently from those
without a stand.

   Further indication that world views influence reading comprehension
is found in Marlene Schommer's study showing that the epistemological
beliefs of college students affect their comprehension of social science and
physical science texts (Schommer 1989). Students who believe in quick,
all-or-none learning (who spend 10-12 minutes working on a problem and
then, if they don't get it, assume they never will) are less likely to be
able to integrate knowledge from text than those who do not believe in
quick, all-or-none learning. Also, students who believe in the *certainty* of
knowledge as opposed to the *tentativeness* of knowledge are more likely to
distort information in order to be consistent with this belief.

   Instructional strategies aimed at intervening and preventing self-
defeating epistemological beliefs are described in Chapter 4.

   In brief, reading comprehension as process involves actively constructing meaning among the parts of the text and between the text and personal
experience. The text itself is but a blueprint for creating meaning. Comprehension and retention are enhanced by strategies for intergrating text with
personal knowledge and experience.

People differ with respect to whether the meaning generated by readers must correspond to the author's intended meaning. Academicians usually emphasize text rather than background knowledge; they want readers to be able to reproduce important facts and ideas from text. Aestheticians respect the reader's background as much as the author's, anticipating, for example, that the reader of literature will create personal meaning that may depart from the author's.

When reading poetry or other inspirational work, the reader is often invited to generate unique feelings and insights. Although one might think that reading for the purpose of following directions or understanding a legal document (especially the fine print and bottom lines) would require strict interpretation of text, this is not always the case. Lawyers recognize that the law can be read as one reads literature; that is, legal interpretations are partly subjective. Defining an author's intention in law, as in literature, is a way to establish meaning of a text. In defining the author's intentions, readers shape the meaning of a legal text by imposing their own values and make inferences about what the author would have intended if apprised of existing factors.

SCHEMA THEORY

Schema theory for teachers? Is it really necessary? How does it apply to my teaching? These might be questions you ask as you read this.

Margaret Mead once said that education needs a new theory every few years. The theory does not have to be really novel or absolutely correct, but it must have at least some elements of novelty and correctness. A new perspective on reading is needed every once in a while to challenge you as a teacher to reconsider what you are doing—to rethink your purposes and methods, to review the latest research (even if the findings seem only to confirm the obvious), to examine new teaching practices, and perhaps to refresh you with the thought that you will be better able to solve some instructional problem that previously seemed unsolvable.

Schema theory has special relevance for teachers of reading comprehension in that it questions the conventional view that pupils should learn to reproduce the statements found in text. It also casts doubt on the idea that books have explicit meanings that can be understood without the need for interpretive frameworks. According to schema theory, text is gobbledygook unless the reader can breathe meaning into it.

Schemata are the reader's concepts, beliefs, expectations, processes— virtually everything from past experiences that are used in making sense of things and actions. In reading, schemata are used to make sense of text; the printed word evokes the reader's experiences, as well as past and potential relationships.

Teachers of reading are concerned with three kinds of schemata. One kind is *domain*: knowledge of specific topics, concepts, or processes for reading particular subject matter. Teachers of science, math, social studies, and other content areas help students develop the background knowledge required for reading textbooks in the given field. Another kind of schema is *general world knowledge:* understanding social relationships, causes, and activities that are common to many specific situations and domains. General world knowledge allows readers to make appropriate inferences while reading and to identify with persons and events. One's schema for reading, which establishes the reader's role and sets expectations of what should follow from reading (a concept of comprehension) requires application of a general word knowledge schemata.

A third kind of schema is *knowledge of rhetorical structures:* the conventions for organizing and signaling the organization of texts. The schemata for a story "grammar" and the patterns used in writing expository text reduce the processing demands of reading.

The teaching strategies described in this book seek to develop these three kinds of schemata.

Ideally, students will read for their own purposes, and, in relating the printed text to their own schemata, they will modify the text and their original schemata. It follows that the student who does not apply schemata appropriately is going to have trouble learning and remembering the information found in textbooks because that information will be interpreted and stored in memory in light of the student's past experience. Unless the proper experience or schema is brought to mind, the information will not be assimilated as intended.

Schemata serve several functions:

1. They are the slots for assimilating additional information. By using a schema for *dessert,* it is easy to augment the familiar *ice cream* and *cake* with the new instance *flan*.

2. They help the reader see what is important. A schema for reading word problems tells us how to decide which operations to use in finding the answer.

3. They permit inferential elaboration. With a sports schema, we can mentally differentiate the size of the balls in sentences such as *The golfer hit the ball* and *The batter hit the ball*.

4. They aid in summarizing by helping the reader separate important from less important ideas. Schemata represent knowledge at all levels of abstraction—from major truths to the meaning of particular words. High-level schemata tend to be the more important ones. Readers with a schema for fable would in their summary of a fable give the moral more weight than any particular character, action, or event.

5. They aid in memory. It is our *interpretation* of what we read that is stored in memory. Hence, it is the interpretation rather than the text

itself that we will recall. Our schema influences the interpretation in the first place and also helps us recall what we have stored from our reading.

Schemata represent knowledge at all levels of generation—from perspectives on the nature of the world, to views of what is meant by reading, to knowledge of patterns of written expression, to the meaning of a given term. Schemata are imbedded within schemata. For example, a schema for attending school would include top-level, global generalizations about studying to learn and about socialization. Beneath this level would be more specific schemata—assignments, grades, teachers, principals, and peers. At the bottom level, there would be schemata for unique events—a first-grade teacher, a favorite book, a dear classmate. The powerful thing about schemata is that once any element in a network of schemata is introduced, it can be understood as related to the entire complex. If *test* is mentioned within the schema for school, it will immediately be understood as a measure of someone's knowledge or aptitude and not confused with a trial, a shell of a mollusk, a reaction to a chemical, or a touchstone.

HOW SCHEMATA OF READING INFLUENCE COMPREHENSION

Students' concepts of reading may determine whether they comprehend the text. A major difference between good and poor comprehension is the extent to which the reader is aware of the need to make sense of the text. Better readers understand that stories and other forms of writing should make sense and that reading instruction is a means to enhance their comprehension.

Beginning readers often do not know that reading is a communication process and that it can be used to fulfill their own needs. Their schemata for reading may include slots for reading materials, for being read to, and for notions of how one should read (e.g. fast, fluently, and with expression). However, many children do not seem to know that an effort to make sense of the text is essential in reading.

Several investigators have ascertained children's reading schemata at various grade levels. Denny and Weintraub asked first graders, "What is reading?" (Denny and Weintraub 1966). These researchers found that most first graders did not know or gave an object-related response—for example, "It's reading a book." Only a few referred to reading as a process of learning new information. In answer to the question, "What must you do to learn to read?" most children described a passive type of obedience or dependence on someone else. Only a few indicated that they had to take some action in learning to read, such as "read to myself" or "look at the pages."

Jerry Johns conducted studies to describe the relationship between pupils' concepts of reading and their reading achievement (Johns and Ellis, 1976). He asked three questions: "What is reading?" "What do you do when you read?" and "If someone didn't know how to read, what would you tell him to learn?" Johns found a positive correlation between the maturity of concepts of fourth- and fifth-grade children and their reading achievement.

The results of other studies also indicate that, across grades 2 through 6, many students have little or no understanding of reading, most children identified word-attack skills as the central concern in reading, and only a few referred to getting meaning from reading.

You may wish to see for yourself how reading achievement correlates with a child's schema for reading. Activity 2.1 will enable you to note the correlation.

In her study of how the reading schemata of first graders are influenced by type of instruction, Penny Freppon found that children whose teachers used a whole-language approach held schemata that were more meaning based; that is, they were more aware of when print did not make sense and they gave more importance to understanding the story (not just getting the words right) than children in classrooms where the teacher focused on systematic teaching of phonic skills (Freppon 1989).

SCHEMA THEORY APPLIED TO THE TASK OF ACQUIRING NEW KNOWLEDGE

As indicated in Chapter 1, reading comprehension is multi-dimensional, ranging from using the text for communication (understanding the author, deriving and recalling information in text) to self-actualization (creating meaning in the presence of text) and social emancipation (recognizing power-knowledge relations). In the school context, the "academic ideology" of reading comprehension has endorsed the notion that meaning is in the text, is literal, and has only one interpretation—that of the teacher or the textmaker. Hence, teachers have tended to use schema theory in designing instruction to help students learn the conventional interpretation of selected texts. Accordingly, much comprehension instruction has focused on *teaching* strategies that will increase learning from particular texts as opposed to *learning* strategies that improve students' ability to comprehend future texts on their own and to read for their own purposes.

Successful teaching strategies consistent with schema theory center on two types of activities: (a) the teaching of organizational patterns of texts or rhetorical structures (schemata for text) so that students can better understand the ideas of authors, and (b) interventions aimed at developing and activating a schema that relates to a particular reading selection. The latter practices facilitate the drawing of "appropriate" inferences from text, control the learner's attention, and anchor details encountered in reading to the schema so they take on significance and are more likely to be remembered.

Activity 2.1   Ascertaining Pupil's Schemata of Reading

Try to ascertain some of your pupil's knowledge of the purposes and nature of reading (their schemata for reading).

Use the following interview questionnaire. You will note that the first two questions are presented to relax the pupils and to affirm that you are interested in their ideas, not in "correct" responses. Question 3 attempts to tap the pupils' perceptions of themselves as readers and the understanding they have about how they might improve. Question 4 asks about the applicability of reading skills to materials other than books (signs, cereal boxes, T-shirts). Question 5 seeks to learn the students' awareness of how people learn to read. The last two questions are critical for determining whether the children see reading as a meaningful activity.

1. Are there some some things you like about reading?
   Yes   No   What are they?
2. Are there some things you don't like about reading?
   Yes   No   What are they?
3. Are you a good reader?
   Yes   No   Why do you think so?
4. Can you read if you don't have a book?
   Yes   No   Why?   Why not?
5. What things does a person have to learn how to do in order to be a good reader?
6. What is reading?
7. Why do people read?

Question 6 provides information on the pupils' schema for reading. Responses such as "reading means reading a book" should be grouped under the heading *object focus*. Responses referring to the mechanics of reading may be grouped under *decoding focus*. Responses that fall under a *meaning focus* are of two types: (1) activities that stress bottom-up strategies for getting information (learning word meanings, putting words together, understanding sentences and stories, remembering what is read); and (2) activities that imply a critical or reflective approach to text (interpreting signs and symbols, thinking about what is read, enjoying other peoples' lives, learning about people and the world).

Once you have the responses categorized under object, decoding, or meaning focus, think about their implications. Is there more need for frequent reading outside school, for expanding vocabularies, for increasing the knowledge base, or for personal involvement with text?

Exhibit 2.1 reproduces responses to the interview questionnaire from children 6 to 12 years of age who attend a two-teacher rural school. From the children's comments you may perceive that the school's reading program features a commercially prepared, structured. sequenced treatment of reading skills with basal readers and pupils' record books. This explains the children's references to the program, tests, and practice books.

Exhibit 2.1   Responses to Reading Concepts Questionnaire

1. Are there some things you like about reading?

I like reading because it is fun trying
to solve the mystery in some novels.

when I read books
to myself.

The practice book and the tests.

2. Are there some things you don't like about reading?

No because it's fun.

decause it annoys me   Sometimes it's
                          boring

when we do hard pages
in our practice book

3. Are you a good reader?

(No) Because I sound like a robot and
      I stop in the middle of a sentence

Yes I think I am a good reader
because I read every night

Source: Deakin University Open Campus Program, ECT 401 *Classroom Processes—Task, Pupil, and Teacher,* 1981, p. 48. Copyright© Deakin University, Victoria, Australia. Reprinted by permission.

4. Can you read if you don't have a book?

You find words
in books and
if you don't love
books then no
words to read

because

there are

Signs to read

I can't see the words

5. What things does a person have to learn to do in order to be a good reader?

If you want to be a good reader
you would learn how too work out
words that you don't no
To stop at a full stop and to
put expression into it.

6. What is reading?

Something that is thought
of and is writen on
paper and is said
again in by being read

A program

the time when you
read your books

7. Why do people read?

people read to fill in time and find
out things .

to learn about
something or for
the joy.

to hear Stores

Schemata for Communicating with Authors

Although the main variable determining whether a reader will comprehend a specific communication is background knowledge relevant to the content, schemata that match the author's organizational pattern also help the reader interpret the message by enabling him or her to anticipate the author's purpose. In Activity 2.2 and again in Chapter 9, you will have

---

Activity 2.2   Recognizing an Author's Pattern and Adjusting Your
                   Reading Approach to It

Check the answer that correctly corresponds to the author's pattern and then read the selection at the speed appropriate for the pattern.

1. sharing-experience ☐   question-answer ☐   imparting-information ☐
   opinion-reason ☐   substantiated-fact ☐
       My bet is that "The Stewarts" will prove a success on public television as did "The Sandland Saga" nearly ten years ago. For one thing, the series is better than the "Saga," just as Jay is a superior novelist to Scott. Consider, too, that "The Sandland" series was filmed in black and white, and "The Stewarts" is in faultless color.
       The script, written by Doulglas Hunter, performs miracles in translating the intricate plots of five novels, set in the period 1735–1765, into a seamless tapestry. The acting is nearly impeccable, at least in the four episodes I saw.

2. sharing-experience ☐   question-answer ☐   imparting-information ☐
   opinion-reason ☐   substantiated-fact ☐
       Intake air temperature varies widely from cold on starting to hot during regular operation. The density of the air varies with temperature change. Unfortunately, automotive carburetors are not able to meter fuel to match density changes and to maintain a near ideal air/fuel ratio. Since engines operate most of the time with warm or hot air, carburetors' jetting is set to give the proper ratio under these conditions. This leaves the cold range somewhat lean. To compensate, a method was devised to provide warm air more quickly. Under cold operating conditions intake air is drawn over an exhaust manifold to warm it prior to mixing with fuel.

3. sharing-experience ☐   question-answer ☐   imparting-information ☐
   opinion-reason ☐   substantiated-fact ☐
       The slow learner—what are his characteristics and needs? The slow learner tends to have poorer reasoning ability than the normal child. He is slow to see cause and effect relationships, to make inferences, and to generalize.
       Short attention span seems to typify this group of learners. However, the short attention span is often due to poor instruction rather than to a defect in the slow learner. When materials are interesting and when success is possible, the attention span of the slow learner increases. Unlike brighter persons, slow learners do not learn incidently, as a rule. Careful planning by a teacher is a must to facilitate their learning. The slow learner needs immediate goals rather

than deferred ones. He must see a reason here and now for engaging in a task. He needs a stimulating environment where he has many things to talk about.

4. sharing-experience ☐   question-answer ☐   imparting-information ☐
   opinion-reason ☐   substantiated-fact ☐

I heard some singing coming from the bathroom, or perhaps I should say reverberating. In the past when this had happened, I had been very disturbed about it and outlawed the music because it is Lucy's most glaring symptom and the one that made me realize that there was something wrong with her. She would listen to her records sometimes all day, during which time she would be in a trancelike state, unable to speak, hear, or eat. This time I paid attention to the words and was surprised to learn that the song tells the story of a girl who runs away from home, and the chorus tells of the parents' consequent bewilderment. I then knew that the songs I had forbidden probably contained important messages and clues to Lucy's problems.

5. sharing-experience ☐   question-answer ☐   imparting-information ☐
   opinion-reason ☐   substantiated-fact ☐

Language is the source of logic. In fact, the logic of the logicians is it-self nothing but generalized syntax and semantics. Evidence for this conclu-sion is found in studies comparing normal children with deaf mutes, who have not had the benefit of articulate language but are in possession of complete sensory-motor schemes, and with blind persons, whose situation is the oppo-site.

The results indicate a systematic delay in the emergence of logic in the deaf mute and an even longer delay (up to four years) among blind children. Being born blind hampered the development of sensory-motor schemes and verbal co-ordinations are not sufficient to compensate for the delay.

Answers

1. The first passage is in the opinion-reason pattern. You should have read it quickly.
2. The second passage is an instance of imparting-information. It should have been read slowly and with attention to details.
3. The third passage is an example of the question-answer pattern, a pattern that frames the question for you, making it easy to read quickly for the answer.
4. The fourth passage is in the sharing-experience pattern, to be read at your highest speed.
5. The fifth passage is an example of the substantiated-fact pattern. You should have read the selection slowly and decided whether or not the author gave sufficient evidence for the conclusion presented.

---

the opportunity to develop your own schemata for patterns commonly used in narrative, expository, and documentary texts. By way of example, the importance of your children having a "story grammar" schema expecting stories to begin with a setting, characters, and develop through a prob-lem or problems, goals, actions, and outcomes has been shown. Teaching students to construct a story map recording the "grammar" of the story while reading results in greater understanding and recall of the story (Idol and Croll 1987). Five frequently found patterns of value to older readers are the sharing-experience pattern, the question-answer pattern, the imparting-information pattern, the opinion-reason pattern, and the substantiated-fact pattern. Each pattern signals a purpose, thus indicating how the material should be read—slowly, with careful attention to details; quickly, to gain general impressions; or merely to answer a specific question.

We can recognize the sharing-experience pattern by asking whether the author is relating some first-hand experience. The use of personal pronouns (I, we, our, and us) indicates that the material represents this schema ("I shall never forget that most frightful hurricane"). Once children recognize this pattern, they should know that they may read it as rapidly as they wish, for there are no detailed facts to recall. With material written in the sharing-experience pattern, we may relax and read quickly, enjoying the author's experiences.

The question-answer pattern is easy to recognize and easy to read. We just have to read the question and then glance through the text until we find the answer. The use of the question helps the reader understand the author's purpose at once, making it unnecessary to formulate personal questions and motives for reading. Whenever titles, headings, or paragraphs are in question format, you know that the author's purpose is to answer the question. An example of the question-answer pattern is: "Why test? To ascertain where one is, to chart progress, and to identify areas that remain to be explored."

A third pattern is the imparting-information pattern. Unlike the previous two patterns, it requires careful, detailed reading—that is, if the reader decides the material is important enough to read this way. As implied by the name, material written in this pattern contains many factual details. The following example, which summarizes the way heat recovery systems retrieve and reuse heat, illustrates the pattern. Notice the many different details packed into a single passage.

> The system creates a thermal path that transports heat escaping up an exhaust duct to a cold incoming air stream. The key component is the heat pipe. The pipe is a closed metal envelope containing a capillary wick and a small amount of liquid within a sealed cylinder. When the end of the pipe is heated, the energy changes the liquid to a gas and drives it to the opposite end. There the vapor condenses, releasing it for warming incoming cold air. The liquid then returns to the wick to repeat the cycle.

The opinion-reason pattern can be read with little time or effort, providing one can recognize it. Clues to this pattern are found in phrases such as *in my opinion, as I see it, I believe, I think,* or *common sense suggests.* Material written in this pattern should be read rapidly to first get an understanding of the author's opinion and to then find the reasons the author offers in support of the opinion. An example follows:

> If you want children to feel at home in school, put them in an old building, not a spanking new one. I think only an older building gives the impression of

having been lived in long enough to understand the troubles of life. It has gone through and survived a lot. That is why it is preferable to adapt an old building with a lived-in feeling for the purposes of a school.

The fifth pattern is the substantiated-fact pattern. You can identify it by looking for a conclusion or statement of fact followed by substantiation in the form of observation, experiment, or other data. Material written in this pattern should be read carefully and slowly. A suggested reading procedure is to (1) understand the author's conclusions, (2) challenge the author to prove it, and (3) read on to see if the proof is sufficient.

Now that you have considered five commonly used patterns, see if you can recognize the patterns in text and can read each sentence at the speed demanded by its pattern (see Activity 2.2).

INTERVENTIONS FOR DEVELOPING AND ACTIVATING SCHEMATA

Previewing

Previews of text by skimming, looking at pictures, and examining the title and subheadings increases students' comprehension of explicit and implicit information (Graves, Cooke, and LaBergh 1983). Similarly, story previews have been found to be helpful when orally presented by the teacher and accompanied by group discussion and prediction (Neuman 1988).

Building Background Knowledge

In contrast with the old idea of building general background about the topic and theme of a reading selection, it is in some instances better to build specific knowledge about key ideas in the selection.

The teacher is a powerful influence in shaping students' text reconstructions. A study of first-grade teachers revealed that students who had more story-related discussion, moving from general features of books (title, author) to discussion of content and theme, recalled three times the amount of theme-related events than students whose teacher emphasized self-expression and application of the story ideas to one's own experiences (Golden 1988).

If teachers provide specific background knowledge to reading selections, students will remember more of the material. By way of example, children in various grades were given information about a fictitious tribe called the "Targa"; while others learned about people in Spain. Later, all the children read a story about a young boy from the Targa tribe, and no mention was made of what they had studied previously. Those who had received the relevant background information recalled more from their reading (Brown, et al. 1977).

Reconciled Lessons. As a technique for developing background knowledge, consider the Reconciled Reading Lesson. Although schema theory points to the importance of the prereading stage in the reading lesson, teachers who follow a basal textbook lesson spend more time on evaluation activities than on instructional activities preceding reading (Durkin 1984). D. Ray Reutzel has proposed a way for them to shift emphasis from evaluation to instruction (Reutzel 1985). His Reconciled Reading Lesson reverses the lesson sequence to fit the basic tenets of schema theory. Accordingly, teachers begin by turning to the last section of the reading lesson in their teacher's manual, often labeled "Enrichment Activities" or "Expansion." The activities in this section are an excellent prereading instructional source. Using the enrichment activities and the vocabulary work *prior* to reading, teachers involve students with unfamiliar events and concepts relevant to what they are going to read. By way of example, prior to reading a story in play format, pupils engage in enrichment activities such as writing or talking about the roles involved in play production, actually performing in a play, and discussing new word meanings (story-related vocabulary).

In implementing the Reconciled Reading Lesson, the teacher uses the activities for skill instruction *before* reading so that children know that reading skills should be applied to their reading. Reading-skill instruction is especially tied to the selection; the comprehension skill of predicting outcomes, for instance, is taught through questions about the story prior to reading rather than through isolated paragraphs afterward.

A third step in the Reconciled Reading Lesson is discussing the story through guided questioning. The traditional basal lesson offers questions for discussion and review at the end of each selection. In contrast, the reconciled lesson makes discussion an integral part of the prereading activity. Questions originally listed after the selection are posed prior to reading and prediction regarding content or likely outcomes are discussed. Postreading activities in the reconciled lesson are brief and to the point. Postreading activities focus on the goals of the lesson: Did students comprehend? How well did students predict answers to prequestions? Did students revise their original expectations in light of the reading?

A successful variant to lessons adapting basal readers is the practice of having students write their own story about a situation similar to one in an upcoming story and later comparing it with the author's. Such an activity is associated with improved story understanding.

Linking Word Meaning to Prior Knowledge

A main distinction of effective teachers of comprehension is the ability to link word meaning to prior knowledge. The semantic mapping activities later in this chapter and in Chapter 7 illustrate good ways to assess prior knowledge and to link the knowledge to terms that are crucial to understanding what is to be read. The linking of text and learner entails recognizing key words in the text that are unfamiliar to the learner and finding experiences in the learner's background involving the concepts that underlie the new terms. Knowing that the terms *dividend, divisor,* and *quotient* in an elementary math book are not familiar to prospective readers, a teacher begins by discussing a situation with which the learners are familiar—a birthday party. The children tell whether the pieces of cake at the party are bigger or not when more children are present. They are then led to sense that if the amount of cake is constant (the dividend), and the number of people who share the cake equally is smaller (the divisor), then the pieces of cake are bigger (the quotient). In connecting what they already know to what is new, children are able to comprehend what would otherwise be incomprehensible.

Scaffolding

Teaching practices associated with scaffolding march ahead of the child's development. They rest on the view of Vygotsky that it is important to awaken in the child a variety of internal developmental processes that operate only when the child is in interaction with significant others—parents, teachers or peers (Vygotsky 1979). The process of internalization is gradual. First, the teacher or other person controls and guides the child's activity. Later, the responsibility is shared by the teacher and the child, and finally the transition from full teacher responsibility, through shared responsibility, to full child responsibility is complete.

The effectiveness of using the strategy has been shown by James Baumann in teaching students how to infer main ideas from the text (Baumann 1984). Baumann's procedures consist of these steps:

1. *Introduction and Examples:* Students are told how the lesson will help them become better readers, and a section of the text is presented with the teacher demonstrating how to apply the skill to be taught in comprehending the section.
2. *Direct Instruction:* The teacher tells, shows, models, and demonstrates the skill. The teacher is in command of the learning situation and leads the lesson as opposed to a worksheet, kit, or textbook.
3. *Teacher-Directed Application:* Responsibility for skill acquisition begins to shift to the students. Students "puzzle out" texts that demand use of the skill.
4. *Independent Practice:* Students have full responsibility for applying what has been taught to materials never seen before.

In Baumann's lessons, students are taught that an implied main idea may be inferred from postulating dominant relationships between the superordinate and subordinate topics of a paragraph. Students are taught to identify details concurrently with the identification of main ideas. A number of heuristics are used to help students understand the concept of dominant relations. Exhibit 2.2 is an example taken from a teacher-directed lesson.

Exhibit 2.2   Sample Lesson Employing a Direct Instruction Paradigm

Introduction

"Remember last time when we learned how to find main idea sentences right in paragraphs? We called these main idea sentences *topic sentences.* Today you will learn how to find main ideas in paragraphs that do not have topic sentences; that is, paragraphs which actually do have main ideas in them, but paragraphs in which the main ideas are not stated. You will learn how to figure out these unstated main ideas by looking at the details in the paragraph and determining what all these details are talking about, and that will be the main idea. This is an important reading skill because many paragraphs have unstated main ideas, and if you can figure out what these main ideas are, you will understand and remember the most important information in the material you read."

Example

"Look at the example I have on this transparency."

My father can cook bacon and eggs real well. He can also bake cakes that taste wonderful. He cooks excellent popcorn and pizza. The thing he cooks best of all, however, is hamburgers barbecued on the grill.

"Follow along with me silently as I read the paragraph aloud"(Teacher reads paragraph.) "Notice that there is no single sentence that states the main idea; that is, there is no topic sentence. Rather, the entire paragraph consists of a series of details. That does not mean that there is not a main idea in this paragraph, however, for there is. What we will learn how to do today is to inspect paragraphs like this one that contain an unstated main idea and then figure out what that main idea is."

Direct Instruction

"Let's examine this same paragraph on the transparency and see if we can determine its main idea. Remember in our last lesson, we learned to figure out the topic of a paragraph—the one or two words that tell what a paragraph is about? What would be the topic of this paragraph? Would it be 'father cooking'?" (Student response.) "All right, the topic of the paragraph is 'father cooking.' Now let's list on the board all the ideas that tell about father cooking. Who can help us begin?" (Students respond by stating the four detail sentences in the paragraph, and the teacher writes them on the board in a numbered list.) "Very good. These are the ideas that tell us about father cooking, and we learned already that we can call these ideas *supporting details.* If supporting details go with a main idea, let's inspect these details and see if we can figure out what the main idea of this paragraph is." (Teacher rereads the supporting details on the board.) "Now what would be a main idea sentence we could come up with that goes with all these details?" (Teacher writes student responses on the board.) "Yes, there are several different ways of saying what the main idea is: 'Father can cook many different things' or 'Father is a good cook.' But the main idea tells us about all the details in the paragraph; that is, the biggest, most important, idea in the paragraph."

"Now look at this transparency. Who can tell me what it is?" (Student response.) "Yes, it is a table. Let's use this table to help us understand how main ideas and details go together. Just as a table is supported by its legs, so too, a main idea is supported by details. So let's put the main idea on the table and the supporting details on each of the legs. Who can help us get going? Let's start with the details on the legs." (Students respond and teacher writes details on table legs.) "Now let's put the main idea on top of the table." (Teacher writes main idea on table top.) "Just as the legs of this table support the table top, so too, the details in this paragraph support the main idea of the paragraph. When you try to figure out the main idea of a paragraph, think of a table and legs to help you understand how supporting details and main ideas relate to one another, or go together." (Teacher then works through a second example paragraph in a similar fashion.)

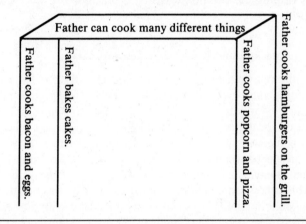

Source: From "The Effectiveness of a Direct Instruction Paradigm for Teaching Main Idea Comprehension" by James F. Buaumann, *Reading Research Quarterly,* Fall 1984, pp. 108–109. Copyright© 1984 International Reading Association. Reprinted with permission of James F. Baumann and the International Reading Association.

A more learner-centered view of scaffolding appears in a successful program for teaching dialect-speaking students to comprehend standard English text (Speidel 1982). Teachers in the program employ live scaffolding strategies:

1. *Listening:* The teacher listens to what children are trying to say and encourages them to take risks with their language and ideas, fostering the view that there is more than one way to look at a situation and to organize ideas.
2. *Cognitive Complexity:* The teacher makes changes in the level of abstraction so that the children can participate in the discussion. For example, in a discussion about dogs none of the children could tell how dogs showed love although many of the children had dogs as pets. At this point the teacher talked about how children might show love to each other, modeling with hugs.
3. *Extension of Language:* The teacher (and often the children themselves) responds to statements that are incomplete or vague. In trying to clarify what the child means to convey, the teacher completes,

substitutes, and adds to the child's response to make sense. Thus children acquire standard English patterns with situations that are meaningful to them.

4. *Prompting:* The teacher gives hints to help children clarify their thinking. For instance, in helping children think of a good title for a story, the teacher might ask the children for the main idea of the story. When the children do not respond, she might humorously suggest that the story is about monsters or something equally incongrous, thus helping the children focus on characters as a way to generate a possible title.

Activating Background Knowledge: Semantic Maps

Having the relevant knowledge structure is not sufficient for comprehension; readers must evoke it. One of the most effective teaching devices for activating appropriate background is the *semantic map*. The map is an arrangement of vocabulary (concepts) about a topic. These concepts are categorized in some way. The making of a semantic map is a procedure for building a bridge between the known and the new. The map informs the teacher what students know about a topic and gives the students anchor points to which they can attach new information and concepts they will encounter. Semantic mapping is consistently associated with higher scores on test items measuring specific comprehension, such as answers to text-based questions, recall of text ideas, and free recall of key concepts.

Guidelines for helping students collectively make a semantic map are as follows:

- Step 1: *Associations*
    Begin by asking students what they think of when they hear the word X (X is the topic they are going to read about). Free association is desirable. As students offer their associations, list the responses on the chalkboard. Try to put the associations into categories. For example, responses to *money* might be categorized into uses of money, kinds of money, denominations, consequences of having money, ways of earning it, and other associations.
- Step 2: *Categories*
    Help the students label the categories and then ask them to read the selection to learn more about X. It is fine to encourage pupils to pose their own questions about what they want to learn about X from the text.
- Step 3: *Read and Revise*
    Next, after reading the selection, the class again addresses the set of categories and prereading questions related to X. At this time, students add new ideas acquired from their reading, correcting and augmenting the original map.

The resulting map is evidence of the students' preexisting schema, their new learning from the text, and the intergration of new and old knowledge.

Discussion, posing of questions, and the relating of students' responses contribute to the success of semantic mapping.

Exhibit 2.3 depicts an initial, incomplete semantic map for the concept *gas*. Note in the exhibit how the more abstract, superordinate concepts of matter to which the concept *gas* is related are placed at the top of the map. Schemata of a more concrete or subordinate level are placed lower.

A semantic map can be used to link students' basic concepts of the topic to both abstract schema and concrete examples. To illustrate, in the basic concept *dog, Fido* is at the concrete or subordinate level and *animal* is at an abstract or superordinate level. More students will be familiar with the term that represents a basic schema; so, in building bridges from the known to the new, we usually start with topics at this basic level, then consider specific examples, and finally relate the term to the superordinate schema. If students need help with the concept of hierarchies, let them classify ideas about their favorite topics (e.g., sports, food, friends). While it is not essential for them to learn the words *superordinate, coordinate,* and *subordinate,* it can be useful. Let students decide why words like *color, texture,* and *shape* are superordinate to *blue, soft,* and *round.* More important, however, elicit the students' associations for the topic.

Additional explanations and illustrations of semantic mapping appear in Chapter 7 of this book. I would like to stress the importance of using the semantic-mapping techniques in classrooms that include students from a variety of cultural backgrounds. You will find that minority group students hold schemata for most topics, even though these schemata are not always conventional. The opportunity to relate their schemata to the topic of the text enables them to see relevance in what might otherwise be viewed as strange and aversive materials.

In order to activate the schematic background of your students and determine its appropriateness for the reading you expect them to do, have your

Exhibit 2.3 Initial Semantic Map for *Gas*

Related to
Molecular movement
Chemical changes   (Superordinate terms)
States of matter
Evaporation and condensation

Gas (basic term)

Uses	*Kinds*	*Properties*	
Healing	Natural	Expands	(Subordinate terms)
Illuminating	Acetylene	Fills space	
Purifying	Helium	No Volume	
Putting people to sleep	Chlorine	No shape	

Activity 2.3   Constructing a Semantic Map

Choose a topic for a selection you want the students to read (e.g., *climate, hap-piness, computers*). Ask students to say what they think of when they hear the chosen word, then arrange responses to form a map. Students should label the categories of responses. Note whether students have schemata at superordinate and subordinate levels.

You may wish to use the map as a means to generate student's questions. You may also wish to have them discuss and revise their map after reading the selection.

class develop a semantic map for a topic in an upcoming lesson (Activity 2.3).

SUMMARY

This chapter introduced schema theory and illustrated how one's schema for reading influences reading comprehension. The importance of having schemata for rhetorical patterns was emphasized, and applications of schema theory in building and activating background knowledge were given. Specific teaching strategies—such as reconciled lessons, scaffolding, and semantic mapping—were featured as effective ways to improve story understanding and to help students derive and recall important content from text.

REFERENCES

Anderson, R. C., and Pichert, J. W. "Recall of Previously Unrecallable Information Following a Shift in Perspective." *Journal of Verbal Learning and Verbal Behavior* 17 (1978): 1–12.

Anderson, R. C., Reynolds, R. E., Schallert, D. C., and Goetz, E. T. "Frameworks for Comprehending Discourse." *American Education Journal* 14 (1977): 357–382.

Baumann, James F. "The Effectiveness of a Direct Instruction Paradigm for Teaching Main Idea Comprehension." *Reading Research Quarterly* 20, no. 1 (Fall 1984): 93–115.

Bransford, J. D., and McCarrell, N. S. "A Sketch of a Cognitive Approach to Comprehension." *Cognition and the Symbolic Process.* W. B. Weiner and D. Palmero, editors. Hillsdale, NJ: Erlbaum, 1974.

Brown, A. C., Smiley, S.S., Day, J., Townsend, M., and Lawton, S.C. "Instruction of a Thematic Idea in Comprehension and Retention of Stories," *Child Development* 49 (1977): 1458–66.

Deakin University Open Campus Program, ECT 401.*Classroom Processes—Task, Pupil, and Teacher,* 1981, p. 48.

Denny, S. T., and Weintraub, S. "First Graders' Responses to Three Questions About Reading." *Elementary School Journal* 66 (1966): 441–448.

Durkin, Dolores. "Is There a Match Between What Elementary Teachers Do and What Basal Reader Manuals Recommend?" *The Reading Teacher* 37, no.7 (April 1984): 734–745.

Freppon, Penny R. "Children's Concepts of the Nature and Purpose of Reading in Different Instructional Setting." Paper presented at the Annual Spring Conference of the National Council of Teachers of English, Charleston, SC, April 6–8, 1989. Educational Resources Information Center ED 313659.

Golden, J. M. "The Construction of a Literary Text in a Story—Reading Lesson." In *Multiple Perspective Analyses of Classroom Discourse.* J. Green and J. Harker, editors. Norwood, NJ: Ablex, 1988, pp. 71–106.

Graves, M. F., Cooke, C. L., and LaBergh, H. J. "Effects of Previewing Difficult and Short Stories on Low-Ability Junior High School Students' Comprehension, Recall, and Attitude."

Idol, L. and Croll, V. J. "Story-Mapping Training as a Means of Improving Reading Comprehension." *Learning Disability Quarterly* 10 (1987): 214–229.

Johns, J., and Ellis, D. "Reading: Children Tell It Like It Is." *Reading World* 16, no. 2 (1976): 115–128.

Neuman, I. "Enhancing Children's Comprehension Through Previewing." In *Dialogues in Literary Research.* J. Readence and R. S. Baldwin, editors. 37th Yearbook, National Reading Conference. Chicago: National Reading Conference, 1988, 219–224.

Reutzel, D. Ray. "Reconciling Schema Theory and the Basal Reading Lesson." *The Reading Teacher* 39, no. 2 (November 1985): 194–198.

Schommer, Marlene. *Students' Beliefs about the Nature of Knowledge: What Are They and How Do They Affect Comprehension?* Urbana, IL: Illinois University Urbana Center for the Study of Reading, 1989.

Speidel, Gisele E. *Oral Language in a Successful Reading Program for Hawaiian Children.* Technical Report no. 105 of the Kamehameha Early Education Program, 1982.

Stein, B., Bransford, J. D., Franks, J. J., Owings, K. D., Vye, N. J., and McGraw, W. "Differences in the Precision of Self-Generated Elaborations." *Journal of Experimental Psychology* 3 (1982): 399–405.

Vygotsky, L. S. *The Development of Higher Psychological Processes.* Cambridge, MA: Harvard University Press, 1979.

Useful Readings

Anderson, R. C., and Pearson P. D. "A Schema-Theoretic View of Basic Processes in Teaching Comprehension." In *Handbook of Reading Research,* P. D. Pearson, editor. New York: Longman, 1984, pp. 225–253.

LaZansky, Frank S., and Johnston, Michael. "Reading to Learn: Setting Students Up." In *Understanding Readers' Understanding,* Robert J. Tierney, P. L. Andrews, and J. Mitchell, editors. Hillsdale, NJ: Lawrence Erlbaum, 1987, pp. 255–283.

Mannes, S. M. and Kintsch, W. "Knowledge Organization and Text Organization." *Cognition and Instruction* 42, no. 2 (1987): 91–115.

Pressley, Michael, Johnson, C. J., Symons, S., McGoldrick, J. A., and Kurita, J. A. "Strategies that Improve Children's Memory and Comprehension of Text." *The Elementary School Journal,* 90, no. 1 (1989): 3–32.

Active Readers

OVERVIEW

In this chapter you are invited to examine teaching practices that aim at helping children become active readers who see reading as useful in pursuing their own purposes. The chapter describes ways to activate student thought before reading and for teaching students to generate questions that will contribute to learning from texts.

In addition to a focus on strategies for academic purposes, there is an introduction to the reading comprehension strategies necessary for workplace literacy, social emancipation, and self-actualization. Emphasis is on the teacher's role in responsive teaching as opposed to the traditional practice of recitation characterized by teacher questions, student response, and teacher evaluation.

FROM ANSWERING TO ASKING QUESTIONS

The late Harry Singer had long been interested in a process for teaching comprehension that departs from the traditional practice of asking students questions before, during, and after reading (Singer 1978). His process of active comprehension taught students to formulate their own questions. The purpose of teaching such a process is to help students acquire a schema of reading that acknowledges their intentions and then encourages a dynamic interaction between reader and author.

In teaching active comprehension, the teacher asks a question to get a question, not an answer. For example, a kindergarten teacher may hold up a picture for the children to look at. Instead of asking questions about the picture that yield predetermined answers such as *Who is on the bike?* or *What is going to happen?* the teacher says, "Look at the picture. What would you like to know about the picture?" The questions children ask in response are often surprising.

Student-initiated questions (made in response to the study of pictures, headings, and other aspects of the text) reflect the students' perceptions, backgrounds, and cognitive development. Some children may first ask about details and then go on to the main idea. Others may start with the theme before progressing to details. In the kindergarten example, children might say, "Why is the boy on the bicycle?" "Does the little girl see the boy on the bike?" "Will they crash?"

Questions may be referred to the class, and then the teacher might ask, "What would you like to know about what happened next?" "How would you avoid the crash?" The latter question directs thinking toward a solution to a problem. After several solutions have been elicited, the teacher might say, "Let's turn the page, read, and see how the person who drew these pictures [the author] solved the problem." After understanding the author's solution, the teacher initiates an evaluation of it: "Is this the best way to stop a crash?" Thus, even in the kindergarten, children develop critical and effective schemata.

Questions can be elicited from students in many ways. One third-grade teacher introduced a book by having someone read the title and then asking students what they wanted to find out about the book. Another teacher arranged a competitive situation in which the class was divided into two groups, with two students at the chalkboard to write down questions. The students filled the chalkboard and then tried to outdo each other answering their own questions, stimulated by the title and first paragraph.

Exhibit 3.1 is a lesson used by Singer in teaching active comprehension.

Russell Stauffer has also advocated teaching students to raise questions in order that they may become reading-thinking scholars (Stauffer 1981). He has proposed a teaching strategy called *group-directed reading-thinking activity* (DRTA). A teacher's plan of action in the DRTA is (1) to activate students' thoughts before reading by asking questions such as, *What do you*

Exhibit 3.1   Lesson in Teaching Active Comprehension

Passage

"Filming a Cannibal Chief" by Osa Johnson

My husband and I wanted to make a moving picture of savages, and Martin finally decided on Malekula, second largest of the New Hebrides Islands. We started from Sydney, Australia on a small ship. Soon a storm of warning broke around us.

Teacher-student interaction

Teacher questions to elicit student questions:

> Look at the title. What questions could you ask just from the title alone?

Student questions on the title:

> How do you film a cannibal chief? (Often implicit in this question is the idea of how do you film a cannibal chief and get away with it.)
> Were they successful?
> Why film a cannibal chief?

Teacher techniques for eliciting questions in the paragraph:

> What would you like to know about Martin?

Student questions:

> Who is Martin?
> Is Martin the husband?
> Why did Martin decide?
> Did Martin have trouble making up his mind?
> Is Martin deliberative?
> Are there many places where cannibals still live?

Teacher question:

> Is there anything you would like to know about the relationship between the writer and Martin?

Student questions:

> Is she frustrated by Martin's indecision?
> Is he the domineering person in their relationship?
> Is she a nagging type of person?

Teacher question:

> Does the ship make you wonder about the trip?

Student questions:

> Why were they going in a small ship?
> How small was the small ship?
> Why didn't the author describe the ship?

Teacher question:

> Look at the last sentence. What questions pop into your mind as you read that sentence?

Student questions:

> What is a storm of warning?
> What kind of danger are they about to encounter?
> Will they survive?

Source: From "Active Comprehension" by Harry Singer, *The Reading Teacher,* May 1978. Reprinted with permission of Harry Singer and the International Reading Association.

think? (2) to agitate reflective thought by asking, *Why do you think so?* and (3) to require evidence in support of the conclusion in the form of references to the text and peer judgments regarding the force of the arguments.

DRTA lessons allow students to work in small groups that read the same material, but from different perspectives and for different purposes. Some purposes may be of group origin, and others may be individual. Students compare and contrast their predictions and paths to answers before reading. Answers derived from the reading and thinking are subject to evaluation.

RECIPROCAL TEACHING: HELPING STUDENTS LEARN TO ASK QUESTIONS

One strategy for attaining the goal of active questioning has been termed the *phase-in-phase-out* strategy, or *reciprocal teaching*. Here, the teacher phases in the questioning process by taking the first step in modeling questions that are appropriate to the content. The teacher also offers additional information about the content to be read or explains more about the topic.

Once students have an idea of the kinds of questions that can be asked about different types of content (expository writing, narrative prose), they are formed into groups to ask each other questions regarding the material to be read. Final phasing out occurs when the students ask and answer appropriate questions on their own.

Palincsar and Brown have had success in teaching questioning routines to children who were adequate decoders but poor comprehenders (Palincsar and Brown 1984). Their procedures were based on A.V. Manzo's *request method,* by which the students and the teacher take turns in asking each other questions regarding a passage (Manzo 1968). Palincsar concentrated on two types of comprehension questions to use while reading: *interpretations* (What is happening now? What is causing it?) and *predictions* (What will happen next?).

Working with individuals, she took turns with each child in leading dialogues over segments of text. Both the teacher and the child read a paragraph, and then one assumed the role of dialogue leader, asking questions about the main idea and about how the information might be grouped together. The dialogue leader also asked questions about what was presently happening in the selection and what might occur in remaining passages. Then the roles were reversed.

At first students had difficulty assuming the role of dialogue leader when their turns came. The teacher had to construct paraphrases and questions for the students to mimic. Only after several sessions did students themselves provide sophisticated paraphrases and questions.

Children who received training in the questioning routines greatly improved their ability to answer comprehension questions. This training was even more effective when it followed a procedure by which students first read silently and then answered questions. Subsequently, the teacher praised correct responses and guided the students back into the paragraphs in which the answers could be found.

The technique of teaching questioning by a reciprocal game need not follow the teacher-and-one-child approach taken in the studies discussed, which may not be practical for classroom use. Instead, a few teacher-trained students can be paired with naive peers for playing the questioning game.

Reciprocal teaching ranks as one of the most successful teaching practices for reading and comprehension. This procedure results in sizable gains on criterion tests of comprehension and on standardized tests of performance. It is an effective procedure with students at all ages. Even when delivered by peers, students maintain the strategies taught through reciprocal teaching over time and are able to transfer them to novel tasks (Palincsar, Brown, and Martin 1987). Unlike many teaching procedures, reciprocal teaching aims at increasing the learners' independence from the teacher. Accordingly, students learn to apply four general strategies consistently to text segments as they read, to generate self-testing questions about the content after reading a passage (What questions might a teacher ask about the passage?), to summarize the passage (Remember a summary is a shortened version, it doesn't include detail), to clarify points (Which part doesn't make sense?) and to ask predictive questions (What will the author talk about next?).

The choice of strategies is deliberate. Postreading questioning is both a check on comprehension and focus on main ideas. Clarifying questions require critical evaluation and a sensitivity to deficiencies in text or content incompatible with the reader's prior experience, and predicting questions contribute to the drawing and testing of inferences.

It is important to note, however, that while lack of appropriate prior knowledge impairs reading comprehension, comprehension also suffers when prior knowledge is not activated. Hence students should be taught to generate self-questions that will activate relevant prior knowledge. Chapter 4, "Metacognition," discusses ways of encouraging such self-questioning. Also, people with little prior knowledge presumably activate general schemata that enable them to ask questions (Van der Meig 1990).

Activity 3.1 will help you find out what is involved in eliciting prereading questions from students and to assess the value of the practice.

CONSEQUENCES OF QUESTIONING BY STUDENTS

In classroom situations there is sometimes a problem with self-generated questions. Students may focus on one detail or aspect of a comprehension test or quiz on the material. Although it is important that students answer their own questions, a teacher may want evidence that they comprehended what others have found valuable and what the teacher expects readers to learn from given material. Hence, students are taught to generate questions

Activity 3.1 Student-Initiated Questions versus Teacher-Initiated Questions—a Classroom Study

Select a fresh story or other reading material for your students. From this material prepare four questions, two of which are factual or literal (the reader should supply or recognize some item of information given in the passages) and two of which require the making of inferences (the reader should state a relationship between elements of the passages that is implied but not explicitly stated). These four questions will constitute the teacher-initiated questions for the selection.

Randomly choose half of your students to generate their own questions to be answered by reading the selection. Introductory paragraphs, titles, pictures, and other features of the selection may be used to help these students generate four questions, which will constitute the student-initiated question. Summarize the student-generated questions and then let the students who proposed them read the selection. Next present the teacher-generated questions to those students who did not participate in posing questions and ask them to read the selection. After a day's delay and without allowing the children an opportunity to reread, administer a test consisting of both the teacher-generated and the student-generated questions. Both groups of students should get the same test.

Score this eight-item test and then analyze the results. What questions might these results answer? Here are some questions you could ask: Was there any difference between the recall scores of the students who were in the question-generating group and those who were given the teacher-generated questions? Did the students in the question-generating group answer more of their own questions correctly than students who were not in this group? Did the prereading focus on generating questions interfere with the question-initiating students' ability to answer teacher-generated questions-that is, did the narrower focus interfere with concomitant or incidental learning?

As an alternative to the general procedure of this study, you may have each child in one group generate his or her own questions. You might then compare responses to one child's questions with responses to the questions generated by the teacher or by other students. Other studies have found that, compared with answering questions asked by other children, asking one's own questions facilitated memory. Also, manipulation of instruction might be undertaken to see how the learners perceive their task. For example, you may wish to compare the effect of telling children to read *only* in order to answer the given questions with the effect of telling them to answer the questions but also to learn as many other things as possible from the selection. Students' questions might be compared with teachers' questions with respect to whether or not they can be answered by reading the selection and whether or not they show a balance between factual (literal) and inferential levels of comprehension.

Examination of the kinds of questions posed by students and teachers alike might reveal whether those of either origin would lead learners to process the information so that it would be learned and retained.

that will be most useful in deriving commonly expected meanings from given subject matter. Chapter 9 contains illustrations of the kinds of questions that will help students organize and integrate text content as well as the kinds of questions that illuminate ideas of central importance to the author.

There is research supporting the idea that students who are taught to actively comprehend resist the narrowing effect of some teacher-posed questions. Active readers have been found to perform better on literal, interpretive, and general comprehension tests than students who have been restricted to teachers' prereading and postreading questions (Rhodes 1977). Fifth-graders using the reciprocal questioning procedure (the students asked the teacher a question for each teacher-posed question they answered) performed better on an interpretation test than students in a group in which only the teacher posed questions (Helfeldt and Lakik 1976).

Students learn to imitate teachers' questions. Questions asked at interpretive and applicative levels stimulate higher cognitive processes than do factual questions. It might be better, therefore, to help students initiate broad questions that have several acceptable answers instead of only narrow questions that have a single right answer. One cautionary note, however, is that the use of broad, divergent questions with children who do not have the schemata for answering these questions will result in little understanding.

EFFECTS OF QUESTIONING BY TEACHERS

The topic of prereading and postreading questions and their effect on comprehension is treated differently by cognitivists, who see the reader as creating a context for interpreting the author's message, and behaviorists, who favor reinforcement for correct responses and antecedent manipulations such as modeling and prompting.

The practice of questioning before reading (prequestioning) is a common one. Studies evaluating the practice from a behavioristic view show that students do better at answering test questions after reading if they have been asked the *same* questions earlier, the prereading questions serving as attention-getting devices or hints on what to look for (Reder 1980).

The cognitivists emphasize the use of test questions that elicit more general responses, not verbatim recall or direct matches to prequestions. Prequestions are regarded by the cognitivist as aids to processing what is read. Accordingly, the questions should force the student to process relevant aspects of the text in useful ways (How will you use the information in your own project?). Questions that force a child to review or summarize the material improve comprehension. Many teachers have intuitively helped children acquire the schema of reading as a meaningful activity by asking questions such as *Can you get into an argument about what you read? On whose side of the argument are you? Why? When you read this, what ideas are not actually put into words? What is the story* really *about? Who might like it and why?*

The use of prequestions as a device to activate the learner's schema is another way in which questions aid in the processing of information. Asking students to find details that support or refute a general idea makes for more effective processing than asking students to recall specific details. Just as comprehension of a selection is improved when the reader attends to a description title, picture, or heading before a passage, so questions make the selection more comprehensible.

Bernice Wong has suggested that we match the type of self-questioning with specific needs of students. Children with deficient selective attention might be taught to generate self-questions to focus on key words in their reading; children who fail to establish connections among ideas learned from text might be taught to ask questions about how they would use information gained in solving a problem—for example, in reading biology, "What is the functional significance of arteries having properties of thickness, being muscular, and elastic?" (Wong 1985).

In brief, it is not self-questioning per se, but the cognitive processes that are induced by one's own questions (inferencing, monitoring, attending) that matter.

To understand better how questions can direct selective attention, first try to derive meaning from the drawing in Exhibit 3.2 without reading the question that accompanies it. Then read the question and see whether the drawing means something different.

RELATING CHILDREN'S BACKGROUNDS TO THEIR READING

Children need to be aware that it is necessary to use what they already know in order to understand the text—that the knowledge they already have can help them in reading.

The attitude that one knows nothing about what is to be read has been described by Pearson and Johnson as the "Charlie Brown syndrome" (Pearson and Johnson 1978).

> Recall what Charlie Brown does whenever he gets a new book. Before he even looks at the book, he counts the pages—625 pages—"I'll never learn *all* that!" He is defeated before he starts, before he has had a chance to realize that he does not have to learn *all* that. It is not *all* new. He already knows something about it. He has not given himself the chance to learn what he already knows about what he is supposed to know.

The Charlie Brown syndrome is common with readers from non-English-speaking cultures, who often regard activities in English as strange and incomprehensible.

Exhibit 3.2   Activating Schemata

Can you see both an old woman and a young woman in this drawing?

A good way to overcome students' reluctance to apply what they know to the unfamiliar is for the teacher to elicit from the students their ideas about the topic, theme, concept, or other organizing element in the selection to be read. The semantic mapping activity in Chapter 2 serves well in this connection. When students tell what a topic means to them and relate their experiences with the topic, they establish an anticipatory set. It enables them to state the questions they want answered by the selection, to say what they expect to find, and to guess about the way the information will be presented.

However, it is not enough for students to relate their experience to a topic before reading. Their background must be brought to bear at all phases of the reading process. Kathryn Au has had unusual success in helping minority children achieve in reading by making the children's past experience an integral part of the entire lesson (Au 1979). Au's cognitive training lessons are composed of three different kinds of sequence—an *experience* sequence for eliciting background, a *text* sequence for determining what sense children are making from the text, and a *relationship* sequence by which children contrast their own experiences with what they read.

Exhibit 3.3 describes and illustrates a lesson (taught to second graders who are members of a minority group) that uses the experience-text-relationship (ETR) method.

In Au's ETR method, the children practice expressing complex thoughts; during the process, the teacher gets an idea of which steps are easy or difficult for individual children. The teacher's interaction with students helps them integrate features of the story with their existing store of knowledge. Over time the children learn to apply the method by themselves. Those who have interacted frequently with a teacher in ETR lessons show better comprehension when reading on their own than children who have not had this opportunity.

Recently, Project Keep has focused on *Responsive Teaching* or *Instructional Conversations* where the teacher's role is to use student input into discussions and student interpretations of texts so that all students move to higher levels of comprehension than they would attain independently. (Tharp and Gallimore, 1989). Instructional conversations mirror the natural learning of the home in that activities are goal directed, as when children and parents work together and with enough help (scaffolding) so that even young and poor readers can participate in complex tasks (like reading and discussing a whole text) before they can do it on their own. The teacher and peers may offer new knowledge or demonstrate strategies, but only in response to the learner's attempts to make sense of his or her world.

What children learn about reading is as much a function of teacher-students interaction and student initiation of questions as it is a function of teacher-directed interventions and teacher-posed questions (Green, Harker,& Golden 1987). There is evidence that students attend more to text and increase their locus of control when teachers discard the old practice of initiating an interaction by asking a question, getting a student response, and then evaluating that response, in favor of empowering students by giving them responsibility for initiating topics, monitoring the relevancy of comments, taking turns, and deciding when to shift discussions to another matter (O'Flahavan 1989).

DIFFERENCES BETWEEN STUDENTS' AND AUTHORS' PURPOSES

Active readers seek printed material in order to meet a variety of needs— to solve problems, to further their interests, to escape psychologically, to help others, to protect economic stakes, to seek knowledge, to satisfy curiosity, to improve themselves, to find spiritual inspiration. In so doing, they bring many purposes to their reading. On the other hand, authors have their own purposes in communicating certain information. The problem of getting the purposes of the reader and the purposes of the author to interact is a real one.

Exhibit 3.3   Lesson Using the Experience-Test-Relationship Method

Experience

In an *E* experience sequence, the teacher has the children discuss experiences they have had, or knowledge they have, which is related in some way to the story. In the following example of an *E* sequence, the teacher is having each of the children talk about what she would do if she had a frog.

Teacher:	Okay, let's think if we could do anything else with a frog. What would you do Shirley?
Ann:	I wouldn't touch the legs. Yuck.
Shirley:	I would put it in a bucket.
Teacher:	You would put it in a bucket. Okay, that's something different. What would you do with it?
Shirley:	Inaudible
Ann:	Yeah, you eat the legs?
Teacher:	Okay, Shirley might even eat it. Good, you can eat frog, can't you?

Text

After this first part of the lesson, in which the children share their experiences, the teacher has them read short parts of the story, usually a page or two, asking them questions about the content after each section is read. These are the *T* or text sequences. Sometimes the children show misunderstandings which the teacher must work hard to correct, as in the following *T* sequence.

Teacher:	Shirley, why did you say Freddy laughed? Okay, read the part that you said—when Freddy laughed.
Shirley:	[Reading] "I would take it fishing. Freddy laughed."
Teacher:	Okay, who says, "I would take it fishing"?
Nathan:	Mr. Mays
Teacher:	Mr. Mays. And why did Freddy laugh?
Ann:	Because maybe he didn't—maybe he didn't know that he was going to use the frog.
Teacher:	No, he laughed for another reason. Ellie? Who can read that?
Ellie:	Because—'cause Mr. Mays didn't know what to do with the frog. That's all he could think was— he didn't know that he could use frogs was—was a bait. That's why Freddy laughed.
Teacher:	Okay, wait a minute. That's not the reason Freddy laughed.
Nathan:	Frogs can't fish.
Teacher:	Right. Okay. Mr. Mays says, "I don't have a frog, but if I did, I'd take it fishing." and Freddy thinks, hah, going

fishing with the frog
sitting down with the
fishing pole?

Relationship

The final category is the *R* or relationship sequence. In *R* sequences the
teacher attempts to draw relationships
for the children between the content
of the story discussed in the *T* sequences and their outside experience
and knowledge. In this example of an
R sequence, the teacher provides the
opportunity for the children to contrast their own knowledge about what
can be used as bait in fishing with an
idea presented in the story.

Teacher:	Did you know before this that fish like to eat frogs?
Group:	Nooo.
Teacher:	I didn't—I never heard of using frogs

for bait. Do you
think they really do?

Nathan:	Yeah.
Teacher:	You think so.
Ann:	My daddy—my daddy—use bread.
Teacher:	Yeah, some people use bread. What else do you use for bait?
Shirley:	Fish.
Teacher:	Sometimes you use smaller fishes.

The *E,T* and *R* sequences show
the teacher's efforts to guide the children systematically through the cognitive processes related to understanding a written story. The teacher in the
examples is a skillful questioner, particularly adept at leading the children
to the...answers, rather than telling
them the answers.

Source: From "Using the Experience-Text-Relationship Method with Minority Children" by Kathryn Au, *The Reading Teacher*, March 1977. Copyright ©1977 International Reading Association. Reprinted with permission of Kathryn Au and the International Reading Association.

F.D. Flower tells how he failed to find what he wanted in a particular work, even though he was convinced that the author had something to say relevant to his purposes (Flower 1970). Flower was interested in interpreting the symbols poets use in describing dreams. Flower sought a copy of Freud's *The Interpretation of Dreams*. He looked down the list of contents and referred to the index. Then he saw that in spite of the title the work was no handbook to the meaning of dreams, as might be found in some popular magazines from time to time, but a very full account with many examples of what dreams are and why they occur. Flower read through Chapter 3, "A Dream is a Fulfillment of a Wish," and glanced at Chapter 6, "The Dream's Work," especially section E, "Representation by Symbols in Dreams." Although he found these parts interesting, he did not discover anything to help him interpret the symbols used by poets. Obviously, Flower had to make up his mind whether to continue digging into the book to see if he could find what he was looking for or to give up and look elsewhere. Freud's book is fascinating, but Flower's time was limited, so he put *Interpretation of Dreams* to one side until another time.

Some authorities recommend that when readers' purposes for reading have been frustrated, they should not do as Flower did but should modify their goals and adjust their original purposes as they read. Perhaps the reading goals of children are not well formed; in continued reading, they may be able to find better purposes.

Readers can satisfy their own purpose even when the author has a different one. Mature readers have learned, for instance, how to "raid" texts for the information they want, selecting only information that meets their special purposes. They know when raiding is appropriate and when it is not. They may use the technique of scanning, in which they anticipate what type of answer to their question is likely to be found in the text. When scanning, they don't look for or recall any information other than the answer to the predetermined question. Indexes, tables of contents, titles, and headings are used in searching for the right places to scan. "Leafing through a text" and sampling introductory and concluding paragraphs are all part of the technique.

What responsibility do teachers have for helping children pose questions that are answerable from the reading selection at hand? What should children be taught about how best to seek answers to their own questions through printed materials? Comprehending different types of discourse addresses these questions in detail. At this point, however, it should be recognized that much school-based instruction is aimed at helping students understand simple narrative and acquire strategies for answering questions about subject matter as presented in school textbooks. Efforts to develop workplace literacy and comprehension as social emancipation are few, and the teaching of reading for self-actualization is only beginning in most schools.

Workplace Literacy

Reading in the workplace is more reading *to do* than reading *to learn*. Reading is undertaken to accomplish tasks—locating information in documents and diagnosing problems by following trouble-shooting guides.

In contrast to what many teachers and employers believe, achievement in school-based reading does not predict that one will be able to read effectively at the worksite. The differences between job literacy and school literacy—different concepts, different reference systems, different writing styles—mean that there is little transfer in what is learned (Duffy 1985).

The most promising programs for preparing students for workplace literacy are those that teach the particular technical vocabulary, concepts, and materials in occupation-specific settings, using the reading materials while solving workplace problems (Mikulecky and Drew 1991).

Critical Reading

Empowerment is the aim of critical pedagogy and reading. The goals are to help students take risks, to struggle with ongoing relations of power, to understand how writing persuades, and to determine whether one should celebrate or undo a text. The development of critical stances in readers—

reflective skeptics, questioners, doubters, and arguers—may require a classroom or other community that values critical thinking and social change.

Critical reading is a pedagogical model that promotes the goal of emancipation. Students are taught to consider each reading selection (article, book, advertisement, chapter, political document) as having a given stance toward an important social issue or discourse. Background information from the field of discourse and familiarity with the social issue addressed by the particular reading selection are important and are developed through the social network of the classroom with its discussions, projects, and inquiries. The practice of helping students understand texts in terms of other texts (intertextual links) develop social and literary knowledge. For example, to conceive text as a genre type makes students more likely to define specific aspects or attitudes related to themata and discourse issues (Beach, Appleman, and Dorsey 1991).

Self-Actualizing

Readers read in accordance with their "identity themes" and re-create literary works in accordance with their own psychological predispositions. Radway's analysis of women's responses to romance novels indicated that novels reinforced their nurturing role as housewives (Radway 1984). Similarly, seventh-graders have been found to read romance novels as a way of anticipating their immediate future life and helping them deal with their fears about their expectations. Literature gives readers the opportunity to see themselves in their reading—to observe their own responses and thereby better understand themselves (Willinsky and Hunniford 1986).

Reading as self-actualization, with its emphasis upon responses to literature, has many instructional implications. For one thing, it means providing materials that will likely relate to student concerns, personal contacts, and student purposes. For another, teachers share their roles as expert interpreters and listen to the responses and interpretations of the students. Reading should occur in small groups where discussion is encouraged and where groups can pursue ends of their own choosing. Among the techniques for eliciting student problems, feelings, and thoughts about the text is *story theatre* (Moffett and Wagner 1983). Students perform an aspect or adaption of the text or a complete poem. The performance can be live or recorded. There are no stage trappings, and voice is favored over action. Discussion of the performance by classmates should include spontaneous questioning and exchanging of responses.

SUMMARY

It is clear that verbal behavior—questioning, clarifying, and discussing—influence learning. Students can be taught to generate particular kinds of questions, each making a difference in what is learned or comprehended from reading. This chapter began with ways a teacher could encourage questions that activate schemata and thinking. The practice of reciprocal teaching and its usefulness in preparing students for independent learning from academic texts was featured. There were also suggestions for enhancing other types of reading comprehension: workplace literacy, critical reading, and self-actualization through responses to literature. The emphasis was on ways of helping students initiate questions and relate text to their own backgrounds and purposes. Responsive teaching, where the teacher listens and builds upon student-initiated questions and comments, was favored over the traditional reading-recitation constraints.

REFERENCES

Au, Kathryn. "Using the Experience-Text-Relationship Method with Minority Children." *The Reading Teacher* 32 (March 1979): 678–679.

Beach, R., Appleman, D., and Dorsey, S."Developing Literary Knowledge through Intertextual Links." *In Developing Discourse Practices in Adolescence and Adulthood,* R. Beach and S. Hynds, editors. Norwood, NJ: Ablex (in press).

Duffy, T. M. "Literary Instruction in the Military." *Armed Forces and Society* 11 (1985): 437–467.

Flower, F. D. *Reading to Learn.* London: British Broadcasting Corporation, 1970.

Green, J. L., Harker, J. O., and Golden, J. M, "Lesson Construction: Differing Views." In *Schooling in Social Context: Qualitative Studies,* G. N. Noblit and W. T. Pink, editors. Norwood, NJ: Ablex, 1987.

Helfeldt, J. P., and Lalik, R. "Reciprocal Student-Teacher Questioning." *The Reading Teacher* 3 (1976): 283–287.

Manzo, A. V. "Improving Reading Comprehension Through Reciprocal Questioning." Doctoral Dissertation, Syracuse University, 1968.

Mikulecky, Larry and Drew, Rad. "Basic Literacy Skills in the Workplace." *Handbook of Reading Research,* vol.2, R. Barr, M. L. Kamil, P. B. Mosenthal, and F. D. Pearson, editors. New York: Longman, 1991, pp. 669–689.

Moffett, James, and Wagner, Betty Jane. *Student-Centered Language Arts and Reading K-13 A Handbook for Teachers.* Boston: Houghton Mifflin, 1983.

O'Flahavan, J. O. "Second Graders Social, Intellectual, and Affective Development in Varied Group Discussions about Narrative." Unpublished doctoral dissertation. University of Illinois, 1989. Cited in P. David Pearson and Linda Fielding, "Comprehending Instruction." *Handbook or Reading Research,*vol. 2, R. Barr, M. L. Kamil, P. B. Mosenthal, and F. D. Pearson, editors. New York: Longman, 1991,p. 843.

Palincsar, A. M., and Brown, Ann. "Reciprocal Teaching of Comprehen-
    sion." *Cognition and Instruction* 1, no.2 (1984): 117–175.
Palincsar, A. M., Brown, Ann, and Martin, S. M. "Peer Interaction in Read-
    ing Comprehension Instruction." *Educational Psychologist* 22 (1987):
    231–253.
Pearson, P. David, and Johnson, Dale D. *Teaching Reading Comprehension*.
    New York: Holt, Rinehart and Winston, 1978.
Radway, J. *Reading the Romance: Women, Patriarchy, and Popular Litera-
    ture*. Chapel Hill, NC: University of North Carolina Press, 1984.
Reder, L. M. "The Role of Elaboration in the Comprehension and Retention
    of Prose: A Critical Review." *Review of Educational Research* 50 (Spring
    1980): 5–53.
Rhodes, A. "Active Comprehension." Unpublished research; University of
    California, Riverside, 1977.
Singer, Harry. "Active Comprehension." *The Reading Teacher* 31, no.8
    (1978): 901–908.
Stauffer, Russell G. "Strategies for Reading Instruction." *45th Yearbook*,
    Malcolm Douglas, editor. Claremont, CA: Claremont Reading Confer-
    ence, 1981, pp. 58–74.
Tharp, R. G., and Gallimore, R., "Rousing Schools to Life." *American
    Educator* 13, no. 2 (1989): 20–25, 46–52.
Van der Meig, Hans. "Question Asking: To Know That You Do Not Know
    Is Not Enough." *Journal of Educational Psychology* 82, no.3 (1990):
    502–512.
Willinsky, J., and Hunniford, R. M. "Reading the Romance Younger: The
    Mirrors and Fears of a Preparatory Literature." *Reading Canada* 4, no.1
    (Spring 1986): 16–31.
Wong, Bernice Y. "Self-Questioning Instructional Research." *Review of Ed-
    ucational Research* 55, no.2 (Spring 1985): 227–268.

Useful Readings

Gallagher, M. and Pearson, P. D. *Discussion, Comprehension and Knowl-
    edge Acquisition in Content Area Classrooms*. Tech. Report No.480.
    Urbana, Il: University of Illinois, Center for the Study of Reading, Au-
    gust 1987.
Palincsar, A. S., Brown, A. C., and Martin, S. M. "Peer Interaction in Read-
    ing Comprehension Instruction." *Educational Psychologist,* 22 (1987):
    231–253.
Wong, B. Y. L. "Self-Questioning Instructional Research: A Review." *Re-
    view of Educational Research* 55 (1985): 227–268.
Yopp, R. E. "Questioning and Active Comprehension." *Questioning Ex-
    change* 2 (1988): 231–238.

Metacognition in Reading Comprehension

Self-Knowledge
Task Knowledge
  The Strategy of Self-Instruction
  Strategies Used at Different Phases of Reading
  A Question-Recognition Strategy
  Reading to Remember
  Need for Abductive Logic
Self-Monitoring
Summary

OVERVIEW

One of this chapter's central purposes is to look at promising approaches to the difficult task of teaching students both to be aware of the reading strategies they are using and to monitor their own reading. These approaches relate to *metacognition*. The original Greek prefix *meta* gave a transcendent character to whatever it qualified. Metacognition refers to the ability to reflect on one's thinking (awareness). It also includes the ability to manage one's learning actions (executive features). In our times, newly coined words beginning with *meta* reflect a view of things from the outside, a more abstract level, and a mature understanding.

In reading, metacognition transcends cognition by enabling individuals not just to use particular strategies, but to select appropriate ones, that is, to be aware of the importance of these strategies and how to appraise them. Metacognition emphasizes broad control processes rather than highly specific task strategies. It addresses the problems of students who have been taught appropriate strategies for comprehending but fail to employ them. It enables students to monitor their comprehension on their own—to achieve conscious control of effective strategies independent of the teacher. There are three interrelated metacognitive processes that relate to reading.

1. *Self-knowledge:* recognizing one's strengths and weaknesses in comprehending. The child's view of self as a reader is an instance.
2. *Task knowledge:* knowing the importance of matching a comprehension task with an appropriate reading or memory strategy. Appreciation of having a perceived purpose for reading, a plan for action, and ways to assess progress and to revise are important parts of task knowledge.
3. *Self-monitoring:* being aware whether one has or has not understood the text and knowing the value of what to do when failing to comprehend. The so-called "debugging" practices of backtracking and reading ahead when incomprehensible text is encountered are examples of self-monitoring.

SELF-KNOWLEDGE

Learners have perceptions and feelings about themselves as readers that affect their performance. "Learned helplessness"—the perceived inability to overcome failure—is particularly self-defeating. After "helpless" children experience failure, they tend to attribute their failure to lack of ability. In contrast, successful readers deal with failure in other ways— namely, self-monitoring and reanalysis of the task at hand (Dweck and Licht 1980).

Knowing that learning-disabled children lack context sensitizing, Pascarella and Pflaum (1981) developed a program to teach such children, ages eight to twelve, how to use context information to raise their level of comprehension. The program had two parts. One set of 12 lessons featured error detection. Students learned to identify oral errors that another person made on tape and then to identify their own. (An example of a serious error would be one that caused the meaning to be altered—*back parent* for *back porch*.) Children determined the seriousness of an error first by judging errors made by others while reading and then by judging their own.

The second set of 12 lessons focused on integrating knowledge of meaning from context with phonic cues to identify words and make self-corrections. The results were an increase in the use of context clues, especially for those who read at second-grade level or better.

Inasmuch as the program encouraged students to decide whether errors were serious and self-corrections accurate, we might wonder if such a program would have a different effect on children who do not have a sense of control over their learning. Would students who attribute success to external forces, who see no connection between their efforts and success, be helped or confused when given control in deciding about errors?

Pascarella and Pflaum wondered about this question (Pascerella and Pflaum 1981). They tried to find out whether differences in orientation regarding the sources of success and failure would interact with the strategy. The original program was revised to provide a version in which the teacher determined errors, as well as a version in which the student determined errors. The results were that children who were internally oriented achieved more when the student determined the procedure; externally oriented students had higher scores when the teacher determined errors. However, the results of this study provoke more questions. Can externally oriented children be helped to acquire an internal sense of control that would have long-term learning benefits? Was the training program long enough to effect a change in student's attributions?

I know of no simple solution to the problem of learned helplessness. There are exhortations about the importance of having teachers and students expect success. In addition, the literature of self-worth and school learning offers general principles. Some of the most interesting literature in this area is by Martin Covington and Richard Berry (1976), Richard de Charms (1976), and Bernard Weiner (1971).

Covington and Berry stress the importance of students being free to make errors, to reveal (temporary) ignorance, and to risk trying their hardest. They recommend that students learn to organize their own learning by dividing tasks into manageable subparts, making hard tasks easy by pinpointing the sources of difficulty, and setting performance goals in light of their own purposes.

De Charms and Weiner also point to the positive consequences of giving students control over their own learning. De Charms refers to students who are *origins*—in personal control of events—in contrast with those who are *pawns*—helpless in the hands of others. A person becomes an origin partly because of skillful goal setting, planning, and acceptance of responsibility for actions. Weiner has drawn attention to *locus of control*—whether a person sees achievement as caused by external forces, such as task difficulty and luck, or by forces within, such as ability and effort. Successful students do not view failure as a threat, for it does not necessarily reflect on their ability and can be set right by effort.

Initiation of questions and other behavior associated with the active reader as presented in Chapter 3 are steps toward helping pupils become success-oriented origins rather than pawns. In addition, it is important to let students know the value of asking their own questions and understanding the rationale for particular learning strategies, not just carrying them out.

The child's schema for reading bears on locus of control. Children who perceive the importance of actively seeking and creating meaning from text before, during, and after reading are more likely to enjoy reading than are the students who see themselves controlled by the text.

One way teachers can help students with learned helplessness is to focus less on comprehension as a product (on the child getting correct answers) and to focus more on allowing variation in interpretation of text. When the competition associated with postreading questioning is deflected, reading becomes less threatening. Also, teachers advance the self-knowledge of readers by making interesting books available, letting students choose what to read and encouraging them to read for the purpose of enjoyment—whereby students lose themselves in their books rather than remembering something to be tested on.

Self-efficacy is also enhanced by helping students develop realistic goals, more systematic use of strategies, and a realization of when effort does and doesn't pay off. Students who use multiple tactics to monitor and improve ther comprehension know how to learn effectively rather than just "trying harder."

Evidence that fifth- and sixth-graders can increase their recognition that success is under their own control through the skillful use of their own efforts is found in the Productive Thinking Program (Covington, Davis, Crutchfield, and Ofton 1972).

This program consists of instructional material in which each lesson introduces a complex problem drawn from a range of subject matters. The student is asked to read a selection and attempt to solve a problem it poses. The problems are accompanied by problem-solving strategies for the student to apply—discovering and formulating problems, organizing incoming information, generating ideas, asking effective questions, and reformulating problems in new ways. A story line is maintained through a narrative involving two school children. These story characters are models for the reader. The reader generates his or her own questions and ideas, then the models respond with theirs. The models are not perfect; they make mistakes, but they also profit from them. Children using the productive thinking lessons acquire a sense of their own ability to think and gain confidence in their ideas. They solve increasingly difficult problems (which require hard work), thereby strengthening the link between effort and outcome and reinforcing an image of self as the cause of success.

Exhibit 4.1, a sample page from the Productive Thinking Program, illustrates one of the strategies featured.

Other evidence that poor performance due to children's negative beliefs can be improved lies in the success of short-term interventions that help students attribute reading success to themselves by teaching reading strategies and stressing the importance of using them (Borkowski, Weghing, and Carr 1988). The strategies taught in this intervention were summarizing paragraphs, including the recognition of main ideas and details.

TASK KNOWLEDGE

Task knowledge as an aspect of metacognition is more than knowing a comprehension strategy; it is understanding the significance of the strategy. The assumption is that if the student can connect the use of the strategy

Exhibit 4.1   The Productive Thinking Program: Basic Lesson 13,
                   "The Puzzle of the Deep-Sea Dive"

Jim and Lila are taking a good first step by reflecting a while on the problem before plunging into it.

Did you do this, too, when you worked on the problem by yourself? If not, here is another chance to reflect a bit—to decide just what the *questions* are before you try to come up with *answers*.

Source: From *The Productive Thinking Program* by Martin V. Covington, Lillian Davies, Richard S. Crutchfield, and Robert M. Ofton, Jr. Reprinted by permission of Charles E. Merrill Publishing Co.

to particular results, he or she will use it in the absence of a teacher. The practice of asking students to state what they are doing and why when learning a strategy is one way to help them make the connection. For example, the following dialogue sometimes occurs in teaching a strategy for making inferences:

> *T:* "What is it that we have been doing before we read each story?"
>
> *S:* "We talk about our lives and our experiences with some of the ideas that are in the story and we predict what will happen in the story."
>
> *T:* "Why do we compare our experiences with the ideas given in the story?"
>
> *S:* "The comparison will help us understand the story."

The use of modeling, as in the productive thinking lessons, is another way to connect the use of a strategy with its consequences. The probability of students' applying a strategy on their own is increased if the teacher has had them generalize for themselves the strategy employed by the model and the results that followed. Of course, students need opportunities to see how well they are implementing the strategy and to find out for themselves the benefits that follow.

Task knowledge also means having broad controlling strategies. Three such strategies are self-instruction, question recognition, and reading to remember.

The Strategy of Self-Instruction

Essentially, self-instruction (self-interrogation, verbal monitoring, or thinking aloud) aims at helping learners be aware of their own cognitive processes. Accordingly, students learn to ask themselves questions: "Why am I doing this?" "What am I to do?" "How shall I do it?" "Did I succeed?"

A student who has acquired the self-instruction strategy might approach a specific reading task—say, finding a topic sentence—by asking and answering questions:

- "What is it I have to do?"(problem definition)
- "I have to find the topic sentence of the paragraph."(focusing attention)
- "The topic sentence is what the paragraph is about. I start by looking for a sentence that sums up the details or tells what the paragraph is about."(plan of action)
- "I haven't found it."(evaluation)
- "That's all right."(self-encouragement)
- "The topic sentence might be a definition or a combination of a question and answer."(revision)
- "I'll try my new plan."(coping)

Another example of a self-instructional learning strategy for comprehension: "I've learned three things. First, I ask myself what the main idea of the story is—what the story is about. Second, I learn important details of the story as I go along. The order of the main events and their sequence are important details. Third, I ask myself how the characters feel and why."

In teaching self-instructional strategies, the teacher first models, talking aloud to the class, while attacking a reading task. Next, the students overtly rehearse the strategy shown by the teacher by telling what they are doing while they do it—defining the task, stating what they have to do, focusing their attention, starting their plan of action, revising the plan when the original plan doesn't work, giving themselves verbal reassurance ("I goofed but that's OK"), revising, and trying again.

The overt rehearsals are followed by covert rehearsals. Here, students attack the reading task, but this time they *think* to themselves the questions.

Finally, students practice using the strategy to approach reading tasks in a variety of other materials. The same procedure (modeling, overt rehearsal, covert rehearsal, practice with other material) is carried out with a number of comprehension tasks, such as finding supporting evidence for generalization, locating specific information, inferring tone or mood, and drawing conclusions. In every case, the elements of problem definition, focus, plan of action, evaluation, and coping should be present, if necessary.

Strategies Used at Different Phases of Reading

Some strategies for independent learning are most appropriate at different points in reading:

1. *Before reading:* Preview the material, skimming and examining the title and subheadings. Self-questioning—as in the K-W-L approach where students learn to ask, "What do I *know*?" "What do I *want* to learn?" and "What did I *learn*?"—helps students think about relevant background information and make predictions about text (Ogle 1986).
2. *While reading:* Generate topic sentences about paragraphs and revise ideas to find the gist; when necessary, backtrack to inspect text already read or use context to clarify meanings and to make sense of the text. Reciprocal teaching as presented in Chapter 3 is the most promising way to help students acquire the critical strategies of predicting, clarifying, stating the gist, and monitoring comprehension while reading.
3. *After reading:* Review and reflect about the text, considering, "Did I meet my goal?", "What did I learn?" "Were my predictions right?" "Did everything make sense?" "Can I summarize the main points?"

A Question-Recognition Strategy

Some years ago Edgar Dale described three levels of reading comprehension: (a) *reading the lines,* by which students obtain information explicitly stated; (b) *reading between the lines,* by which students discover implicit meanings of text; and (c) *reading beyond the lines,* whereby students interpret text in terms of their own personal values (Dale 1966). However, before students can engage in reading at these levels, they must know the difference between questions that are directly answerable from text (explicitly stated in text); questions whose answers can be logically inferred from the sentences in the passage (implicitly stated in the text); and questions that can only be answered if the reader's own experiential background suggests the answers (implicit in schema or script).

Pearson and Johnson have proposed a taxonomy for categorizing questions on the basis of their function and the source of likely answers (Pearson and Johnson 1978). This taxonomy suggests an important way for helping students acquire the metacognitive knowledge needed to determine whether questions are answerable and, if they are answerable, how.

The taxonomy features three categories: *text explicit*, *text implicit*, and *script (schemata) implicit*. *Who*, *what*, *where*, *how*, *when* and *why* questions can fit any category, depending upon the text. For example, *why* usually calls for an answer regarding purpose. Purposes, however, may be directly stated, inferred from the sentences, or inferred from the reader's experiences. *What* frequently demands a fact for an answer. Yet, in some contexts, the answer may be stated; and in other contexts, the factual answer can only come from application of personal knowledge.

You may wish to see if you can categorize questions according to the Pearson and Johnson taxonomy. Read the following paragraph and then classify the four accompanying questions as text implicit, text explicit, or schemata implicit. Then compare your answers with those given.

> First were paraded the Indians, painted to their savage fashion, and decorated with tropical feathers, and with their national ornaments of gold. After these were borne various kinds of live parrots, together with stuffed birds and rare plants. Great care was taken to make a conspicuous display of Indian bracelets and other decorations of gold, which might give an idea of the wealth of the newly discovered region. After these, followed Columbus on horseback, surrounded by a brilliant cavalcade of Spanish chivalry.

What is the newly discovered region?
Why were the bracelets displayed?
How did the writer regard the Indians?
Where does the event take place?

The answer to the first question requires background information—a schema for the discovery of a New World by Columbus (script implicit). The second question requires a text explicit answer—to show the wealth of the new region. The answer to the third question is implicit in the text, as indicated by the writer's use of words such as *savage* (wild, uncivilized, animal). The fourth question can be answered by associating the desire to impress with the presence of Spanish chivalry; the answer—Spain—is text implicit.

A program for teaching young children question-answer relationships as a strategy for facilitating correct responses to questions has been developed and implemented by Raphael and Wonnacott(1981). This four-day intensive program introduced pupils to the concept of how questions are related to answers. Questions and corresponding answers from several different texts at each level of the question-answer taxonomy were illustrated. Pupils learned to explain how each category of questions (explicit, implicit, script) applied and how the response information was located. Gradually, pupils provided responses to questions independently.

All materials were based on familiar topics so as to maximize the possibility of success. Implementation of the program resulted in higher performance on a comprehension test and gave evidence that the question-recognition strategy transferred to reading improvement in the content fields.

Taffy Raphael refers to question-answer relationships as QARs (Raphael 1982). As shown in Exhibit 4.2 in Raphael's program, *right there* refers to text explicit questions, *think and search* refers to text implicit questions, and *on my own* refers to schema implicit questions. Little divergence is expected in answers to *right there* QARs. However, more divergence occurs as pupils deal with *think and search* and *on my own* QARs. In learning QARs, the readers should progress from shorter to longer texts, from group to independent activities, and from the easier task of recognizing an answer to the more difficult task of creating a response from more than one source of information. The following is an outline of the four lessons used in training pupils to find where the answers to questions lie.

- *Lesson One:* The first lesson includes four phases: In the first phase, students are given a passage plus questions whose answers and QARs have already been identified. Students discuss why the questions and

Exhibit 4.2   Three Kinds of Questions

Type 1

Where is the answer found?   **Right There**

The answer is in the story, easy to find. The words used to make the questions and the words that make the answer are Right There, in the same sentence.

Type 2   **Think and Search**

The answer is in the story, but a little harder to find. You would never find the words in the question and words in the answer in the same sentence, but would have to Think and Search for the answer.

Type 3   **On My Own**

The answer won't be told by words in the story. You must find the answer in your head. Think: "I have to answer this question On My Own, the story won't be much help."

Source: From "Question-Answering Strategies for Children" by Taffy E. Raphael, *The Reading Teacher,* November 1982. Copyright©1982 International Reading Association. Reprinted with permission of Taffy E. Raphael and the International Reading Association.

answers represent particular QARs. In the second phase, students are given passages, questions, and responses; but this time they identify the QAR for each. In the third phase, students are given other passages and questions and are required to read the passage, decide on the appropriate QAR, and supply the answer to the question.

- *Lesson Two:* Longer passages (75 to 150 words) with up to five questions per passage are used. Students may work through the first passage as a group and then continue independently.
- *Lesson Three:* Passages about the length of a basal reading story are used. A passage is divided into approximately four sections and is followed by six questions, each from a different category.
- *Lesson Four:* Material found in the classroom is used—basal story or social studies or science chapter. Students respond to a long passage (600 to 800 words) accompanied by six questions for each QAR category. Students read the passage, respond to each question by identifying the QAR, and then give the answer.

Later, Raphael modified the QAR program to provide an easier format for considering developmental differences in teaching QARs (Raphael 1985). Students prior to second grade respond best when introduced initially to two sources of information—the book or story and the reader's background knowledge. Middle school students learn the three categories in a single lesson. Thus the modified version for use with very young children calls for students making distinction between "in the book" and "in my head."

A typical teacher comment that accompanies opportunities for students to recognize questions whose answers are in the book is: "Can you point to where in the story it tells you?" Useful comments to accompany opportunities for recognizing schema implicit questions are: *Does the text tell you that? No, then how do you know? Yes, your own experiences tell you.*

When students have a clear picture of the differences between "in the book" and "in my head," each category is further developed. The "in the book" category is expanded to include two types of situations: (1) when the answer is explicitly stated in the text within a single sentence, and (2) when the answer to the question requires the reader to put together information from different parts (think and search, or putting it together). Raphael recommends that the teacher balance explicit and implicit questions. Think and search QARs should dominate because they require integration of information. That is, QARs can be a useful tool for the teacher in thinking about the types of questions that are most appropriate in guiding students through a selection.

From the metacognitive viewpoint, however, the value of the question-answer strategies is the independence they offer. The strategies help the student locate information and determine when an inference is required. Most important, understanding of QARs helps students understand that information from both texts and their own experiences is important when answering questions. Training in the relationship of questions to where answers lie is facilitative for those of average and lower ability levels (Raphael and Pearson 1985). The effective use of lookback strategies (reinspection of text) in question-answering depends on knowing where the answers are; that is, time is lost and the quality of responses diminishes if students reread to find the answer to a reader-based question (Davey 1988). Activity 4.1 gives an opportunity to demonstrate the ability to recognize the kinds of answers sought by particular questions.

Reading to Remember

Any appropriate strategy for remembering requires identification of main points. These main points may be saved in some form—outline, notes, summary. The points should be mentally rehearsed and the text skimmed at a later time. You and I know that persons are less likely to remember ideas that are of less personal interest or that counter preexisting beliefs. But students may have to be made aware of these facts so that they can give such ideas additional attention.

Knowledge of mnemonics is useful in recalling parts of a text. Examples are: saying the item to be remembered over and over, elaborating upon

Activity 4.1   Recognizing the Sources of Answers to Questions

Using the paragraphs and questions below (or a selection of your own choosing), have pupils tell whether the answer to each question is directly stated in the text (text explicit), inferred from the relationships among several sentences (text implicit), or generated primarily from the reader's own background (script implicit).

An animal and a plant are both living things. How can you tell which is which? Do both move? Yes, a daisy folds its petals together at night, and the sunflower moves its head from one side to the other as the sun goes across the sky. How then can you say that a cat is an animal but that the daisy and sunflower are not?

We know that the cat is an animal because it can't make its own food. The green plant can make its own food. An animal like a cat (or a human being, for that matter) can't.

The cat eats all sorts of things—fish, milk, mice, and birds. But that food is already "made." The cat can't join water, gas, and salts together to make the fish and milk. But green plants can make foods, just as complex as these, from the air and from what comes by its roots with the water from the soil.

1. How do we know that a cat is an animal? (answer is text explicit)
2. Why can't animals make their own food? (answer is script implicit)
3. Why do animals have to move about in order to find food while plants can feed best by staying in one place? (answer is text implicit)

the item (making up a meaningful context in which to remember it), and categorizing the information.

Young children tend to overestimate what they will be able to remember. Therefore, one function of metacognitive instruction is to help the child learn about his or her capacity to remember and see how the application of a plan for remembering increases recall.

A generalizable study procedure in most plans is to read until feeling ready for testing and then to self-test. Obviously, the child should recognize that the self-testing must match whatever is important to remember.

Need for Abductive Logic

Abductive logic is a type of reasoning that yields an explanatory hypothesis from a given set of facts. Thus far it is clear that metacognitive strategies have aimed at equipping students to read in ways that agree with the teacher's logic and to use deductive logic in completing set tasks. Even the celebrated Reciprocal Teaching Method has been harnessed to the idea of teaching students how to derive the meanings that teachers value. The questions students are usually taught to ask are "teacherlike" questions prompted by the internalized voice *What question do you think a teacher might ask?*

Metacognitive intervention could be conducted so that students could make abductions, perceive anomalies in test, and generate their own hypotheses. To this end, reciprocal teaching can be modified in several ways:

1. Instead of responding to single paragraphs, students can predict, pose questions, clarify, and summarize the complete text or several texts— or treat a common theme or issue.
2. In their predictive reading, students may be taught to avoid the confirmation bias that comes from focusing only on content that will confirm their predictions. Instead, they may be encouraged to try to refute their predictions. *Is there evidence that your prediction is false?* (Garrison and Hoskisson 1987).
3. Inasmuch as metacognitivists conceive the learner as motivated to explore and seek explanations, reciprocal teaching might expand its focus from narrow questions in a highly structured environment to the broader context of mature tasks where students learn to generate integrative questions important to them and to the solving of significant problems.

SELF-MONITORING

Being aware that one has not understood and knowing what to do about it are metacognitive matters. Self-checking and correcting are associated with good reading. Researchers have attempted to assess students' awareness that they have not understood by deliberately creating errors in the text—disorganizing passages, adding inappropriate transition words and inconsistent sentences—and then observing whether students noted the errors. For example, one group of investigators manipulated the content of simple stories (Owings, Peterson, Bransford, Morris, and Stein 1980). One version contained logical information: *The hungry boy ate a hamburger.* The other version related deliberately arbitrary information: *The hungry boy took a nap.* Successful readers noted that the stories with arbitrary content were more difficult to learn and regulated their study accordingly. Less successful readers did not. In fact, the less successful readers appeared less aware that arbitrary information is harder to learn and did not spontaneously monitor their reading comprehension. Schema theory helps explain the failure. Readers must have a schema that predisposes them to make sure that text makes sense. Further, they must have the relevant schema for whatever they are reading so that they form expectations about the text. Failure to confirm expectations signals a comprehension failure.

Sometimes students may not report inconsistencies and anomalies in text because they assume the writer made a mistake that can be ignored (children can be very generous); or they may draw on prior knowledge to supplement the information incorrectly presented. Perhaps, too, they have been taught not to question the text.

Evaluating one's own comprehension requires a concern for both standards and the process of comprehending. The degree to which one wants to comprehend depends upon one's purpose for reading. If a person is interested only in filling in some detail—such as a figure or location—the standard for comprehension may be low. On the other hand, to assimilate a point of view, a new procedure, or a concept requires a higher standard.

Monitoring comprehension gets better when students have personal reasons for reading the material and when they improve at processing text, that is, noting whether their reading is confirming or refuting their predictions. Self-questioning also helps by clarifying the relevance of what is read. Unless students try to connect the meanings of sentences, they are not likely to detect contradictions and inconsistencies in text. Hence, attempts are made to improve self-evaluation of comprehension by using cooperative learning and peer tutoring to teach the constructive processes underlying it. The literature about cooperative learning and peer tutoring indicates that it benefits all levels of reading comprehension. In one study of peer tutoring, students shared their question-answering strategies in reading expository text, thereby permitting poor comprehenders to become aware of the strategies used by good comprehenders (Gardner, Wagoner, and Smith 1983).

Activity 4.2 suggests a way to use cooperative learning and peer tutoring in enhancing metacognitive strategies.

Carol Capelli and Ellen Markham taught third and sixth-graders to detect inconsistencies by having them read short stories, one sentence at a time, and answer a set of questions after each sentence (Capelli and Markham 1981).

Activity 4.2   Self-Instruction and Monitoring in Cooperative Learning

Activity 4.2 capitalizes on the principle of cooperative peer teaching. Ask each student to select a reading comprehension task that he or she can do—finding the meaning of an unfamiliar word from context, finding a topic sentence, summarizing, predicting from headings, recognizing emotionally laden words, finding bias in text, and others.

Once the task has been selected, ask the student to write an answer to each of the following questions about the task:

1. What is it I have to do? Student defines problem and identifies focus of attention. For example, the problem may require determining the sequence of events.
2. How do I do it? Student forms plan of action. For example, he or she may decide to go about determining the sequence of events by looking for words indicating sequence (*first, next, last*), by imagining the events unfolding, or by anticipating the structure of the story—setting, events, character reaction, character's actions, consequences of the actions.

Children should be asked to answer question 2 by writing what they would say to themselves while trying to solve their chosen tasks. The statement of task and the plan of action should be reviewed. Class discussion of the plan may lead to additional ideas for accomplishing the task. The student who contributed the strategy should demonstrate its application, talking aloud as he or she attempts the task, using an appropriate classroom text. (An appropriate selection offers opportunity to apply the strategy. If the task calls for identifying a sequence of events, there must be a sequence of events in the selection.)

After the tasks have been defined and the strategies reviewed and demonstrated, students exchange tasks and accompanying strategies.

The children were asked to make hypotheses about who the characters were, what was going on, why the characters did what they did, and where the story took place. Initially, the teacher modeled answers to the questions. Next, the children themselves answered the questions. The explicitness of the questions was gradually diminished until the children were simply describing their interpretations, while keeping the questions in mind. Later, the children read stories with inconsistencies and reported the problems they detected. They were to keep the question in mind and "to think about everything that's going on in the story" as they read it.

Once readers recognize that they do not understand—that their purposes are not being met—what should they do? Common strategies for dealing with such difficulty are rereading, continuing reading, and seeking clarification in subsequent sections of the text. Skilled readers know when to keep reading and when to jump back and reread. These readers carry a set of questions and, if the text suggests that these questions will be answered, they continue to read. If too many questions collect, they jump back to the sentences that led to the questions. These sentences they then reread to form a hypothesis that will allow them to cut down the number of unanswered questions. The hypothesis may be quite specific: Is it that a word is not understood? Is the sentence not understood? Does the difficulty lie in the relationships among sentences? Is it a problem because the text contradicts one's own experience and belief?

Skilled readers who encounter textual inconsistencies also spend more time on portions of the material containing the inconsistency, looking back at inconsistent material and at material immediately preceding the inconsistency (Baker and Anderson 1981).

Poor readers fail to engage in spontaneous critical evaluation of text. Therefore, Annemarie Palincsar designed a training program for poor comprehenders that offered explicit instruction in identifying parts of text that were confusing (Palincsar 1984). The approach was to first stimulate discussion among students as to why text is sometimes unclear. Students usually thought of such factors as "hard words." The teacher added unclear referents, disorganized text, and unfamiliar content. Next, the teacher shared with students parts of a passage that they felt required clarification or places where they reread, looked back, or sought other means of bringing meaning to the text. Examples of students' increased sensitivity to the need for clarifying were, "I don't see how they can say heat lightning occurs on hot summer days." "How could you see it?" and "The word *meter* throws me off in the sentence."

SUMMARY

Metacognition is the conscious control of one's thinking about self, task, and the monitoring of performance. The problem of metacognition is to make readers aware of the difference between what they know and what they don't. In reading, metacognition means being aware of what one's purposes for reading are, how to proceed in achieving these purposes, and how to regulate progress through self-checking of comprehension and self-testing.

In this chapter, one aspect of self-knowledge — learned helplessness — is addressed. Productive-thinking lessons are offered as an instructional answer to this problem.

Task knowledge is treated in this chapter as something more than knowing a comprehension strategy; it involves understanding the significance of the strategy — why it works. Techniques for helping readers acquire task knowledge, such as modeling a strategy for making inferences and helping readers form a self-interrogation strategy, are featured. Considerable attention is given to helping readers learn to recognize where the answers to questions can be found and to be conscious of when answers are text explicit, text implicit, or script implicit. Strategies for remembering — using mnemonics, saving main points, and being knowledgeable about one's own

for midterm :
using neumonics
analogies

capacity to remember—are also considered. Future directions in metacognition, such as emphasis on abductive logic, are suggested.

The problem of monitoring and evaluating one's comprehension is examined in some detail, including ways to help readers independently be aware of when they do not understand text inconsistencies. Suggestions are given for helping readers develop awareness of self-questioning procedures and strategies for dealing with difficulties in comprehending text.

REFERENCES

Baker, A., and Anderson, R. *Effects of Inconsistent Information on Text Processing*. Technical Report No. 2031. Urbana: University of Illinois, Center for the Study of Reading, May 1981.

Borkowski, J. G., Weghing, R. S., and Carr, M. "Effects of Attitudinal Retraining on Strategy-based Reading Comprehension in Learning-disabled Students." *Journal of Educational Psychology* 80 (1988): 46–53.

Capelli, C. A., and Markham, E. M. *Improving Comprehension Monitoring Through Training in Hypothesis Testing*. Palo Alto, CA: Stanford University Press, 1981.

Covington, Martin V. and Berry, Richard C. *Self-Worth and School Learning*. New York: Holt, Rinehart and Winston, 1976.

Covington, Martin V., Davies, Lillian, Crutchfield, Richard S., and Ofton, Robert M. *The Productive Thinking Program*. Columbus, OH: Charles Merrill, 1972.

Dale, Edgar. "The Art of Reading." *The Newsletter* 32 (December 1966): 1–4.

Davey, Beth. "The Nature of Response Errors for Good and Poor Readers When Permitted to Reinspect Text During Question Answering." *American Educational Research Journal* 25, no. 3 (Fall 1988): 399–414.

de Charms, Richard. *Enhancing Motivation: A Change in the Classroom*. New York: Irvington Publishers, 1976.

Dweck, C. S., and Licht, B. G. "Learned Helplessness and Intellectual Achievement." In *Human Helplessness: Theory and Applications*, J. Garber and M.E.P. Seligman, editors. New York: Academic Press, 1980.

Gardner, R., Wagoner, S., and Smith, T. "Externalizing Question-Answering Strategies of Good and Poor Comprehenders," *Reading Research Quarterly* 18 (1983): 439–447.

Garrison, James W., and Hoskisson, Kenneth. "Confirmation Bias in Predicting Reading." *The Reading Teacher* 42, no.7 (March 1987): 482–486.

Ogle, D. M. "K-W-L KWL Teaching Model that Develops Active Reading of Expository Text." *The Reading Teacher* 39 (1986): 564–570.

Owings, R., Peterson, G. A., Bransford, J. D., Morris, C. D., and Stein, B. S. "Spontaneous Monitoring and Regulation of Learning: A Comparision of Successful and Less Successful Fifth Graders." *Journal of Educational Psychology* 72 (1980): 250–256.

Palincsar, Annemarie. "The Quest for Meaning from Expository Text." In *Comprehension Instruction*, G. Duffy, L. R. Roehler, and J. Mason, editors. New York: Longman, 1984.

Pascarella, E. T., and Pflaum, S. W. "The Interaction of Children's Attributions and Level of Control over Error Correction in Reading Instruction." *Journal of Educational Psychology* 73 (1981): 533–540.

Pearson, P. David, and Johnson, Dale D. *Teaching Reading Comprehension*. New York: Holt, Rinehart and Winston, 1978. 157–164.

Raphael, Taffy E. "Question-Answering Strategies for Children." *The Reading Teacher* 36 (November 1982): pp. 186–190.

Raphael, Taffy E. "Teaching Question-Answer Relationships, Revisited." Paper presented at International Reading Association, New Orleans, May 1985.

Raphael, Taffy E., and Pearson, David P. "Increasing Students' Awareness of Sources of Information for Answering Questions." *American Educational Research Journal* 22, no. 2 (Summer 1985): 217–235.

Raphael, Taffy E., and Wonnacott, C. A. "Metacognitive Training in Question-Answering Strategies Implemented in a 4th-Grade Developmental Reading Program." Paper presented at the National Reading Conference, Dallas, December 1981.

Weiner, Bernard. "A Theory of Motivation for Some Classroom Experiences." *Journal of Educational Psychology* 71 (1971): 3–25.

Useful Reading

Baker, L., and Brown, A. C. "Metacognition and the Reading Process." In *A Handbook of Reading Research*, P. D. Pearson, editor. New York: Longman, 1984, pp.353–394.

Garner, Ruth. *Metacognition and Reading Comprehension*. Norwood, NJ: Ablex Publishing Company, 1987.

Johnson, Peter H., and Winograd, Peter N. "Passive Failure in Reading." *Journal of Reading Behavior* 27, no. 4 (1985): 279–300.

Paris, S. G., and Winograd, P. "How Metacognition Can Promote Academic Learning and Motivation." In *Dimensions of Thinking and Cognitive Instruction*, vol. 1. Hillsdale, NJ: Erlbaum, 1991.

Elaboration in Reading

OVERVIEW

Comprehension can be improved by deep processing of text material. One form of deep processing is elaboration—the embellishing of what is read. Strategies for elaborating include using mental imagery, drawing inferences, notetaking, and summarizing text in one's own words. Elaboration rests on the hypothesis that when readers actively integrate new information with existing knowledge, greater storage and use of the new material will result. Although some theorists believe that elaboration works because it increases learners' interests, others attribute its effectiveness to the fact that elaboration strategies draw readers' attention to what is relevant. Still others say that elaboration is effective because it activates learners' relevant schemata, thereby allowing the new information to be incorporated into their sets of past experiences.

In this chapter you will have the opportunity to learn about strategies for encouraging elaboration and to discover for yourself their value in comprehending text.

USING MENTAL IMAGERY IN COMPREHENDING TEXT

Generally, comprehension increases when readers create images for the information they get while reading. Pressley taught eight-year-olds to construct mental pictures for the sentences and paragraphs they read (Pressley 1976). Compared with a control group whose members read the story, the imagery group recalled more of the story's events. Similarly, more inferences were made by older students who were taught to create images of what was happening as they read technical text (Mayer 1980). However, a few researchers report inconsistent results from attempts at imagery instruction. Jeannette Miccinate carried out an imagery program that had both auditory and visual components. She first taught students to draw simple stick figures representing the images generated as they listened to various passages on tape. Then students were asked to draw their own images as they read. This imagery training did not affect the comprehension of students as measured by a standardized achievement test (Miccinate 1982). However, it is not clear whether the tests included high-imagery sentences and passages.

Keys to effective image-making seem to lie in forming mental pictures of persons, events, or information to be learned. Readers must know the purposes of the material, its relationship to their own experiences, and the logical relationships among the ideas expressed. Training students to image *separate* sentences may differ from training them to generate an image that *connects* sentences. As in the case of other elaborating techniques (note-taking, outlining, underlining) successful imaging requires that the ideas singled out for attention be the important ones. Some children comprehend by acting out their reading through drawing or painting. Some close their eyes and "see."

Mind's Eye is a set of procedures for helping students to find out what is important and to transform text into vivid mental images. The materials were developed by persons in the Escondido School District, who report that yearly average comprehension gains tripled after the technique was introduced.

The *Mind's Eye* procedure consists of these elements: (Escondido School District 1979).

1. *Key words:* Children are taught to recognize important words in sentences and passages. Initially, key words are underlined, and students automatically pick up key words and simultaneously create images for them.
2. *Discussion of images:* After silent reading of key words, students are asked questions that help them make clear mental pictures: *What do you see? Tell me about your picture. What else can you see?* The discussion questions may also develop anticipation: *What do you think will happen next?*

3. *Oral reading:* After discussion of their mental images, students read orally for fluency and for verifying that their images fit the text.

Mind's Eye procedure may be used with individuals, small groups, or an entire class. The following accounts were prepared by teachers using *Mind's Eye:*

Teacher X

Preparation

I worked with third-, fourth-, and fifth graders for a period of two weeks to help them with visualization skills. I had them try to get different pictures for different words I would say. I used words such as *apple, rose,* or *peach.* The children were told to form a picture from these words and try to sense the feel, the touch, and the smell of the word. Thus from the word *apple,* the children would get the idea that an apple is big, round, and usually red. If you had never seen an apple, then the descriptive words would be important words; however, the word *apple* should create a mental image immediately in most of us. This way the children will spend less time trying to decode the word and spend more time making pictures as they read only a few words.

Also as part of the preparation, I told the children that they did not need to read every word in the sentence to get a picture. They only needed a few words per sentence or line to form a picture in their minds.

Procedure

I first arranged the children in a group and explained to them about *Mind's Eye.* I then showed them how to underline just a few important words per line, the ones needed to get a picture in their minds. The children underlined a few words per line and were instructed to *read only the words they underlined.* We then discussed the pictures they had in their minds and each student shared his picture. After reading several paragraphs each student then reads aloud. I had each student read some of the material—just read silently and compare oral pictures with silent pictures.

There were some words the children had to be shown to underline, such as negative words; if these words are left out, the meaning of the story is changed.

I found with my third-graders or slower readers that they were having trouble picking out the important words. I took some of the stories that we were reading and blocked out the unimportant words. Then they read the stories with just the important words showing, and they seemed to be able to get better pictures. After we discussed the pictures they had, I then showed them the whole story and we talked about whether or not the pictures were different. They found out that their pictures were basically the same.

My fourth- and fifth-graders were able to pick up underlining much faster, and we were able to move on to the next stage. I then told them as they were reading to themselves to do the same thing as they had been doing with the pencil—only reading the important words.

Observations

I found that the younger the students were, the more beginning instruction was needed. The slower readers spent more time underlining before moving on to the next stage, while the faster readers needed only to underline for a couple of days. When there was a faster reader in the group, he had to wait for the others or be allowed to continue on his own.

Teacher Y

Setting

Begin with a group of four to six students. (Several small groups like these may be combined once the procedure has been learned.) Work with the group for a period of fifteen to twenty minutes. During this time, the rest of the class may be working at their desks.

Day One

Introduction to the Mind's Eye program—Explain to the students that when reading silently, it is not necessary to know every word in order to understand what is taking place in the story. Tell them that they are going to learn to make "pictures" or a "movie" of the stories as they read them. Discuss what is meant by important or key words—those words necessary to for a clear picture in their minds.

The story—Begin with a short story, one or two pages. Have the students underline important words in the first few sentences or first paragraph. Instruct them to form a mental image of what they are reading as they underline. Encourage them to underline as few words as necessary to make a clear picture. When all students are finished, choose one student to explain his picture to the group. When that student is through, ask if anyone has anything to add. At this point, if you notice any students who have underlined too many or not enough words, take the time to review the concept of important words and what makes them important. Continue with underlining the important words and discussing the picture for the remainder of the period. Each time the students complete their picture-telling, you may wish to choose a student to read orally the passage just discussed. Other students may follow along or close their eyes and form a picture. This procedure often helps to clarify if the students have been unable to come up with a complete or accurate picture.

Day Two

If you did not complete the story in the previous session, take a moment to briefly review what took place and recall the pictures. Do not take too much time in review. Continue with the procedure followed in Day One. It is not necessary to ready orally every passage, as this sometimes impedes progress through the story and causes lack of interest. If all of the students develop an inaccurate or incomplete picture, it is helpful to ask them to scan the section for a particular point. Then ask one student to read that sentence of paragraph aloud. You should be increasing the amount read between discussions. The amount the students can read and still get good pictures will vary with each group and is left to the teacher's discretion.

Day Three

Students might be able to stop underlining and simply point to important words with a pencil or card. You will be able to tell if it is too soon for this change by the kinds of pictures the students are making. It may be necessary to go back to underlining with slower groups; however, it is encouraged that the students move away from underlining as soon as they can. This will allow them to begin working in books where they will not be able to underline. Other than this change, the same procedure as in Day One and Two should be followed.

Day Four and Beyond

If the students are making clear pictures, it may be possible to start them in a short book with short chapters. *If you do not feel they are ready, continue with the above procedure for a few more sessions.* It is not necessary that all students read the same book, but in order to get a good idea of the students' accuracy in picture making, the teacher should have read the book. Allow students to read independently, moving their own cards down the page, covering up what they have already read. They are to continue reading until they are called up for a conference. In the conference the teacher allows the student to describe his picture. Then he or she may read a section orally to the teacher.

Children benefit from being asked to make up pictures after reading an entire story. Drawing pictures to illustrate these mental images may help children process text information and relate new information to background knowledge. It is generally better for readers to think of their own pictures than to have pictures given to them. A common practice is for the teacher to give a few examples and then encourage students to form their own. The teacher may help students initially by asking them to suggest more about a central character, situation, or process than is revealed by the author. For example, after reading the sentence, *It was summer and Tony and Carla were going shopping,* students might be asked, "What do you think they were wearing?" "Who is taller?" Obviously, such questions call for inferences as well as mental imagery.

Two final comments on imagery center on spontaneous imagery and the value of imagery training for recognition of textual inconsistencies. There is evidence that students who report using imagery without instruction to do so are more likely to understand complex relationships in prose than students who do not report using representional images (Sadoski 1985).

With respect to the effect of imaging upon the ability to notice textual inconsistencies, experimenters taught fourth- and fifth-graders to construct images representing prose, and later they were asked to read short stories to determine if they made sense: "Make pictures in your mind to help determine if there is anything that is not clear and easy to understand about the story."

Activity 5.1   Assessing the Value of Visual Imagery

General Procedures

1. Select a passage (paragraph, story, article) that you would like your students to know about. The passage should be unfamiliar to the pupils. Try to select a passage that you think give rise to imagery.
2. Randomly divide your class into two groups (assigning every other name in the roll book to the same group works well).
3. Read the entire passage to both groups. Then ask members of one group to draw simple pictures depicting the event described in the passage. Members of the other group may draw pictures of something they like a lot.
4. Collect the pictures and note whether those who illustrated the passage depicted accurate and relevant information or not. Did they relate ideas expressed in the passage?
5. Several days later, ask members of both groups to write a summary of the passage.
6. Score the summaries on the basis of number of central ideas and events recalled.
7. Average and compare the scores earned by the two groups.

Analyzing the Results

According to cognitive theory, the overall performance of the group that drew pictures depicting the ideas and events of the passage should be better than that of the group that drew unrelated pictures. The construction of the image is supposed to help the reader integrate and remember the text. Perhaps the results will not be so clear for children younger than eight years old. Some children below this age have difficulty in generating images when instructed to do so.

You should examine the results to see if children thought to be poor readers did as well with the imagery condition as good readers did without it. When analyzing your data, you may wish to include in your imagery group averages only the scores for persons who were able to depict accurate and relevant images.

After reading the stories, students were probed to determine if they had detected inconsistencies. The results showed that imagery-trained children were more likely to detect inconsistencies than those not so trained (Gambrell and Baler 1986).

Activity 5.1 will enable you to see for yourself how an imagery technique will enhance pupil comprehension.

MAKING INFERENCES WHILE ELABORATING

The poorest performance on reading tests is elicited by items that demand inference—the derivation of some idea that is not directly stated. John Carroll has suggested three ways for deriving inferences from passages (Carroll 1969). First, a reader can infer meaning from the subtleties of verbal expression: *She was a viscountess, but he was only a baron*. Even if you do not know the ranks of the British peerage, you can tell that viscountesses are higher in rank than barons. How? By linguistic awareness of the word *only*.

Similarly, Roger Shank's favorite example of how people make inferences involves the word *but*. He thinks the word *but* basically means *call off the inference*. If you say, "I ate dinner but I'm still hungry," the *but* says that the usual inference (that you are satisfied after eating) isn't true in this case (Shank 1983).

Second, in other instances, a reader derives inferences through reasoning. *Bill isn't as tall as Mary but he's much taller than Steve*. Who is the tallest?

Third, inferences are made by involving the reader's personal experience to determine how characters in text might feel:

> The delight that Tad had felt during his long hours in the glen faded as he drew near the cabin. The sun was nearly gone and Tad's father was at the woodpile. He was wearing his broadcloth suit that he wore to church and to town sometimes. He was doing Tad's work and in his good clothes. Tad ran to him. "I'll get it, Pa."

When Tad saw his father, did he feel (a) disappointed, (b) important, (c) angry, (d) guilty? To infer that Tad felt guilty, the reader must not only understand the surface level of the paragraph but also apprehend the total situation.

Schema theory addresses the question of how we apprehend the deeper facts and relationships that lurk in text. This theory posits that most of what we read represents a stereotyped sequence of actions or events. Our familiarity with the schema allows us to infer the appropriate connections (Reder 1980). *John knew his wife's operation would be very expensive. There was always Uncle Henry. He reached for the phone book.* Comprehension of this passage may rest on a "raising money for important expenditures" schema evoked by the words.

In addition to helping readers infer omitted details, a schema helps them elaborate the text. That is, readers may generate thoughts consistent with the schema invoked but not necessarily supported in any way by the text. In the above example, inferences might be made about how the couple felt about each other and about the nature of the operation; many other elaborations might be based on the reader's own experience with such situations.

Elaborations from inference serve important functions. They help us find connections among sentences; they generate expectations about subsequent information; and they aid retention. To illustrate the inferences children must make when reading, consider this paragraph and then answer the question that follows:

> The Benchley family was out riding with their German Shepherd. After they pulled onto the shoulder to change drivers, young Marie slipped and broke her

ankle. They raced to the hospital and were getting out of the car when they noticed that Shep was missing.

What happend to Shep? If you answered the question at all, you did as well as a kindergarten child whom John Guthrie asked this question (Guthrie 1979). If you could provide details of how Shep got lost, you performed as well as two third-graders and one fifth-grader.

The question and answer seem simple, but the necessary inferences are substantial. Here are some of them: Benchleys had (probably owned) a dog that they cared about. Everyone in the family was healthy and happy. They were riding down the highway in a car and decided to change drivers, which required stopping the car. Two people got out of the car; both walked around it and got back in. While the car was stopped, the doors were opened. Marie got out and slipped hard enough to break an ankle. After they discovered that she had broken her ankle, the Benchleys hurried to a hospital. Getting to a hospital fast is important. Hurried people close doors quickly. In normal circumstances, attention is broadly deployed. When there is no threat, injury, or unbalance in their equilibrium, people attend to many different happenings. When a problem occurs, however, attention is focused on it. Also, people are more important than dogs; an injury is especially important, and an injured person commands more attention than a healthy dog. In an accident, the Benchleys paid close attention to the injured person. As the problem was partly solved by getting to the hospital, attention was broadened to include Shep and to note that he was missing.

The process of elaborating aids long-term retention. If passages are richly elaborated during reading, then only a few statements need be retrieved for the gist of the original text to be recalled. If teachers provide students with information that makes it easier to elaborate a given text, students will remember more about it.

One major difference between poor readers and good readers is the speed with which they make inferences and elaborate. Recommendations for improving their speed include the following:

1. Make sure that children are aware that there is a difference between the literal meaning of a text and the deeper meaning that is found in the inferences drawn from it. Although children constantly draw inferences in real life, they don't seem to realize fully the need for drawing inferences from their reading. Many readers spend much time looking for a directly stated answer in the text when the answer to the question must be inferred.

2. Illustrate the drawing of inferences over and over again, using a variety of textual materials (e.g., literature, newspaper stories, editorials). With repeated exposure to situations, the reader develops stereotyped generalizations that allow formation of a well-constructed causal chain to predict behavior.

3. Give children much practice in drawing inferences so they can automatically infer the important information necessary for comprehending what follows in a text.

Eileen Wood and fellow researchers have shown that the learning of arbitrary facts from texts can be improved by asking students to answer *why* questions about the facts in the text (Wood, Pressley, and Winne 1990). For example, children who were prompted to elaborate upon their reading (e.g., give an explanation of why a particular animal lived in a stated locale) demonstrated more learning of the facts than children who were not asked to elaborate. Although producing any elaborative answer is better than producing no answer, the quality of a student's elaboration influenced recall.

Jane Hansen and David Pearson have shown us an interesting way to help children draw inferences from their reading (Hansen and Pearson 1982). Their strategy and questioning procedure enhanced the ability of children to answer comprehension questions about stories and to become better at drawing essential inferences from text by encouraging them prior to reading to discuss personal experiences related to the topic of the selection and to predict what might happen in the story. Additionally, they discussed with the students why they were doing these activities, "because comprehension is easier when you compare what happens in the text to what you already know." There was no conclusive evidence that the procedures resulted in students' spontaneously applying the strategy in reading unfamiliar stories. However, the procedures have been combined and tried with good and poor readers and in other contexts; the results suggest that inferential instruction may be especially well suited for poor readers.

Similarly, in a study teaching fifth-graders a variety of strategies to improve inferential comprehension, the use of a cloze procedure, whereby students learned to fill in words in a cloze passage using their prior knowledge, was more effective in generating inferences and in helping students apply the strategies in other situations (transfer) than (a) learning to use structured overviews to relate text with prior knowledge or (b) using a self-monitoring checklist (Dewitz, Carr, and Patberg 1987) .

A PROCEDURE FOR HELPING STUDENTS INFER

The intent of inference training lessons is to make students aware of the importance of drawing inferences to link new information with their existing knowledge. To this end, the teacher identifies one or more key ideas implicit in the selection to be read. This idea becomes the basis for discussion prior to reading—a discussion in which children have the opportunity to report their experience with the idea. Often, the idea is presented in the form of a problem or story. The discussion activates schemata for children to use in making inferences as they read. More than that, the knowledge recalled is used to make predictions about what might happen in the story. Students hypothesize about what the protagonist will do in a situation similar to one they themselves have experienced. Next, the children read the selection and then engage in another discussion in which they answer inferential questions suggested by the text. The following illustration involves a lesson in which the students are to read Ouida Sebestyen's *IOU'S* (Sebestyen, 1982).

Key Idea

Before having students read the book *IOU'S*, the teacher identifies two themes: (a) the possibility that a child may have a teasing, affectionate relationship with a parent rather than see parents as adversarial authorities and (b) the way people may dam up their feelings to avoid losing someone's approval and to keep things as they are.

I. *Prereading Discussion*
   A. *Purpose*
   Students know the purpose for the prereading discussion and re-mind themselves of what they are doing and why. "Before we read, we talk about our lives—those parts that relate to what the story is about." "We also predict what will happen in the story." "We compare our experiences with what takes place, so that we will better understand the story."
   B. *Questions for Activating Background Experiences*
   "Have you ever had a friend whose relationship with parents is different from your relationship with your parents?" "How was it different?" "In the story that we will read, Stowie's friend Brownie questions the way Stowie acts toward his mother—and his need for his mother's approval."
   C. *Hypothesis*
   "On the basis of your own experiences, do you think Stowie will pursue his own way even if it isn't what his mother thinks?" "Will his mother help Stowie expose himself to the fear of losing her affection?"
II. *Postreading Questions*
   "Why did Stowie not tell his mother that his grandfather was ill?" "Did Stowie mean it when he said, 'Let me be better to her than they were; I want to make it up to my mother'?"

Similar formats can be followed for expository material. For example, in introducing factual material about three-dimensional shapes, the teacher might activate students' backgrounds by drawing approximations of the shapes—sphere, hemisphere, cube, cylinder, or cone—on the chalkboard and asking, "Of what does each of these shapes remind you?" Prediction would follow, and the teacher might make such comments as the following. "In this chapter you will learn how many sides each shape has and what the sides look like." "On the basis of your experience with cylinders, will the cross-section be circular?" "What will the sides be?" "What shape will the longitudinal section be?"

OTHER WAYS TO ELABORATE TEXT

Merl Wittrock has written extensively on the importance of generative activities that lead students to construct relations among the parts of the text and between the text and their personal knowledge and experience. In one of his studies, 400 sixth-graders were asked to write, in their own words, a sentence about each of several paragraphs immediately after reading them. In addition, some groups of children were given paragraph headings, either to be incorporated into their sentences or omitted from them. The generation of their own sentences was expected to facilitate the students' construction of relationships among experience, knowledge, and the text. The paragraph headings were intended to serve as cues for relevant schemata. Results of the study show that a combination of both sentence generation and use of headings was the most effective in enhancing retention and comprehension, followed by sentence generation, and then use of headings. The use of paragraph headings was more effective with the better readers, whereas the sentence generation was better with the poorer readers. The combination of the two methods doubled comprehension for children of various levels of reading ability (Wittrock, Marks, and Doctorow, 1975; Wittrock, 1990).

It appears that elaboration requires the learner to create a construction that, when combined with new information, gives this information more meaning. Underlining, notetaking, and categorizing are important ways to induce elaborations. This is so at least when the reader is able to identify the main ideas by underlining or otherwise singling out. Rewriting parts of a selection in order to produce different conclusions, giving analogies, providing examples, and writing summaries are other valuable activities that enhance elaboration and comprehension. Similarly, teachers can ask students to identify parts of a selection that are of personal significance by asking, "What important points have been left out?" "Why are these points important?" "What would happen if people did what the author suggests?" "Before we read the story, you told me _____ ; now what do you think about _____ ?"

Asking students questions *after* reading will help them retain both the information that answers the questions and other information addressed while reading the text. Applying information and ideas gained from reading to other situations is a powerful means of elaboration. Providing opportunities for students to relate reading to writings, drama, and discussions is valuable; and encouraging them to use the new content in out-of-school situations, such as reading to the blind and sharing their new knowledge with fathers and mothers, is an effective learning strategy.

Claire Weinstein has recommended that teachers foster the use of elaboration strategies by encouraging a broad list of questions representing a variety of different techniques (analogy, transformation, comparing-contrasting):

> What is the main idea of this story?
> If I lived during this period, how would I feel about my life?
> If the principle were not true, what would that imply?
> What does this remind me of?
> How could I use this information in the project I'm working on?
> How could I represent this in a diagram?
> How do I feel about the author's opinion?
> How could I tell this in my own words?
> What might be an example of this?
> How could I teach this to my dad?
> Where else have I heard something like this?
> If I were going to interview the author, what would I ask her?
> How does this apply to my life?
> Have I ever been in a situation where I felt like the main character? (Weinstein, et al. 1988).

GOING BEYOND THE AUTHOR'S INTENTIONS

Traditional testing in reading usually assumes there is a single right answer to each question. In contrast, an interactive view of reading holds the possibility that other answers may be acceptable, inasmuch as meaning is always a mediation between the worlds of the author and the reader. The reader makes an assessment of the text as a whole using the perspective available to him or her. Yet, collision with the material itself may influence the reader's preconceptions, resulting in what someone once termed "a fusion of horizons." If you accept the idea that meaning is not only to be found in the text but in interaction between the text and the reader, then you are obligated to find out how the child is interpreting the text. A child's answer is not an error just because it does not match someone else's expectations.

What children bring to their reading by way of elaboration is wondrous. Different people may use different logic to connect the same two events. John Guthrie tells about hearing two fifth-graders discussing a story about Robert Frost (Guthrie 1979). Frost was working as a farmer and seemed to be thoroughly enjoying himself by endlessly fiddling around with words. One child said that Frost's fiddling was understandable because Frost was seeking self-expression. The other child said that he did not think that fiddling with words was strange since Frost would probably write some good poems and sell them for a lot of money. These children had distinct but logical ways of interpreting Frost's fiddling with words.

Idiosyncratic responses to text can be dealt with in several ways:

1. Accept initially the child's statement about the text and then explore with the child the ramifications of the statement. In the process, the statement may be modified by the child. However, this does not mean that it is necessary for the children to abandon their own perceptions or to ignore their feelings and associations. Readers may find different themes in the same selection that reflect both the content and a reader's unique viewpoint. In admitting the validity of alternative interpretations, teachers allow the story to have more personal significance for the child and to influence the child's perceptions.

2. Accept an emotional reaction to the text, but have the child examine the assumptions underlying the reaction.

3. Teach the child procedures to better understand what the writer was trying to say. By way of example, Alan Purves offers a schema by which one can derive meaning from a literary work (Purves 1979). The schema consists of seven heuristics (problem-solving strategies) for deriving the theme for a difficult text, *The Heart of Darkness:* (a) Assume the importance of Marlowe and look at all his generalizations; (b) assume the importance of the title and examine the use of *heart* and *darkness;* (c) look for juxtaposition and stated or implied comparisons; (d) look for repetitions of word or event; (e) look at the motif of the story and for analogies in other journeys; (f) look at the structure of the story (the frame tale) and determine the relationship of frame to tale; (g) explain a particular character and see if he or she embodies a theme.

The issue of multiple interpretations of text is considered in Chapter 6, which includes the structuring of schemata and the social construction of texts in classroom discussion. The importance of using other texts, personal experiences and other students' interpretations in forming one's own interpretations has been shown (Rogers 1988).

Activity 5.2 is designed to illustrate the idea that individuals derive different meanings from the same text material, to give you an opportunity to practice dealing with differences in interpretation, and to explain these differences in terms of individual schemata.

SUMMARY

Elaboration is especially important *while* reading, although in the form of orienting instructions, priming questions, and summaries, it can be applied *before* and *after* reading. The more elaborations generated, the greater the recall of what is read. The amount of elaboration can be influenced by instructions—the giving of background information, the encouraging of imagery, and the preparation of summaries. Relevant background knowledge

Activity 5.2 Deriving Meaning from Print—Individual Variations

Are you entitled to read into a poem or other text material anything you choose? While no two people respond in exactly the same way and while one person may see deeper meanings in a text than another, we should be able to support what we get out of a text by reference to what it actually says.

By looking very closely at what authors literally say and the way they say it, you may perceive meanings, fully supported by the texts, that the authors themselves have not seen. However, in making you own meaning, you have to stick to what is on the page.

General procedures

(Note: Elementary school teachers may select a poem that is more appropriate for their pupils.)

1. Read William Wordsworth's *The World*. Pay regard to (a) the main idea of the poem; (b) the attitude toward nature; (c) the attitude toward humankind; (d) the form, language, and manner of expression; and (e) the relevancy of the poem to your own condition.

   The World
   The world is too much with us; late and soon,
     Getting and spending, we lay waste our powers:
   Little we see in Nature that is ours;
   We have given our hearts away, a sordid boon!
   This Sea that bares her bosom to the moon;
     The winds that will be howling at all hours,
     And are up-gather'd now like sleeping flowers;
   For this, for everything, we are out of tune;
   It moves us not.—Great God! I'd rather be
     A Pagan suckled in a creed outworn;
   So might I, standing on this pleasant lea,
     Have glimpses that would make me less forlorn;
   Have sight of Proteus rising from the sea;
     Or hear Triton blow his wreathed horn.

2. Compare your response with those of your colleagues. What concepts and inferences account for your differences in interpretation? Did you or your colleagues use any of Purves' seven heuristics in determining the main ideas? Which did you use? Was each person's interpretation supported by the text? Do some persons have literary schemata that enabled them to gain more meaning from the poem than others? Describe some of these schemata.

---

is a prerequisite to drawing the required inferences, and inferences and elaborations made during reading should relate to what is to be remembered. Elaboration should focus on critical statements in a text, not on unimportant ones. Readers who learn to automatically draw inferences and elaborate upon key aspects of text will greatly improve their comprehension.

REFERENCES

Carroll, John B. "From Comprehension to Inference." In *Claremont Reading Conference,* Malcolm Douglas, editor, 33rd yearbook Claremont CA: Claremont Graduate School, 1969.

Dewitz, P., Carr, E., and Patberg, J. "Effects of Inference Training on Comprehension and Comprehension Monitoring." *Reading Research Quarterly* 29 (1987): 99–119.

Escondido School District, *Mind's Eye.* Escondido, CA: Board of Education, 1979, p. 55.

Gambrell, C. B., and Baler, R. J. "Mental Imagery and the Comprehension-monitoring Performance of Fourth-and Fifth-Grade Poor Readers." *Reading Research Quarterly* 21 (1986): 454–464.

Guthrie, John. "Purpose and Text Structure." *The Reading Teacher* 32 (February 1979): 315, 624–626.

Hansen, Jane, and Pearson, P. David. "An Instructional Study: Improving the Inferential Comprehension of Fourth-Grade Good and Poor Readers." *Journal of Educational Psychology* 75 (1983): 821–829. Technical Report No. 235. Urbana, IL: University of Illinois, Center for the Study of Reading, 1982.

Mayer, R. E. "Elaboration Techniques That Increase the Meaningfulness of Technical Text: An Experimental Test of the Learning Strategy Hypothesis." *Journal of Educational Psychology* 72 (1980): 770–784.

Miccinate, J. "The Influence of a Six-Week Imagery Training Program on Children's Reading Comprehension." *Journal of Reading Behavior* 14, no. 2 (1982): 197–203.

Pressley, G. M. "Mental Imagery Helps Eight-Year Olds Remember What They Read." *Journal of Educational Psychology* 68 (1976): 355–359.

Purves, Alan. *Putting Readers in their Places: Some Alternatives to Cloning Stanley Fish.* ERIC Document ED 1799 74 (1979).

Reder, L. M. "The Role of Elaboration in the Comprehension and Retention of Prose: A Critical Review." *Review of Educational Research* 50 (Spring 1980): 5–53.

Rogers, T. "Students as Literary Critics: A Case Study of the Interpretive Theories, Processes, and Experiences of Ninth-Grade Students." Ph.D. diss., University of Illinois, 1988.

Sadoski, M. "The Natural Use of Imagery in Story Comprehension and Recall: Replication and Extension." *Reading Research Quarterly* 20 (1985): 258–667.

Sebestyen, Ouida. *IOU'S.* Boston: Little, Brown, 1982.

Shank, Roger. "A Conversation with Roger Shank." *Psychology Today* 17 (April 1983): 28–36.

Weinstein, Claire E., Ridley, D. S., Tove, D., and Weber, S. "Helping Students Develop Strategies for Effective Learning." *Educational Leadership* 46, no. 4 (Dec. 1988 Jan. 1989): 17–19.

Wittrock, M. C., Marks, C. B., and Doctorow, M. J. "Reading as a Generative Process." *Journal of Educational Psychology* 67 (1975): 484–489.

Wittrock, M. C. "Generative Processes of Comprehension." *Educational Psychologist* 24, no. 4 (1990): 345–376.

Wood, Eileen, Pressley, Michael, and Winne, Philip H. "Elaborative Interrogation Effects on Children's Learning of Factual Content." *Journal of Educational Psychology* 82, no. 4 (1990): 741–748.

Useful Reading

Carr, Eileen, Dewitz, Peter, and Patberg, Judythe. "Using Cloze for Inference Training with Expository Text." *The Reading Teacher* 42 (1989): 380–385.

Cunningham, James A. "Toward a Pedagogy of Inferential Comprehension and Creative Responses." *Understanding Readers' Understanding: Theory and Practice*. R. J. Tierney, P. L. Anders, and J. Mitchell, editors. Hillsdale, NJ: Lawrence Erlbaum, 1987, 229–255.

Weinstein, Claire E., and Mayer, R. E. "The Teaching of Learning Strategies." in *Handbook of Research on Teaching,* 3rd edition, M. C. Wittrock, editor. New York: Macmillan, 1986, 315–327.

6

Restructuring Schemata

OVERVIEW

Thus far this book has emphasized schema theory as it contributes to *assimilation,* by which new information from reading is fitted into existing schemata, the adding of information to what one already knows and believes; that is, "new wine is placed in old bottles." Now we consider *accommodation*—the restructuring of schemata, modification of one's beliefs, and refutation of one's knowledge—"new bottles for new wine."

Assimilation in reading demands that the reader interpret something using an existing schema, answering questions such as *How does this add to what I already know?* On the other hand, accommodation demands suspending judgment, or withholding interpretation. Accommodation implies the possibility that the reader's schemata may shift. It requires answering questions such as *What is the author's perspective? What evidence does the*

88

author offer for the new propositions? Do the new propositions address my fundamental concerns better than my present way of thinking and acting?

Students come to school with schemata acquired from many cultural sources (TV, parents, friends) and with the capacity to be involved in what they read. Sometimes the schemata based on the students' everyday experiences conflict with the concepts met in reading, as is clear from the ways students conceive of the phenomena they read about in science classes. Thus the teacher is faced not with a problem of helping the student absorb new information but with a problem of modifying the whole or large parts of the student's cognitive structure. Children rarely use the text to update their knowledge if the new information conflicts with their present views (Lipson 1984). In addition, Donna Alvermann and others have found that, if children's prior knowledge is incompatible with the ideas in the text, activating it will interfere with reading comprehension (Alvermann et al., 1985).

When there are discrepancies between the knowledge structures of the readers and reality as perceived by the author, the readers either fail to learn, forget what they have read (but only after they have completed the examination on the material, of course), or unknowingly misinterpret what they have read so that the new information does not conflict with their earlier ideas. This is not to say that children's own thinking is to be disregarded or that children must be forced to correct schemata. In this chapter, emphasis is placed on readers' viewpoints and, where appropriate, on procedures to modify them. Most of these procedures are not designed to puncture a child's theory, but to offer opportunities for gathering evidence so the child will revise schemata without outside intervention.

IDENTIFYING CONFLICTING CONGITIVE STRUCTURES

The late Roger Osborne and John Gilbert explored the scientific understandings of students that differ from scientists' viewpoints (Osborne and Gilbert 1980). They found that students hold incongruous beliefs. For example, when asked about the forces on a person in a satellite, many students, even some as old as 19, said there was no air in space and, therefore, no gravity. Such informal knowledge (or schemata), which conflicts or interferes with subsequent learning from text, has been described by a variety of terms: intuitive conceptions, misconceptions, naive theories, and alternative frameworks. The difficulty of modifying these schemata has been shown in many studies (Anderson and Smith 1987).

In one study it was found that after six to eight weeks of instruction on the topic of photosynthesis, only 7 percent of 229 fifth-graders were able to explain that plants get their food by making it themselves (Roth and Anderson 1990). Students won't change their beliefs about plants by simply *adding* information about photosynthesis to their prior knowledge.

The knowledge structures of students are frequently not the structures authors and teachers assume students have. Readers' views of the world and meanings for words are not isolated ideas but conceptual structures by which the readers make sense of their lives. The more teachers know about and appreciate the cognitive structures of their students, the more they will be able to provide learning opportunities for modifying the structures.

The reader's schema has a big effect on what is remembered, as indicated in schema-consistent distortions. In a study of the biasing effects of beliefs on memory, people who were either strongly for or strongly against nuclear power read a text about a fire at a nuclear power plant (Read and Rosen n.d.). Although both groups of readers showed little difference on a test given immediately after the story, they did remember different facts about the reading when the test was given two weeks later. Those who were opposed to nuclear power correctly rejected spurious pronuclear statements but accepted incorrect antinuclear statements. Those who favored nuclear power produced the opposite pattern of results.

In Chapter 2 we referred to Marlene Schommer's finding that students' beliefs about the nature of knowledge affected their comprehension in important ways. Other studies have shown that dogmatic learners with closed minds are less likely to be affected by the content and implications of text than less dogmatic, open-minded learners (Richards and Slife 1987). It is not clear whether highly dogmatic persons can become more flexible to change through the use of, for example, supplementary materials that provide views that contrast with those in the textbook.

FORMING AND CHANGING SCHEMATA

There are three views of how schemata are formed and changed. Exhibit 6.1 outlines a classification of these views proposed by David Rumelhart and Donald Norman (1976).

Accretion and Fine-tuning

Much of our present teaching practice is based on the notion that schemata are usually developed by *accretion* and *fine-tuning*. Accretion is merely putting new information into a schema we already have. When you read a newspaper account of an election, you probably fill your election slot with information about who won and which issues were favored. However, your basic schema for election doesn't change much. Fine-tuning refers to changing the categories we use in interpreting new information. It involves minor modifications in existing schemata. In fine-tuning, irrelevant aspects of a schema are dropped and new variables are added. Examples include the little child who learns that not all animals are "doggies" and the person

Exhibit 6.1   The Acquisition of Schemata as Learning Tasks

Learning

Accretion	*Restructuring*	*Fine-Tuning*
Matching new information with previously available schemata; adding to the data base of knowledge when it corresponds with existing schemata	Restructuring existing schemata when new information does not fit currently available schemata or when the organization of existing data structures is not satisfactory	Adjusting to terms to improve accuracy, improve generalizability, improve specificity, and make inferences from text

Source: From *Accretion, Tuning, Restructuring: Three Models of Learning* by David Rumelhart and Donald Norman, La Jolla, CA: Report 7602, La Jolla Center for Human Information Processing, August 1976. Reprinted by permission.

who modifies his schema of an automobile after seeing a car with only three wheels. Teachers engage students in tuning by sharing a broad experience with them, asking them to list the components of the experience, categorizing and labeling the components, and discovering the reasons why only members of each category belong.

Restructuring

Reconstructuring is a major change in an individual's schema system. Usually it occurs when the person's broad perspectives are remodeled—when he or she comes to see things very differently. A shift in a politician's views from conservative to liberal is an example. Richard Anderson (1977) has speculated on how large shifts in perspective—such as religious and political conversions—occur. He believes that a teacher's critical questions can cause a person to modify world views, ideologies, and theories.

Through questioning, students come to recognize differences between their currently held schemata and alternatives; questioning may lead students to appraise the power of an alternative. To the extent that students engage in critical discourse, they open themselves to persuasion. Conceptual change is usually gradual—over years rather than over lessons—and occurs as the learner gives the new view higher status than the old one.

Students must first be dissatisfied with their preconceptions and must find the alternatives intelligible and useful in addressing new problems (Posner et al. 1982). Successful attempts to promote conceptual change involve direct confrontation of naive conceptions. However, the scientific views presented in textbooks frequently fail to address the student's naive beliefs, so students fail to connect the new knowledge with their beliefs. In order to make the connection, students must first recognize that the new information is related to what they already know, and then this information must be linked to two types of prior knowledge: (1) that which is consistent with the textbook knowledge, and (2) that which is incompatible with the new notions.

Summaries of social-psychological research indicate that new information will likely be resisted if its acceptance requires major cognitive reorganization. We resist new information when it requires that we change a large number of other logically related beliefs in order to maintain consistency among them. Resistance to a new schema takes the form of counterarguing with the learner's current framework, treating anomalies in current thinking as exceptions that prove the rule, and keeping incompatible schemata separate.

Students' schemata are not reconstructed merely by laying on a new set of propositions. You have known students who appear to have changed their ideas when in fact they have merely assimilated the information into old schemata. "Playing the game of school" is recognized as meeting surface expectations for tests and the classroom but holding fast to schemata from out-of-school experiences that conflict with the classroom view. Faced with statements from teachers and texts that are not in keeping with their own conceptual frameworks, students have to either modify their views or keep the new schemata separate from existing generalizations. Indeed, it may be desirable for a student to have both everyday meanings and scientific meanings, provided that the student is aware of which context is appropriate for each.

The problem of restructuring is particularly acute in schools where tension is created between individual or family views and the views of a larger society. In confronting some types of cognitive conflict, students cannot simply adopt new schemata, or even consider what is true or accurate, because acceptance of the newer views would have too severe personal and social consequences.

In his moving autobiography, Richard Rodriguez, the son of poor Mexican immigrants, tells how, in order to succeed academically, he had to move from the environment of the home to the environment of the classroom at the opposite cultural extremes (Rodriguez 1981). Without extraordinary determination and the influence of others—at home and at school—there is little chance poor minority children will advance in academic studies. Rodriguez found that his academic success distanced him from a life he loved, even from his own memory of self. Initially he wavered, balanced allegiances, and used much from both home and school. Gradually, the balance was lost. Rodriguez needed to spend more time in the world of school. As he advanced in his studies, his parents became figures of lost authority. He grew embarrassed by their lack of education and, to evade nostalgia, concentrated on the benefits education would bestow. A primary reason for his success in the classroom was that he allowed schooling to change him and to separate him from the life he had enjoyed before becoming a student. The school bid him to trust reason, while parents had taught him to trust spontaneity and nonrational way of knowing. The allegiance Rodriguez might have given his mother and father was transferred to his teachers.

> I began by imitating their accents, using their diction, trusting their every direction. The very first facts they dispensed I grasped with awe. Any book they told me to read, I read—then waited for them to tell me which books I enjoyed. Their every casual opinion I came to adopt and to trumpet when I returned home.

In an early grade Rodriguez was baffled by the isolation reading required. He felt lonely when reading. Only after a teacher playfully ran through complex sentences, calling the words alive with her voice, making it seem that the author somehow was speaking directly at him, did he sense the possibility of fellowship between a reader and a writer—not intimate like the words spoken at home, but nonetheless personal.

In the upper grades, Rodriguez read a great deal and had favorite writers. But often the writers he enjoyed the most he was least able to value. Reading helped him sense something of the major concerns of Western thought and brought him academic success. But he wasn't a good reader—merely bookish. He lacked a point of view when he read. Rather, he read in order to get a point of view.

For Rodriguez, education required radical self-reformation; his story centers on how great is the change any academic undergoes as well as how far one student had to move from his past. For him, education was a long, unglorious, even demeaning process—until he came to trust the silence of reading and the habit of abstracting from immediate experience. It was education in the end that allowed him to confront his desire for the past and to speak and care about that fact.

MODELS FOR RESTRUCTURING SCHEMATA

Teaching models that have demonstrated effectiveness for restructuring schemata are hard to find. However, approaches involving the deliberate creation of cognitive dissonance are promising. (Cognitive dissonance occurs when the student feels dissatisfied upon experiencing disequilibrium in ideas and must reduce the dissonance, incongruity, or conflict between the opposing schemata.) Promising, too, are methods that involve analyzing a text and reading a given text from different perspectives. Communication theory that emphasizes the importance of perceiving the writer as truthful and that stipulates the conditions necessary for accepting the views of others provides a fresh direction for the teaching of reading. Response-based approaches to literature instruction also may alter individual perceptions.

The Dialectical Method

Allan Collins offers a dialectical model in which the teacher plays devil's advocate, applying a strategy to counter the student's resistance to arguments and evidence—resistance that results from conflict with currently held schemata (Collins 1977). Some of the rules in Collins' strategy are as follows:

1. Bring out any facts the student knows about the issue.
2. Determine what causal factors the student knows.
3. Determine if the student knows how causal factors are related.
4. Help the student determine which factors are insufficient.
5. Give the student a counterexample for an insufficient one—"Why doesn't the cause hold good in this case?"
6. If the student overlooks a fact, ask why the factor does not apply.
7. Pose a misleading question in order to free the student to learn about exceptions to the general rule.
8. Ask for a prediction about an unknown case.
9. Ask for consideration of other factors.

The following "Fragments of a Dialogue on Growing Grain" is an illustration of the strategy used by Collins:

1. **T:** Where in North America do you think rice might be grown? (Rule 1: Ask about a known case.)
2. **S:** Louisiana.
3. **T:** Why there? (Rule 2: Ask for any factors.)
4. **S:** Places where there is a lot of water. I think rice requires the ability to selectively flood fields.
5. **T:** OK. Do you think there's a lot of rice in, say, Washington and Oregon? (Rule 5: Pick a counterexample for an insufficient factor.)
6. **S:** Aha, I don't think so.
7. **T:** Why? (Rule 2: Ask for any factors.)
8. **S:** There's a lot of water up there, too, but there's two reasons. First the climate isn't conducive, and second, I don't think the land is flat enough. You've got to have flat land so you can flood a lot of it, unless you terrace it.
9. **T:** How about Japan? (Rule 5: Pick a counterexample for an unnecessary factor.)
10. **S:** Yeah, well they have this elaborate technology I suppose for terracing land so they can flood it selectively even though it's tilted overall.
11. **T:** Do you think they might grow rice in Florida? (Rule 8: Ask for a prediction about an unknown case.)
12. **S:** Yeah, I guess they could, if there were an adequate fresh water supply. Certainly a nice, big, flat area.

13. **T:** What kinds of grains do you think they grow in Africa, and where, then? (Pause) Well, where would they grow rice if they grew it anywhere? (Rule 8: Ask for a prediction about an unknown case.)

14. **S:** If they grew it anywhere, I suppose they'd grow it in the Nile region, and they'd grow it in the tropics where there was an adequate terrain for it.

15. **T:** What do you think they live on (in West Africa)? (Rule 8: Ask for a prediction about an unknown case.)

16. **S:** I guess they grow some kind of grain in West Africa.

17. **T:** What kind is most likely?

18. **S:** Wheat.

19. **T:** You think wheat is the most likely grain?

20. **S:** Wheat or some combination of wheat and rice if they can grow it, and I suppose they could. I don't really know much about the geography there, but I suppose there are places, like Nigeria is pretty fertile.

21. **T:** OK. It's fertile but what are its other qualities? Is the temperature warm or cold? (Rule 9: Ask for consideration of different factors.)

22. **S:** Yeah, the climate's temperature and . . .

23. **T:** Do they have rain or not? (Rule 9: Ask for consideration of different factors.)

24. **S:** Yeah.

25. **T:** They have a lot of rain. OK. What do kinds of configurations predict as far as grain goes? (Rule 8: Ask for a prediction about an unknown case.)

26. **S:** Rice.

(Collins 1977, pp. 351–352)

Note how Collins' strategy forces students to deal with counterexamples and face contradictions. Note, too, how it is the student who is constructing the new schema, instead of being handed the teacher's schema. The teacher keeps the students working until they have constructed a framework that will stand up to criticism.

Promoting Changes in Students' Ideas About Science Through Cognitive Conflict

Joseph Nussbaum and Shimshon Novick have proposed an instructional strategy for accommodating conceptual conflict (Nussbaum and Novick 1982). The strategy consists of three phases: (1) exposing alternative frameworks, (2) creating conceptual conflict, and (3) encouraging cognitive accommodation. Nussbaum and Novick knew that many students have the misconception that matter is continuous. Students sometimes say, for instance,

that between the particles in the air there are more particles (bacteria, pol-
lutants, oxygen, or the like) or simply "more air." In the teacher's view, it
is desirable for students to replace this misconception about the nature of
matter with the notion that a gas is composed of tiny invisible particles and
that there is an empty space (a vacuum) between the particles. To this end,
Nussbaum and Novick designed an "exposing event": the evacuation of air
from a closed flask by use of a hand pump. This event forced each student
to take a position with regard to the possible existence of "empty space"
(a vacuum). The following is an account of what happened (Nussbaum and
Novick 1982).

Lesson 1: *Exposing Alternative Frameworks and Creating Conceptual Conflict*
Our lesson opens with the presentation of a flask containing air and an
evacuating hand pump, whose operation is demonstrated.... Learning set
is established when students feel the pump's sucking effect against their
fingers (the laughter generated contributes to a relaxed atmosphere in the
classroom).

Phase 1: "Which part of the flask is left without air?" "Where do you
place the 'empty space' (vacuum) in your model?"—setting an "exposing
event."

> ...We would need a much better evacuating pump to take out most of the air
> from this flask. Let's connect the flask to the pump and push the piston in and
> out about ten times. Let's assume we've removed half the air from the flask.
>   Of course, we can't see the air in the flask. Let's pretend that each of us is
> given a pair of "magic magnifying spectacles" through which we can actually
> see air. I want each of you to imagine you're looking at the air in the flask
> through our "magic spectacle." What would you see? I am giving each of you
> a sheet of paper with two drawings of a flask in outline—one for the air before
> we used the pump and one for the air remaining after we removed half of it.
> Draw the air in the two flasks on the sheet, as it would look through the "magic
> spectacles," before and after the partial evacuation. (pp. 190–196)

The teacher, moving around the classroom, selects representatives of
each type of drawing. Each representative is sent to the blackboard to reproduce his or her speculated picture of the state of the air in the flask "before"
and "after." Several flask outlines were prepared beforehand on the blackboard by the teacher. Soon we have three to seven different depictions of the
air in the evacuated flask on the blackboard. The teacher writes each contributor's name above his or her drawing and adds a very short description
of the drawing. At this point the blackboard looks like Exhibit 6.2 without
the "reasons," which are filled in later in the lesson.

A few procedural comments are in order here. In order to create an
atmosphere of free debate, somewhat analogous to one that may exist among
a group of scientists, we propose the following:

1. The teacher is advised to refrain from any hint of value judgment—all
   drawings are accepted equally. The teacher may say, "That's interest-

Exhibit 6.2   Blackboard Array of Students' Preconceptions

	1 David	2 Sarah	3 Ruth	4 Gideon	5 Miriam	6 Dan	7 Benny
Description	The air that is left is on the top; below it there is a vacuum	Air remains on the bottom; above it there is a vacuum	Air fills the flask, but there is less of it	The air remains near the side arm	Most of the air is on the bottom, then less and less and on top—a vacuum	Air fills the flask, but there is less of it	The remaining air is in the middle and around it there is a vacuum
before evacuation / after	after	after	after	after	after	after	after
Reasons	The air sinks because its specific gravity is greater than the vacuum	A gas flows, so the air flows to fill the flask	Air has nearly no weight; very light things rise	We pulled the air from this opening; the remaining air concentrates there and wants to push out	It's like what we learned about the atmosphere in our geography lessons	This is like the second drawing but it would look like this if a little dwarf could get in and see	I can't give a reason; I just feel it should be that way

Source: Joseph Nussbaum and Shimshon Novick. "Alternative Frameworks: Conceptual Conflict and Accommodations." *Instructional Science* 11(1982): p. 192. Reprinted by permission.

ing," or, "Here's a new idea." The teacher should not say, "Good," "fine," or the like.

2. Neat, accurate drawings and descriptions using chalk of different colors definitely help students to differentiate meaningfully between the alternative suggestions, thereby contributing to more active and meaningful class participation.

3. It is desirable that the teacher always refer to drawings by the contributor's name: "Who wants to support David's drawing?" "Who thinks Benny's drawing isn't right?" "According to Gideon's theory, the air wants to burst out." "Sarah's theory doesn't show us from where the evacuated air is missing."

4. A class will not always offer as many as seven conceptions; more generally four or five alternatives will surface. While the teacher should try to encourage many suggestions, it is not necessary to labor the point. We have found that as few as three conceptions are sufficient to start a very interesting discussion.

Phase 2: "Give reasons for your description"—deepening awareness of the component of each alternative preconception:

> ...Now that we have all these interesting descriptions, I suggest we go back and ask each contributor just why he thinks the air looks like that after we took out half of it with the pump. Anyone else is also welcome to add reasons for the drawing that looks the best to him.

The reasons offered for the drawing are shown in Exhibit 6.2, as they appeared on the blackboard array. During this phase, arguments develop in a lively give-and-take atmosphere—there is a heightening of intellectual and emotional tension. We tell the students, however, that we want to concentrate first on reasons supporting each hypothesis and delay counterarguments for the next phase of the lesson—the open debate.

> Now that we clearly understand each of your drawings, we have a problem. We received quite different suggestions from you. Can we accept all of them? Is there one which is better than the others? Which one is most reasonable? How shall we find out? Shall we take a poll? (Students explain why a democratic poll is not a scientific method.) It is true that a poll is not the right way to find out. Nevertheless, let's find out how you all feel about this—just to see "which way the wind is blowing."

By taking a poll, one gets of course a different distribution in each class, but we have noticed a pattern. In the sixth- and seventh-grade classes we have taught, drawings 1, 3, and 4 received the most support. What do they have in common? Well, they all picture the air as one big "chunk" that is found in some defined part of the flask, and where the air was removed (by the pump) a vacuum is left.

Another comment on classroom "atmosphere" is in order here. With this "poll of public opinion," pupils become more involved and very curious to find out who gave the "correct" description.

Phase 3: "Pros and cons"—debating the issue. Sharpening awareness of alternative preconceptions.

> Well, it seems you're all very eager to find out how the air should really look through our magic magnifying spectacles. We should look at the logic of each position and try to see how it fits with other experiments we could do with air. Now break up into groups and see what you can come up with to defend or refute each of the drawings.

In classes used to working in small groups, the argument is especially lively and sometimes heated. At this point, even the more reticent students become involved. Interestingly enough, no critical remarks (pro or con) were made about Dan's drawing (No. 6). Why? It would seem that at this stage, the idea that the air could be in "chunks," with empty spaces between them, is so foreign that no need is felt to argue against it.

At the conclusion of Phase 3, after students have had a chance to give considerable thought to the key question of where the vacuum exists in the evacuated flask, we judge that all the students in the class have become aware of their own conceptions by presenting them verbally and by confronting other conceptions of their peers. This confrontation, we believe, introduces the seeds of "conceptual conflict" or "cognitive dissonance" that will mainly build up later in the lessons. We are now ready for the next phase.

Phase 4: "What makes air compressible?—preconceptions in conflict with a reexamined phenomenon—a "discrepant event."

Our first lesson ends with the demonstration of a phenomenon that will hopefully lead to an accommodation in students' cognitive structures—that is, get them to see the need for the existence of empty space inside any sample of air (or other gas).

> Let's leave our "hot debate" for a moment. I'd like you to recall what we found out about compressing gases, liquids and solids. Let's compress some air in this syringe . . . (demonstration) . . . You all remember that we couldn't compress a liquid or solid like that. I wonder—does compressing a gas like this raise any questions for you . . . does it make you wonder . . . ?

Either on their own initiative or with some help from the teacher, students arrive at the following query: How can you force one half of the air, which is in the cylinder, into the remaining space which is already occupied by air?

> After all, we know from everyday experience with things that aren't gases that you can't take their place without moving them away (two pupils can't sit at the same time on the same seat). So how does the air in the bottom of the syringe allow more air to occupy the same space when we push down the plunger?

What in the nature and the structure of air makes it so compressible?

> We've come to the end of our lesson today. Shall we continue with this problem next time? (A chorus of assent.) OK. Then think about it until tomorrow. I

suggest you try to see which of the drawings on the blackboard could help you to best explain how we can compress air in a syringe.

Lession 2: *Cognitive Dissonance Leads to Accommodation and the Invention of a New Model* Our second lesson begins with a review of the various descriptions of the air left in the flask, with the help of duplicated sheets showing the blackboard array of descriptions, drawings, and reasons (see Exhibit 6.2).

> Let's go back now to our discussion about air in a syringe, which I hope you've thought about since our last lesson. Here you see how I can easily make 100 cc of air occupy only 50 cc (teacher demonstrates). What questions can be asked about this peculiar phenomenon?

Students talk about this in small groups or in class discussions and the following three questions emerge on the blackboard: (1) How can two quantities of air in the syringe, each occupying 50 cc (together, 100 cc) occupy only 50 cc after the plunger is pushed in? (2) Why can this be done only with a gas, like air, and not with a liquid or a solid? (3) What is special about the structure of air that allows it to be compressed?

> Now, as you remember, I asked you at the end of our last lesson to think about which of the seven descriptions of the air in the evacuated flask might help us to answer these questions.

Students begin to search for some relationship among the various speculated "structures," represented by the drawings, and the observation of a phenomenon unique to gases: their compressibility. The kinds of responses offered will of course vary from group to group. However, in every class that we have taught, at least one student suggests something to the effect that,

> Maybe air is always like Dan's drawing (number 6)—even when we don't remove any of it. Maybe air is made of little pieces with empty space in between.

In one class a student suggested this model (basically not too different from a particle model):

> Maybe air is like a sponge. Maybe the air is like the sponge material itself and between the chunks of air there is empty space like holes in the sponge.

The discussion now becomes very lively; students are personally very involved in the debate. They try to show how their own drawings could explain the air's compressibility and to deal with the criticism of their classmates. Students are seen using paper and pencil and hand gestures to help their arguments for their picture of air's structure and behavior in the flask and in the syringe. We have found that the suggestion that drawing 6 explains the air's compressibility is at first rejected by many students. For them the idea that there is a "vacuum" in ordinary air is just too strange. The teacher, while refraining from expressing preference for any one drawing, presses the "antiparticle" students to offer a better explanation of the air's compressibility. Most pupils begin to realize that despite the strangeness of the "particles in a vacuum" idea, it does explain both phenomena—the evacuation and the compression of air. More and more students join the "particle camp" and even volunteer to argue against their previous opinions. One argument against the particle idea should be noted. Some students said:

> If we assume there is empty space among particles, then why doesn't water rise into a glass of air inverted in a bowl of water?
>
> What holds the particles separated from each other if there is just empty space between them? Why don't the particles just fall down and pile up at the bottom of the flask?

The teacher acknowledges these questions and even writes them on the blackboard as good questions to be kept in mind. These responses show the need to introduce inherent motion of particles as part of the model, to explain pressure phenomena. This additional aspect is developed in subsequent lessons by again invoking "cognitive dissonance" and accommodation.

After the particle picture has become the focus of discussion and its supporters are increasing, the teacher intervenes to demonstrate the compression once again, but this time compressing 100 cc of air to just 20 cc.

> If we assume the air is really composed of particles what does this compression suggest about the amount of space taken up by the particles compared with the empty space between them?

Students suggest the empty space is much larger than the space taken up by the particles:

> If I had pressed much harder on the plunger, I could have compressed the air even more. But even if we used a steel syringe and exerted tremendous force, we still couldn't compress the air to zero volume. We always reach a minimum volume. Why?

Students suggest that the limit of compression is reached when there is no more empty space between the particles.

Our second lesson ends with the teacher's statement:

> Indeed the picture scientists have accepted is that of air composed of particles and empty space among them. The question which now arises is why the air resists being compressed. Why do we have to press on the plunger to keep the air compressed? We'll talk about this problem next time.

The Inquiry Method for Acquiring a New Schema

Observation and guided questioning can help students acquire new schemata.

Teacher's Statement	*Student's Response*
1. List what you observed. Tell me what you saw, tasted, heard, read.	Describes the observed phenomena.

2. What facts or events go together?	Groups the items.
3. What is the common thread among these items?	Gives common factors for grouping.
4. What do you call each of the groups?	Labels the groups.
5. Do the items belong to one group only?	Examines the grouping.
6. Let's try to find another way to group the items.	Considers alternative ways to group.
7. What is the common thread among the items in the new grouping?	Identifies a common factor for the new grouping.
8. In the light of these groupings, what concepts (labels, schemata) do we now have?	Summarizes by giving final grouping.

When the outline above is used, students' responses constitute the cognitive process that develops the schema. For instance, if you wanted to introduce a schema for democratic government, you might ask pupils to read about governments such as those of ancient Egypt and Mexico and those of modern Japan, France, and Britain. Once students have information, you may begin the questioning. Students should group the various governments (step 2), examine the groups (step 5), offer alternative grouping (step 6), and give final labels (step 8). When students perform these processes, they have a strong stake in the schema. *They* have manipulated the data by grouping and labeling the various features of governments and by defending their suggested groupings and final concept. Inasmuch as the concept and categories that are developed reflect a way of structuring the world, you must ask for and accept alternative ways for grouping the various governments and elicit suggestions according to a variety of vantage points.

The construction of inductive towers has been found to be an effective learning activity at the secondary level (Clarke, Raths, and Gilbert 1989). To build a tower, students follow four steps of the inquiry model:

1. Collect facts from observations, text, interviews.
2. Link two or more facts to create a new proposition.
3. Link two or more positions to create a generalization.
4. Link generations to create a theory or value statement.

Exhibit 6.3 is an excerpt from a student tower on AIDS education in the United States. The tower was created by high school seniors in a history class as a way of coming to terms with the issue of who should make national policy. Students scanned newspapers and magazines for facts related to the AIDS controversy. Next, they linked the facts and made interpretive statements in group settings, creating the higher tiers of the tower. The figure does not show the difficulties the students experienced in resolving

Exhibit 6.3 Excerpt from a Student Tower on AIDS Education in the U.S.

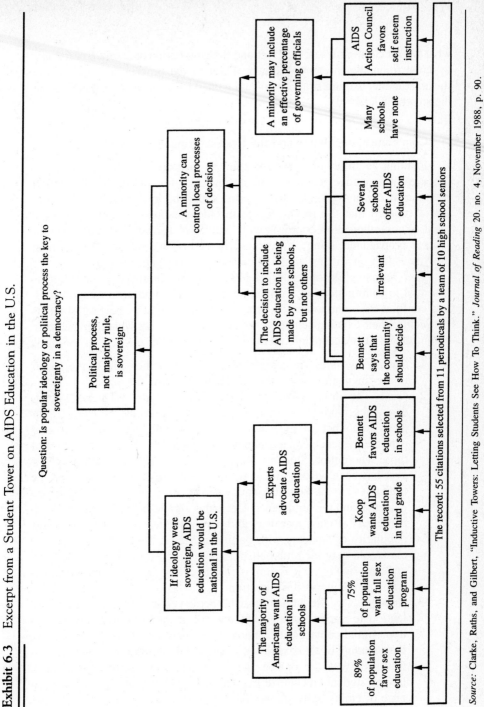

Question: Is popular ideology or political process the key to sovereignty in a democracy?

Political process, not majority rule, is sovereign

A minority can control local processes of decision

A minority may include an effective percentage of governing officials

AIDS Action Council favors self esteem instruction

Many schools have none

Several schools offer AIDS education

The decision to include AIDS education is being made by some schools, but not others

Irrelevant

Bennett says that the community should decide

If ideology were sovereign, AIDS education would be national in the U.S.

Experts advocate AIDS education

Bennett favors AIDS education in schools

Koop wants AIDS education in third grade

The majority of Americans want AIDS education in schools

75% of population want full sex education program

89% of population favor sex education

The record: 55 citations selected from 11 periodicals by a team of 10 high school seniors

Source: Clarke, Raths, and Gilbert, "Inductive Towers: Letting Students See How To Think." *Journal of Reading* 20. no. 4, November 1988, p. 90.

what would count as a relevant fact and the negotiations that were necessary to agree upon the inferences drawn. Through the process of building the tower, students learned from others and gained some critical perspectives on their own beliefs.

Communication Theory and the Restructuring of Schemata

Reading as an art of communication is governed by the same rules as other communicative acts. Certain norms exist for successful interaction between reader and author. These norms stress the importance of the truth and a concern that the reader accept the ideas expressed. This normative ideal of communication contrasts with "strategic" forms of communication, such as propaganda, lying, misleading, deceiving, and manipulating, which are "parasitic" on writing aimed at creating sincere understanding.

The German philosopher Jurgen Habermas has summarized the elements essential to communication. Further, he has discussed procedures for resolving conflicts in communication procedures that apply in helping students restructure their existing schemata when confronted with what they perceive as untruthful or unacceptable ideas (McCarthy 1981):

1. *Comprehensible.* The author should be comprehensible to the reader in the linguistic sense—the reader must follow the syntax.
2. *Truth.* The author must have knowledge to share. Whatever knowledge, observation, or interpretation is stated should be true. If students do not believe the statements, they should be instructed to compare the evidence and arguments of the author with the arguments of those who doubt. Students must feel free to call into question whatever has been written and to try to arrive at a decision regarding the truth or falsity of the statement by considering only the strength of the evidence and the arguments. Decisions should be based on a rational consensus of class members and not on the teacher's position or the popularity of students with particular views. Such rationality in the classroom may seem unrealistic, and its occurrence is probably most unusual; however, it is impossible to arrive at true communication without moving in this direction.
3. *Truthfulness.* The author must be perceived as truthful, with no intention to deceive readers. If readers do not perceive truthfulness upon initial contact with a book, they should continue far enough in their reading of the text to see if the author shows the implications— truth—of what he or she is saying. The conventional practice of having students recognize bias in writing is relevant here. The presence of emotionally laden words, the omission of facts, and the use of overgeneralizations are grounds for doubting truthfulness.
4. *Acceptability.* In order to communicate, whatever the author says or recommends must be right and acceptable in terms of the reader's normative schemata. At times a teacher may have to help students

see how the author's ideas are consistent with their norms and values and their social context. It may also be necessary to have a critical discussion of the students' norms. This point has much to do with restructuring schemata. When differences in beliefs and values block communication, the reader has three options: stop reading the text, continue to read the text and feign agreement with the points made in order to please the teacher (a strategic form of communication), or enter into a discussion for the purpose of arriving at rational agreement.

As a basis for helping students deal with the problem of truthfulness in communication, use Activity 6.1.

Teachers who organize a critical discussion when students are unable to accept the writer's point of view may try to restructure schemata in several ways. First, they may try to see what is present in the students' situations that makes the author's ideas appropriate. Perhaps the author is saying something that is really consistent with the readers' norms. What are the consequences of the beliefs held by the readers? To what extent do these beliefs contribute or fail to contribute to the concerns of human life, to generally accepted needs and wants (physical and mental well-being, self-respect, self-actualization, control over aspects of one's life)? Critical discussion will work only if the participants know and say what they really want.

Why is it important to engage in critical discussion of the ideas in text that appear to be unacceptable? Because the author may offer a better response to some of the readers' central concerns than their existing schemata. Comprehending text means making sense of it by relating it to one's own situation and seeing how it contributes to the needs of human life.

Children come to school with the symbolic universe of the family — as Rodriguez says, the language of intimacy. Increasingly, the school will

Activity 6.1 Reading for a Different Purpose — Perceived Truthfulness

Pick any selection you use in your classroom. Ask students first to read the selection for *what* the author says. Then ask them to reread for the purpose of deciding *how* and *why* the author said it. Was the author truthful?

Help the students reread by asking them to provide instances of the author's logical and emotional arguments, facts, and allegations. Ask them to identify the author's values with respect to honesty, friends, nature, money, and so on. Does he or she make fun of persons and manners?

Ask these kinds of questions: What does this character do that is connected with the author's values? How does the author tell what honesty or some other value means to him or her? Why does the author think the value is important? What reasons does the character give for valuing *X*? Is the author ashamed or proud about the value *X*? Why do you think the author has this value? Do you perceive the author as truthful? Why? Why not?

introduce content that challenges the norms of the home and the local community. In making the transition, children must examine norms in light of new ideas about the human situation.

The practice of reading and writing in combination contributes to revision of one's position on an issue. Tierney and others, for example, found that when given topics such as the ethics of transplants (Baby Fae) and sexual discrimination (women in the movies), students are more likely to revise their original positions on the issues when they both read and write on the issues than when they only read about the topics (Tierney et al, 1989). Typical comments about reading and writing tasks show individual differences in openness and rigidity of belief:

- *Reading an article:* "opened me to other opinions on the subject"; "made me think twice about mine"; "I could see which stands I agree with."
- *Writing on the topic:* "helped me realize my opinion on the subject"; "didn't help all that much because I was already set in my views."

Reading from Multiple Perspectives

Unlike the preschool child, beginning readers have the ability to distinguish between fantasy and perception, between impulse and obligation. They can learn to look at reading selections from the perspectives of others representing the familiar roles of family and community members. They can learn that different persons see the same situation from different perspectives, with different intentions, wants, feelings, and meanings. Activity 6.2 is useful in developing alternative frameworks.

Students in late childhood can apply an even wider range of perspectives. They are ready to consider how those with different perspectives are responding to human needs. As adolescents, most readers are capable of reading from a number of perspectives based on various theories and views about religion, politics, education, economics, art, psychology, medicine, and the like. Adolescents are able to treat their own views and the author's as hypothetical and can separate themselves from inherited roles, norms, and values. They are at a stage when it is appropriate to engage in critical discussion. They are open to the beliefs of others and can weigh evidence in support of new ideas and the inherited norms with which they appear to conflict.

Activity 6.3 is an invitation to look at familiar materials in a different light—how the materials might conflict with the students' broad or world views.

Reading Response and the Changing of Schemata

Both isolated reading of a literary text and discussion of texts with friends or classmates have the potential for restructuring one's beliefs and can result in rejection of previously held assumptions and negation of the

Activity 6.2 Reading from Different Perspectives

A device for restructuring schemata is the repeated reading of text from different perspectives. The requirements are (a) a text that is relevant to the schemata to be restructured and that allows for alternative interpretations; (b) the assignment of pupils to various viewpoints; (c) a discussion by the readers; and (d) a switching of points of view.

Select one story, article, or book. Have pupils first read it to get the gist of the material. Then do the following:

1. Decide upon the perspectives that would give rise to important dimensions of the topic or theme. Young children may use the frameworks of those with different social roles — father, mother, sister, doctor, driver. Mature readers may use theoretical frameworks with which they are familiar — a Marxist or a Freudian perspective, for example. You may want to demonstrate the way in which a person with a given perspective would respond to a class of situations.
2. Have students briefly state the perspective they will use. The statement should include major concerns, arguments, and values associated with the perspective. Assumptions underlying the viewpoint may be given by mature readers.
3. Have students identify the essential features of the selection from the perspective chosen.
4. Have students, using the perspective, tell how the selection is different from or similar to other familiar selections.
5. Have students decide if there are elements missing in the selection that would be important to the perspective.
6. Have students tell why the missing elements are important to the perspective.
7. Have students give their judgment of the selection.
8. Repeat the steps but from another perspective. (This activity may occur at a subsequent time.)
9. Have students make an overall conclusion about the selection after considering the points raised from the perspectives taken.

In assessing the value of this activity, note changes in students' schemata as indicated by their conclusions and points of view about the selection analyzed.

---

familiar. The voices of significant others (authors as well as classmates) may help form the individual. A reader's identity may be clarified or transformed by engaging the psychological themes generated by text and recreating the work in accordance with the reader's own psychological predispositions.

Restructuring may be advanced by the practice of regarding the classroom as an interpretative community where readers share their responses to a work and then discuss their individual reactions in efforts to reach a consensus on meaning and significance. Such discussions provide opportunities to resolve conflicts by filling in gaps in knowledge structures, correcting misunderstandings, and reconciling conflicting views. The social coordination of conflicting views can lead to the restructuring of knowledge (Bearison 1982).

Activity 6.3   Identifying Conflicting Preconceptions

Students sometimes find it difficult to accept ideas in their reading because of conflicting preconceptions of a moral, cultural, or physical nature.

Take a selection—complete text, chapter, or article—that you intend to use in your classroom. Identify the major assumptions underlying the author's conclusions or main ideas. Before asking students to read the selection, present the assumptions and ask students whether they agree with them or not, giving their reasons. These responses will reveal ideas that need restructuring if the reader is to accept the information given. The following categories and examples illustrate typical assumptions underlying various materials.

Moral Assumptions (social studies, literature)

Relativism: There are different points of view. Things are not black or white, right or wrong. Rules are made by people and can be modified to fit circumstances. Behavior should be judged in terms of motive and consequences.

Authority: There are those who have authority over our behavior (legal authority). This authority should restrain our actions. On the other hand, there are equals (peers and friends) with whom we cooperate because we identify with them. Sometimes the values of the peer society conflict with those of persons in positions of authority.

Cultural Assumptions (social studies, literature)

Children's role: Children should participate with adults in the serious concerns going on about them. Pupils should be able to effect change and set standards for themselves.

Social class: There is a rank-order among people striving for social recognition— upper class, middle class, and lower class. People in different classes hold different values. Social class affects children's motives, actions, and long-term development.

Conflict: The presence of multicultural patterns in our society accounts for confusion about acceptable standards.

Historical time: The Peruvian Indians had extensive systems of religion, farming, and industry nearly 5,000 years ago that lasted until Pizarro arrived in 1532. Using the analogy of a clock, we can say that Peruvian Indian culture shows 24 hours while United States history from the time of George Washington to now shows less than an hour.

Physical Assumptions (science, social studies)

Nature: We should not see nature as our enemy—something to be feared and destroyed. Neither should we worship nature. We should strive to understand nature and the human conditions within it.

Cause: Most explanations of physical phenomena are based upon reason and logic rather than upon direct observation of forces within the phenomena.

Variability: The attempt to make persons uniform—biologically, emotionally, or intellectually—is a betrayal of the evolutionary thrust that has put human beings at the apex.

Uncertainty: All knowledge is limited—everything is at best a guess. (Granted there is a high probability that the chair you are sitting on is indeed a chair, even though it might be changed in some way from yesterday or last year.)

Interpretive communication promotes a style of thought, a common approach to seeing the world. Kathy Short has described classrooms that foster interpretive communication through literature-circle discussion groups (Short et al. 1990). Groups of third-graders read different books that were related in some way. Each group used different strategies for dealing with their sets of books, focusing on characters, problems, themes, genres, setting, and the like. The war-and-peace group, for example, compared how the different books portrayed war and peace. Sets of books in each classroom were compiled from the interests and needs of the children, such as books about war and peace, books about native Americans, books about Japanese culture, and books about dragons. The sets ranged from 5 to 30 books. Students signed up for the set they wanted to read and discuss, read one or more books from the set, met with their group to share what they had read, made comparisons across texts, and then presented their sets to the class. Presentations to the class varied among groups as well and included plays, reports of interviews, learning centers, a mural, letters, and other written material.

Pertinent to reconstruction is that the activities of the interpretive community influenced the understandings of individuals. As students read the books in the sets, they created their own stories based on these texts; these stories, in turn, changed as students shared them and searched for connections among the different texts treated. Dialogue supported both the creation of text and the process of intertextuality. Reading and discussion caused students to rethink what they thought they knew and to grow beyond it.

SUMMARY

The influence of students' preconceptions and misconceptions on their reading of texts has been underestimated. Readers do not often really change their ideas as a consequence of their reading. It takes energy to unlearn a misconception. Just giving the student an explanation for how and why something is true is not enough; the student must actively create meaning from that explanation. Teachers need to find out the views that students bring with them to reading lessons. Critical misconceptions must be restructured. Classroom practices that facilitate the restructuring of readers' ideas generally call for (a) creating a situation that requires the students to invoke their preconceptions, (b) encouraging students to state their preconceptions, (c) encouraging confrontation to bring out in discussion the difference between the student's view and those of others, (d) creating a conflict between exposed preconceptions and some situation that the preconceptions cannot explain, and (e) supporting the student's search for resolution and accommodation.

Among the teaching practices that may contribute to reconstruction and the changing of schemata are the dialectical method, alternative framework strategies, inquiry and inductive methods, reader response approaches consistent with communication theory, and the establishment of an interpretive community that values the generation of new meanings rather than the superficial acceptance of a correct reading.

REFERENCES

Alvermann, Donna E., Smith, L. C., and Readence, J. E."Prior Knowledge Activation and the Comprehension of Compatible and Incompatible Text." *Reading Research Quarterly* 20, no. 4 (Summer 1985): 420–437.
Anderson, C. W., and Smith, E. L. "Teaching Science." In *Educators' Handbook: A Research Perspective*, V. Richardson Koehler, editor. New York: Longman, 1987, pp. 84–111.
Anderson, R. C. "The Notion of Schemata and the Educational Enterprise." In *Schooling and the Acquisition of Knowledge*, R. C. Anderson, R. J. Spiro, and W. E. Montague, editors. Hillsdale, NJ: Erlbaum, 1977, pp. 415–431.
Bearison, D. J. "New Directions in Studies of Social Interactions and Cognitive Growth." In *Social Cognitive Development in Context*, F. C. Serafica, editor. New York: Guilford, 1982, pp. 199–221.
Clarke, John H., Raths, James, and Gilbert, Gary L. "Inductive Towers: Letting Students See How to Think." *Journal of Reading* (Nov. 1989): 86–94.
Collins, Allan. "Processes in Acquiring Knowledge." In *Schooling and the Acquisition of Knowledge*, R. C. Anderson, R. J. Spiro, and W. E. Montague, editors. Hillsdale, NJ: Erlbaum, 1977, pp. 350–354.
Lipson, M. Y. "Some Unexpected Issues in Prior Knowledge and Comprehension." *The Reading Teacher* 37, no. 4 (Summer 1984): 760–764.
McCarthy, Thomas. *The Critical Theory of Jurgen Habermas*. Cambridge, MA: MIT Press, 1981.
Nussbaum, Joseph, and Novick, Shimshon. "Alternative Frameworks: Conceptual Conflict and Accommodation." *Instructional Science* 11 (1982): 183–200.
Osborne, Roger, and Gilbert, John. " A Technique for Exploring Students' Views of the World." *Journal of Physics Education* 15 (1980): 376–379.
Posner, G. S., Strike, K. A., Hewson, P. W., and Gertzog, W. A. "Accommodation of a Scientific Concept: Toward a Theory of Conceptual Change." *Science Education* 62 (1982): 211–227.
Read, S. T. and Rosen, M. B. "Remembering History: The Biasing Effects of Belief on Memory." (unpublished paper).
Richards, John P., and Slife, Brendt D. "Interaction of Dogmatism and Rhetorical Structure in Text Recall." *American Research Journal* 24, No. 4 (Winter 1987): 635–641.
Rodriguez, Richard. *Hunger of Memory: The Education of Richard Rodriguez*. Boston: David R. Godine, 1981.

Roth, K. J., and Anderson, C. W. "Promoting Conceptual Change Learning from Science Textbooks." In *Improving Learning: New Perspectives,* P. Ramsden, editor. London: Kogen Page, 1990, pp. 140–166.

Rumelhart, David, and Norman, Donald. *Accretion, Tuning, Restructuring: Three Modes of Learning.* La Jolla, CA: Report 7602, La Jolla Center for Human Information Processing, 1976.

Short, K., Hanssen, E., Harste, J. C., and Short, K. G. "In Conversation: Theory and Instruction." In *Beyond Communication,* Deanne Bogdan and Stanley B. Straw, editors. Portsmouth, NH: Boynton/Cook, 1990, pp. 259–281.

Tierney, Robert J., Soter, Anna, O'Flahavon, John F., and McGinley, William. "The Effects of Reading and Writing Upon Thinking Critically." *Reading Research Quarterly* 24, no. 2 (1989): 134–169.

Useful Reading

Anderson, C. W., and Smith E. L. "Teaching Science." In *Educator's Handbook: A Research Perspective,* V. Richardson-Koehler, editor. New York: Longman, 1987, pp. 84–111.

Ramsden, P., editor. *Improving Learning: New Perspectives.* London: Kogen Page, 1990.

Vosniadov, S., and Brewer, W. F. "Theories of Knowledge Restructuring in Development." *Review of Educational Research* 57, no. 1 (1987): 51–67.

7

Teaching Vocabulary from an Interactive View of Reading Comprehension

---

OVERVIEW

The strong relationship between vocabulary knowledge and reading comprehension has long been known. What isn't known is why word knowledge is such a powerful factor in comprehension. Three hypotheses have been proposed: The *aptitude hypothesis* states that people score high on a vocabulary test because of their mental agility, which also enables them to comprehend text well. The instructional implication of this hypothesis is that, since vocabulary training won't affect mental ability, the difference in comprehension between high- and low-aptitude readers will remain the same in spite of such training.

The *instrumental hypothesis* claims that knowledge of individual word meaning is the primary factor responsible for reading comprehension. The instructional implication is that teaching vocabulary will improve reading comprehension. The more word meanings known, the better the comprehension.

The *knowledge hypothesis* holds that a person who knows a word well knows other related words and ideas. It is this network of ideas that enhances comprehension. When a person reads a particular word in text, it activates word associations that allow the reader to create meaning. Accordingly, vocabulary should be taught in the context of subject matter or situations so that word meanings are related to each other and, where possible, to the prior experience of the learner. The knowledge position is taken in this chapter. It is consistent with schema theory in that it is an interactive approach by which new words are related to each other and to the learner's schemata.

In this chapter, you will examine (a) prereading and culminating vocabulary instruction aimed at improving the reader's comprehension of particular selections (teacher-led strategies), and (b) interactive instruction by which students become independent in acquiring vocabulary and in deriving the meaning of unfamiliar words.

KINDS OF WORD MEANING

Words have different kinds of meanings. A word's denotive meaning refers specifically to a theory, a quality, an action, or a relationship. The teaching of vocabulary in the past often centered on this level of meaning: "Circle the word that matches the definition." However, from an interactive view of reading, it is more important to focus on the associative meanings of words (connotations). By way of example, the word *farm* may call to mind *field, row, fertilizer, plow, barn,* and much more. In this way a word is a central point for a chain of images. As indicated in Chapter 2, these complexes of associative meaning constitute a semantic field, which is important in making references and comprehending text.

In addition to representing objects and eliciting associations, words have the function of conveying the essential property of an object and relating it to other words in a category. This is the categorical or conceptual meaning of a word. For example, the essential attribute of *pet* is domestication; of *fruit,* seed enclosure; of *myth,* conveyed picture of a shared ideal. Different things are categorized as equivalent or similar because they share essential properties. When new words and their referents appear to belong to a known class or category, the reader generalizes from knowledge of the category to the new term. Thus, conceptual meanings become a primary basis for communication and learning. If, for example, an author refers to a particular role, and the reader does not grasp the general sense of the word *role* (expected action in an interactive situation of one in a given position), there is little comprehension. With knowledge of the general meaning of the term, the reader already knows a great deal about the role the author is talking about, even if the role is an unfamiliar one. The reader knows, for example, that the role is not dependent upon personality, that there are social consequences for departing from the expected action, and that others have a corresponding set of responses to the role. Knowledge of essential attributes of a category and the ability to generalize these properties to particular and novel words in the category make understanding new words possible.

A little black humor gives a different view of the importance of context in the meaning of words. George Orwell once told an anecdote about the Spanish Civil War and the Army's use of double passwords. Usually, these passwords were of an elevating and revolutionary nature—*cultura-progreso.* Illiterate sentries had a problem in trying to remember these unfamiliar words. One night the password was *cataluna-eroica,* and a peasant lad named Jaime Domenech asked, *"Eroica*—What does *eroica* mean?" He was told that it meant the same as *valiente.* A little while later as Jaime was stumbling up the trench in the darkness, a sentry challenged him. *"Alto! Cataluna!" "Valiente,"* yelled Jaime, certain he was saying the right word. Bang!

ASSUMPTIONS ABOUT LEARNING WORDS

Newer techniques for teaching vocabulary are based on four assumptions:

1. *Words are constantly being redefined.* By way of illustration, a very young reader understands *store* in terms of a precise object referent—a place where one can buy something—or perhaps in terms of the positive emotional connotations of toys and candy that *store* evokes. On the other hand, a mature reader has many concepts for *store,* including economic ideas of exchange (money, goods) or forms of exchange (capitalistic, cooperative). In other words, redefinition comes with developmental growth. One implication of this fact that with very young children, vocabulary instruction should encourage developing affective associations and relating new terms to actual situations. When students begin to read in the content fields, the categorical meanings of words—abstract concepts—must receive attention. Indeed, the teacher must help the students form hierarchies of connected categories.

2. *There are many meanings for a single word.* Polysemy refers to cases in which there are multiple meanings of a word. Texts with many polysemous words, especially seemingly simple and unambiguous words, create comprehension difficulties.

The fact that there are so many meanings for a single word suggests that the teaching of vocabulary must help students see that it is not so important to learn *the* meaning required from several candidates. Inasmuch as context often determines the meaning of a word, the traditional practice of teaching context clues to word meaning is warranted. Students should practice using both syntactic and semantic cues in determining word meaning. It is helpful for students to learn how to use appositives and statements of contrast as clues to word meaning, together with guesses based on the situations described in the text.

Active processing is a desirable basis for increasing vocabulary and integrating word meaning with other words and the reader's schemata. Asking questions that demand applications of the new term in a variety of contexts is a technique for encouraging active processing. For example, in teaching the term *altercation,* you might ask, "Do you ever have altercations with your brother?" "What altercations do you have with your opponents?" "Would you expect more altercations at your birthday party?"

3. *We should teach entire conceptual frameworks related to a word, not just the individual word.* Anderson and Freebody (1981) suggest that the child who knows the word *mast* is likely to have knowledge about sailing. This general knowledge, not familiarity with the word *mast,* is what enables the child to understand text in which the word *mast* appears. The child who knows *mast* as a part of a conceptual framework can also comprehend such statements as: "We jibed suddenly, and the boom snapped across the cockpit." Instead of learning *mast* independently of concepts such as boat and sail, readers should learn sailing jargon in the context of sailing and sailboats. Trying to teach naive children a single sailing concept in isolation from related concepts (as is encouraged by authors of spelling workbooks) is inefficient.

One idea for teaching vocabulary so that it improves reading comprehension involves increasing the child's precision of word knowledge. Accordingly, words that share a common conceptual basis are taught together. For example, the words *hurl, thrust,* and *nudge* might be compared and contrasted with one another. The teaching of word families and their roots (e.g. *community, communicate, common*) has enjoyed long popularity.

4. *When the conceptual meaning of a word is taught, the framework used should represent a hiearchy of terms.* Having said that concepts do not exist in isolation but as a part of a set of related schemata, it is necessary to say something about how one decides upon the set to which the new word is to be linked.

Often, in a reading selection, the set is already present in the narrative or in the circumstances described in connection with the new term. For example, the new term *plane* (a tool for smoothing wood) may appear in the context of a description of furniture-making along with words for related tools, purposes, standards, directions, and the like.

At other times, the teacher may help the students relate the new word to a hierarchy of related concepts. Some of the concepts should be superordinate (more abstract than the new word); others should be subordinate (instances of the target concept, perhaps); and others should be coordinate (of equal importance and degree of specificity). Coordinate terms may share many of the same attributes as the new term. By way of example, in teaching the meaning of *liquid,* coordinate terms to introduce might be *solid* and *gas.* Subordinate terms might be *water* and *oil.* Superordinate terms might be *states of matter* and *effects of heat.*

I suspect that many teachers will have difficulty in selecting sets of concepts that should be taught together. Textbooks are not always helpful in this regard. Most textbooks introduce one concept at a time and give only a denotive meaning for the terms followed by a simple example. The following vocabulary is meant to stimulate your own thinking about conceptual networks that might be appropriate for reading in your content field.

- *Art*—concepts related to materials, composition, and organization of elements, such as level, color, value, volume, depth, perspective, plane.
- *Math*—element, set, equality, sum, product, difference; logical concepts such as *is a member of, not, all, such that, if-then, or-and;* relations, functions, variables.
- *Physical science*—facts, hypotheses, principles, generalizations, laws, theories, models; energy, interactive particles and their organization; elements.
- *Biology*—species, genus, family, order, class, phylum, kingdom; evolution, inheritable variation, adaptation, natural selection, structural analysis, functional analysis; organization, organism, compound.
- *Sociology*—group, norm, role, status, institution, conformity, deviation, culture; value, need, conflict, change.
- *Economics*—land, population, specialization, goods, service, exchange, market system, supply and demand, price, competition, monopoly, money, partnership, corporation, labor, wage, collective bargaining, conditions of work.

TEACHING VOCABULARY AS A NETWORK OF IDEAS

William Nagy has identified *integration* as an important property of vocabulary instruction that is effective in increasing reading comprehension (Nagy 1988). Integration refers to relating ideas and a new concept to what we already know. Scott Koeze has created a dictionary game for his chapter one students that helps them relate the meanings of words to their own interests (Koeze 1990). The game is played by groups of children in a circle. One person selects a word that everyone knows. The person on the left gives a word that he or she predicts will appear in the dictionary definition of that word. Articles or prepositions are excluded. Play continues around the circle. For example, the word *dinosaur* is selected. The first player predicts *reptile* will appear in the definition. The second player predicts *brontosaurus*, the third says *extinct*, and the one who originally chose the word *dinosaur* predicts *animal*. Students learn that just because their words don't appear in the dictionary doesn't mean they shouldn't or couldn't appear there.

Other practices that foster integration are conceptual mapping, semantic mapping, and feature analysis.

Conceptual Mapping

An illustration of how children can be helped to relate new vocabulary to both their background and other concepts has been provided by M. Buckley

Hanf (Hanf 1971). Hanf described a situation in which students were to read a selection from their science textbooks on the topic of black widow spiders. She first had students tell all they knew about the subject and then decide what they expected to find in the chapter. (She was, of course, activating and channeling purpose to guide the processing of text.) Next, she had students say what aspects of black widow spiders they expected the chapter to tell about, and then they checked the accuracy of their guesses by skimming the chapter. Headings and the section labels also helped to identify categories for information. The categories became the start of a cognitive map, which was drawn on the chalkboard. With the larger view of the chapter in mind, students read for details and later restated details from memory (the recall of details from memory is one way to monitor comprehension). They also reread for poorly understood details. The students discussed new words met in the chapter, such as *abdomen*, *organs*, and *nocturnal*, by (a) referring to the examples given in the text, (b) asking each other for nonexamples of each term, (c) defining the terms in their own words, and (d) deciding where each new word should be placed on their map. Exhibit 7.1 shows the map. Note how it relates the topic to a hierarchy of concepts and details as well as relating the new words to the old.

Semantic Mapping

The semantic map was introduced in Chapter 2 as a tool for relating new concepts to a child's background knowledge. As a vocabulary-building device, mapping is frequently used to connect the conceptual meanings of new words to a hierarchical organization of concepts of schemata. One advantage of teaching words for their associative and categorical meanings — as opposed to their denotive meanings — is that it enhances recall. Whenever a particular concept in memory is activated, the whole structure of concepts with which it is associated is activated and becomes available for use in remembering and comprehending.

As mentioned, in the subject matter fields new terms should be related to other concepts at different levels in a structural hierarchy. Semantic maps make possible a graphic description of these levels. Exhibit 7.2, an example of a semantic map for *city*, illustrates how vocabulary terms are related at different levels of abstraction. This semantic map was used for comprehending a social studies assignment. Terms such as *city, state,* and *nation* were treated as labels for particular objects with whatever associations they brought to mind (denotive and associative meanings of the words). As information about a variety of cities accumulated, students abstracted and generalized their common properties and relationships (categorical or conceptual meanings of the words). The terms were then organized as shown on the map so that students could see how terms such as *nation, state, suburb,* and *city* are related to each other. Subsequently, in reading text in which these words appeared, the readers could draw upon their mental images of this map in constructing appropriate responses to the terms.

Exhibit 7.1   A Conceptual Map Relating New Vocabulary to Old

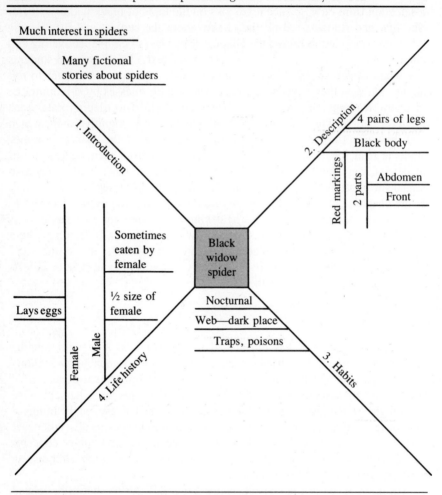

Source: Hanf, "Mapping: A Technique for Translating Reading into Thinking." *Journal of Reading* 14, no. 4 (1978–1979):228.

Student discussion is necessary in the preparation of a semantic map. Students should talk about the meanings and uses of new words, new meanings for old words, additional meanings for known words, and of course, the relationships among words.

Dale Johnson and others have introduced *refocused semantic maps* for helping students become familiar with text-specific meanings associated with a central concept (Johnson, Toms-Bronowski, and Pittleman 1981). The teacher initiates refocusing by centering on a textbook term that has a specialized meaning as well as several common associations. The students start the map with known examples, properties, and classes. After reading the selection, they revise the map to incorporate the new meanings.

Exhibit 7.2 Semantic Map for City

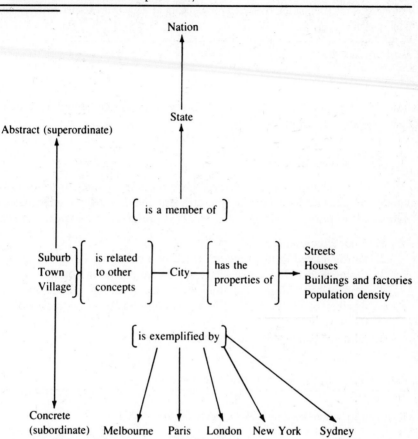

The map shows that a city has such features as streets, houses, buildings, factories, and population density. Examples of cities are Paris, New York, London, Melbourne, Sydney. *City* is also related to other schemata, such as *suburb, town,* and *village.* Finally, *city* can be subsumed under a more abstract concept, such as *state,* which in turn is subsumed under the concept *nation.* Thus, in the semantic map the upward direction is toward more abstract and more inclusive schemata and the downward direction is toward a more concrete and less inclusive level. But note that even though particular cities are exemplars of the concept *city,* they themselves are schemata with their own properties and relationships. For example, Paris has such features as the river Seine, Notre Dame cathedral, and the Eiffel Tower. Thus, the semantic map is a hierarchical organization of concepts or schemata within a reader's long-term memory.

The reader can draw upon the properties in his or her semantic map for constructing a response to the stimulus or printed word *city.* One response may be an image of a city. Whether an image forms of a particular city depends on the information in the text. If the text provide constraining information for a particular city, the reader is likely to respond with the exemplar that fits the stated characteristics—provided, of course, that the exemplar is within the reader's memory. For example, given the sentence, "The city with its famous Eiffel Tower and historic buildings along the river Seine was lit up at night," the reader is likely to think of Paris.

Source: Semantic Map of a City, p. 49 ETL821 *Nature of Teaching and Learning*. Deakin University Open Campus Program. Copyright©1982 Deakin University, Victoria, Australia. Reprinted by permission.

Exhibit 7.3 is an example of a refocused semantic map incorporating a text-specific meaning for the word *boom*.

Semantic Feature Analysis

Semantic feature analysis is a procedure for helping students to see how words within a category are alike and different and to relate the meanings of new words to prior knowledge. Vocabulary is presented in a logical manner:

1. A topic is selected.
2. Words related to the topic are listed in a column.
3. Features shared by some of the words are placed in a row.
4. Students put pluses and minuses in the resulting grid to indicate whether or not each word in the column has each feature listed in the row.
5. Students add words and features.

Exhibit 7.3   Refocused Semantic Map for *Boom*

Text: During a thunderstorm a *boom* might become dislodged.

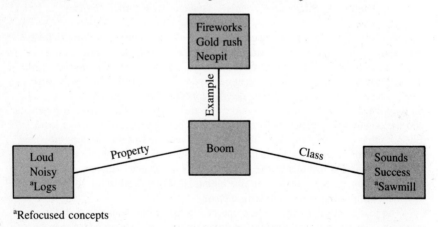

[a]Refocused concepts

Source: Dale D. Johnson, Susan Toms-Bronowski, and Susan D. Pittleman, *An Investigation of the Trends in Vocabulary Research and the Effects of Prior Knowledge on Instructional Strategies for Vocabulary Acquisition* (Madison: Wisconsin Center for Educational Research, University of Wisconsin), November 1981, p.151.

As students examine the patterns of pluses and minuses they discover that no two words have identical patterns and hence that no two words have exactly the same meaning. Exhibit 7.4 is an example of a partially completed semantic feature analysis of shelters.

Ezra and Vardà Stieglitz (1981) use semantic feature analysis as a culminating activity to a lesson when students have a base knowledge of a topic in a content field. Exhibit 7.5 is an example of a semantic feature analysis grid completed as a group activity in a math class under the direction of the Stieglitzes.

Disagreements about the qualities of concepts are opportunities for learning. One student who placed a plus next to *parallelogram* and beneath *sides equal* supported his choice by stating that the rhombus is a parallelogram that has four equal sides. Grids can be made more complex by replacing the + and − notations with numerical ratings (1–5). As a child's experience increases, the differentiations become more precise.

VOCABULARY INSTRUCTION IN THE TEACHING OF NEW CONCEPTS

In beginning reading, children learn to recognize words they already know, making instruction of word meaning often unnecessary, but soon they will encounter words for which they have no concepts or meaning. Vocabulary instruction is chiefly the teaching of new concepts. The teaching of a new concept is not the same as having students learn new words or labels for familiar concepts, for example, learning more elegant words or labels for commonly used words, such as *attire* for *clothes*.

William Nagy offers an example of vocabulary instruction focused on concepts rather than labels where the teacher starts discussing the meaning of a word without mentioning the word itself. "Have you ever had the feeling that something was going to go wrong or that something bad was going to happen? Not that you had any reason to think that—just a sort of feeling. Has anyone ever had such a feeling? Did something bad actually happen? After some discussion for a minute or so, the teacher introduces the actual term. Well, that sort of feeling is called a premonition."

Activity 7.1, *Developing Conceptual Vocabulary*, is an opportunity for your students to use the semantic feature analysis as a way to show the changing conceptual meanings of words.

Frayer Model

The Frayer model for attaining conceptual meanings of words was developed from work by Dorothy Frayer, Wayne Frederick, and Herbert Klausmeir at the University of Wisconsin (Frayer, Frederick, and Klausmeir 1969). The model offers a systematic procedure for conceptualizing words. These are the steps in the model:

Exhibit 7.4 Partial Semantic Feature Analysis of Shelters

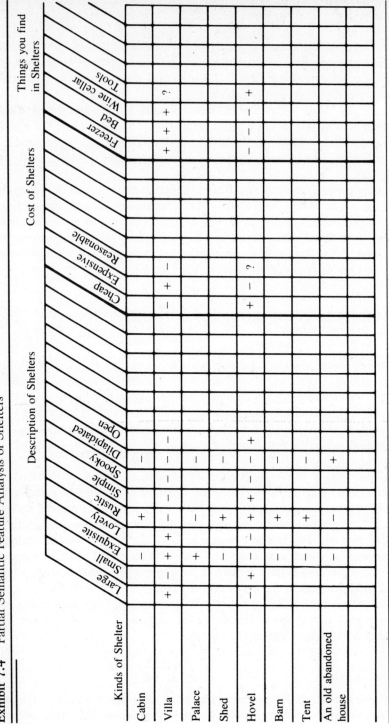

Kinds of Shelter	Description of Shelters									Cost of Shelters			Things you find in Shelters			
	Large	Small	Exquisite	Lovely	Rustic	Simple	Spooky	Dilapidated	Open	Cheap	Expensive	Reasonable	Freezer	Bed	Wine cellar	Tools
Cabin		−		+			−									
Villa	+	+	+	−	−	−	−	−		+	−		+	+	?	
Palace		+		−			−									
Shed				+			−									
Hovel	−	+	−	+	+	+	−	+		−	?		−	−	+	
Barn				+			−									
Tent		−		+			−									
An old abandoned house		−		−			+									

Source: Dale D. Johnson, Susan Toms-Bronowski, and Susan D. Pittleman, *An Investigation of the Trends in Vocabulary Research and the Effects of Prior Knowledge on Instructional Strategies for Vocabulary Acquisition* (Madison: Wisconsin Center for Educational Research, University of Wisconsin, November 1981), p. 40.

Exhibit 7.5 Semantic Feature Analysis of Shapes

	Four-sided	Curved or rounded	Line segment	All sides equal length	Right angle
Triangle	−	−	−	+	+
Rectangle	+	−	+	−	+
Parallelogram	+	−	+	+	+
Circle	−	+	−	−	−
Trapezoid	+	−	+	−	−
Semicircle	−	+	+	−	−
Square	+	−	+	+	+

Source: "Savor the word to reinforce vocabulary in the content areas" by E. L. Stieglitz and V. S. Stieglitz, *Journal of Reading,* October 1981. Reprinted with permission of E. L. Stieglitz and V. S. Stieglitz and the International Reading Association.

1. Discriminating the relevant qualities common to all instances of the concept. For example, the relevant attribute of *globe* is *spherical.*
2. Discriminating the relevant from the irrelevant properties of instances of the concept. For example, *large* or *small* is an irrelevant attribute for *globe.*
3. Providing an example of the concept, such as a classroom globe.
4. Providing a nonexample of the concept, such as a chart (non-spherical).
5. Relating the concept to a subordinate concept, such as *ball.*
6. Relating the concept to a superordinate term, such as *global.*
7. Relating the concept to a coordinate term, such as *map.*

In the event a concept cannot be defined by its relevant attributes, steps 1 and 2 are omitted and an antonym and a synonym are substituted for the defining relevant and irrelevant attributes (for example, for the concept *lovely,* a synonym might be *pretty;* an antonym, *ugly*).

The Frayer model is very useful in preparing students for a reading assignment. First, the teacher reviews an upcoming reading assignment to identify new words central to the topic. Together teacher and students supply the denotative meanings for the new words (usually the author states this meaning the first time the word is introduced, or it may appear in a glossary). Then, students try to provide both an example and a nonexample of the concept. Comparing examples and nonexamples leads to identification of relevant and irrelevant attributes. I don't want to slight the difficulty that may occur in determining essential attributes. Sometimes there are overlapping attributes among members of a category rather than a single critical feature. Among democratic countries, for example, one country may have the features *a* and *b;* another *b* and *c;* and a third, *c* and *d.* Members of

Activity 7.1 Developing Conceptual Vocabulary

Exhibit 7.6 below is an incomplete semantic feature analysis grid for musical instruments. If this topic is appropriate for your students, you may wish to have them add more words and features and then indicate which features apply to each word. If the topic is not appropriate, select a topic from a textbook used by your students. Together you and your students determine the instances and the qualities or attributes to place on the grid. Complete the grid by placing + or − in the appropriate squares. Completion of the grid should involve discussion that will illuminate the changing conceptual meanings of words. As jazz symphonies and other musical innovations occur, there are corresponding changes in the meanings of our words for musical instruments.

Exhibit 7.6 Incomplete Semantic Feature Analysis of Musical Instruments

	Description						Musical quality			Musical group		
	Wind	Strings	Percussion	Large size	Deep tone	Low pitch	Soft	Shrill	Mellow	Marching band	Orchestra	Wind ensemble
Violin		+										
Trumpet	+	−									+	−
Piano	−	+	+	+								
Bass					+	+						
Drum											+	

categories with overlapping features have been described as sharing "family resemblances" (Mervis 1980).

Once the essential attribute is identified, students may supply coordinate, subordinate, and superordinate terms. Upon completion of this step, students are ready to read the assignment. When teaching children the critical attributes of categories, it is best to use the most perfect example (a robin, for instance, is a better example of a bird than a penguin). Poor examples often lead to an unreliable generalization or to a failure to generalize at all. Further, a category is not always defined by a perceptual attribute, but sometimes by a function—what it can be used for and what it can do.

As an illustration of children's conceptual development, consider the story of children playing a game of "odd out," where they were to find one of three items that didn't belong. Adults were puzzled why, when given the words *dog*, *car*, and *cat*, the children selected *cat* as odd. Interviews revealed that the children regarded *car* and *dog* as the only two items that required a license.

Charles Peters compared the reading comprehension of students who used conventional social studies textbooks and students instructed according to the Frayer model (Peters 1974). Both good and poor readers who used materials organized in accordance with the Frayer model comprehended better than comparable pupils who used materials with the conventional features of textbooks. The textbook materials in Peter's study differed from those following the Frayer model in these ways:

Textbook	*Frayer Model*
Definition of term and example	Definition and example
No nonexample	Defining attribute
	Nonexample
Concept is introduced in context of historical period	Concept is related to superordinate, coordinate, and subordinate terms

Peters also tried to relate key terms to the students' background. For example, in including the concept *diplomacy* in the context of setting a territorial dispute between nations, he referred to the territorial disputes of street gangs—but only if the students had a schema for street gang warfare. Activity 7.2 can be used either as a preteaching vocabulary lesson or as a summary lesson.

A gifted teacher and reviewer of this book who was teaching Mayan culture to children combined the Frayer Model with imagery to produce a most effective lesson.

> I passed out word cards with definitions on the back—hard words that we didn't know but we'd need for the unit. I formed the pupils into groups of four, and each group had to perform their words: first, a careful dramatized example; second, a careful dramatized nonexample; third, they inductively got attributes through discussion of what they'd done; fourth, they insisted on nonattributes for what they'd done. Example, *chac,* a term for old men in the culture, keepers of the children, officiates in the ceremony to convert child to adult and (I fear) officiates at human sacrifices. Wow! What nice dramatization followed by a drama.

EFFICACY OF DIRECT INSTRUCTION AND LEARNING WORDS FROM CONTEXT

The number of words to be learned for general reading is enormous. (The number of new words the average middle grade child encounters while reading about 700,000 words per year is estimated between 750 and 5,500 words.) Yet teaching a prereading vocabulary for a given text greatly enhances comprehension of that text and contributes something to vocabulary

Activity 7.2   Applying the Frayer Model

Select a key term from a textbook you are using and then complete each of the following steps:

1. *Example.* Provide an instance of the concept.
2. *Nonexample.* Provide a noninstance of the concept.
3. *Relevant attribute.* Name the relevant attribute (or attributes) or the defining properties for the term selected.
4. *Irrelevant attribute.* List any attribute that is associated with the concept but is not indispensable in identifying whether something or someone is or is not an instance of the concept.
5. *Subordinate term.* Name a more specific part or illustration of the term you have selected.
6. *Superordinate term.* Name a term that refers to a related concept (principle, generalization, theory) that is more general and encompassing than the term you have selected.
7. *Coordinate term.* Name a term that often appears in the same context as your selected term and that is neither subordinate nor superordinate to your term. The coordinate may share some of the same attributes.

This activity can be used either as a preteaching vocabulary lesson before a selection is read, or as a summary lesson after reading.

You may decide to try something more ambitious—to encourage students to use the Frayer model on their own. An approach to such a goal is to give many opportunities for pupils to determine relevant attributes, irrelevant attributes, examples, and nonexamples and to select related hierarchical terms for familiar concepts.

---

growth. Independent investigators have demonstrated the value of using expanded networks, applying new terms in various contexts, and explaining answers to questions about new words: "Could a virtuoso also be a rival?" (McKeown, Becker, Amanson, and Perfetti 1983). An alternative to these direct teaching methods is incidental learning of vocabulary by wide reading of natural text.

The learning of word meaning and the ability to derive the meaning of novel words from context improves with age. William Nagy and others have shown that learning from context has long-term cumulative effects (Nagy, Herman, and Anderson 1985). Hence, a most effective way to produce large-scale vocabulary and to independently learn noninstructed words is to read a lot.

It may appear that there is an issue as to whether vocabulary should be taught directly—words targeted for classroom attention—or whether learners develop their vocabulary naturally through wide reading and their own desire to clarify concepts. On the one hand, it has been found that direct instruction is more effective than incidental learning for the acquisition of a particular vocabulary (McKeown et al. 1983). On the other hand, to promote long-term vocabulary growth teachers must aim at increasing students' incidental word learning. Studies reveal that readers learn words incidentally from context, particularly when these words occur frequently (Nagy et al. 1987). The overall influence of normal reading is large because the volume of reading students do allows for an accumulation of many words. Indeed, after third grade, for those who read a reasonable amount, reading may be the single largest source of vocabulary growth (Miller and Gildea 1987).

Contextual Processing

It's almost a platitude to say that the meaning of a word depends on its context. However, context has many dimensions. The situation in which reading occurs is context. The reader as a person with prior experiences constitutes context. So, too, does the purpose of reading. The schema for the work as a whole—exposition, narration—is a contextual variable that will influence the meaning the reader gives to words (one interprets *check* differently when reading an auto mechanic's manual than when reading a historical novel).

Narrower contexts for determining word meaning are paragraphs and adjacent sentences. Techniques for determining word meaning in these narrow contexts are presented in the following discussion.

A study by two Dutch investigators, M. Van Daalen-Kapteijns and M. Elshout-Mohr (1981), throws light upon the process by which word meaning is derived from narrow context clues. In their study, the investigators asked students to find the meaning of unfamiliar words such as *kolper* from serially presented sentences similar to the following:

1. When you're used to a broad view, it is quite depressing when you come to live in a room with one or two *kolpers* fronting a courtyard.
2. He virtually always studied in the library, as at home he had to work by artificial light all day because of those *kolpers*.
3. During a heat wave a lot of people all of a sudden wanted to have *kolpers,* so the sales of sun blinds then reached a peak.

Perhaps you derived from the first sentence a hypothesized schema for *kolper* and used this schema to fill in additional information about kolpers.

Most students hypothesize from the first sentence that *kolpers* are windows. In order to understand what sort of window a kolper is, one must reformulate the sentences so that they relate to the meaning of the new word. For example, sentence 2 may be reformulated to read "Having kolpers in a house means having artificial light all day." Also one must transform the reformulated sentence into something that fits the hypothesized schema. Such a transformation for sentence 2 might be "Kolpers transmit little light."

Good comprehenders make more substantive transformations than poor comprehenders. For example, for sentence 3 a typical response from poor comprehenders is "Kolpers are much asked for during a heat wave" (a literal reformation), while good comprehenders say something like, "Kolpers have a cooling effect" (a generalized reformation).

Support for an interactive model for teaching word meanings in context has been found by Joan Gipe (1978–1979). She reasons that a familiar context will activate a learner's "old information" or schema and that the new meaning will then be assimilated. By relating the new word to an existing schema, the learner is more likely to retain the meaning of the new word.

Gipe's interactive method for teaching word meaning requires that students read a three-sentence passage in which each sentence uses the target word in a defining context. Simple sentence structures and common words are used in the sentences in order to make the context familiar. Students respond in writing after reading the sentences, giving a word or phrase from their own experience that defines the new word. An example adapted from Gipe's materials appears below:

> The *brute* kicked the dog and hit the owner on the nose.
> Any person who acts cruel to anybody or to anything is acting like a *brute*.

A *brute* is a person who is very mean. Write down something that a brute might do at the dinner table.

Third- and fifth-graders comprehended new words better when taught by the interaction context method than when taught by any of the following methods:

1. An *associative method* by which they paired a new word with a familiar synonym or brief definition. Students were told, "Memorize the list of word pairs. Try to write this list again without looking at it."

   Brute—cruel, mean person
   Graphite—pencil
   Colossal—large
   Wretched—happy

2. A *category method* whereby pupils added to a list of words fitting a general category. Each list contained a new word and three familiar words. Students added words from their own backgrounds and recategorized a random list of previously learned words:

Bad people	*Things you can write with*
Mean	Pencil
Cruel	Graphite
Brute	Marker
Robber	Chalk

Words meaning big	*The way you look when unhappy*
Huge	Wretched
Large	Sad
Giant	Frowning
Colossal	Miserable

3. A *dictionary method* whereby students looked up designated words, wrote the definitions, and then wrote sentences containing each new word.

Although each method benefited vocabulary development, the interactive context method was better than other methods for students at both grade levels and for both good and poor readers. Asking students to apply a new word meaning to their own experience was valuable in all instances.

The teaching of strategies for figuring out word meanings from narrow contexts is undertaken so that students can later independently determine the meaning of unfamiliar words. Two such strategies are the SCANR Strategy and Recognizing Context Clues. SCANR (an acronym that summarizes the steps) is a metacognitive strategy whereby the student internalizes these directions: (1) Substitute a word or expression for the unknown word, (2) check the context for clues that might support the idea, (3) ask if the substitution fits all clues, and (4) revise your idea to fit the context (Jenkins, Matlock, and Slocum 1989).

The SCANR procedure coupled with practice in deriving the meaning of 15 unknown words each day over 11 sessions has been found to be helpful in teaching students to derive meanings themselves.

The context clues offered in sentences by direct explanation, appositives, and contrasts can be taught to students through exercises using artificial contexts. Activity 7.3 is such an example.

Although learning from context is an important way to improve vocabulary, it has some limitations. Context clues do not point directly to the meaning of a term. A range of possible substitutions is likely. Often in natural contexts of reading as opposed to artificially constructed classroom exercises, there are less helpful clues. For example, in a random sample of reading materials, investigators found that contexts were often as likely to be misleading as to be helpful (Schatz and Baldwin 1986). Context clues are quite helpful if one already knows what the word means, but it seldom supplies adequate information for one who has no other knowledge about the word. A single context clue is not sufficient for teaching a new concept.

SUMMARY

This chapter emphasizes an interactive approach to vocabulary development by teaching new words in the context of subject matter and related words. It includes suggestions for helping readers relate new terms to their own backgrounds. Chief among recommended teaching and learning strategies are cognitive mapping, semantic mapping, semantic feature analysis, the Frayer model, inference of word meanings from context clues, and use of new vocabulary in a variety of contexts. These techniques emphasize concern for active processing of new vocabulary so that vocabulary development enhances reading comprehension, not just word knowledge.

Activity 7.3   Determining Word Meaning from Context Clues

Typically, three types of context clues are taught in order to help readers derive the meaning of unfamiliar words—*direct explanation, appositive,* and *contrast.* Examples of these clues appear below. Study them and then see if you can use such clues in guessing the meaning of uncommon words. If you determine the meaning of a word and you want to remember it, make a statement (written or oral) in which you use the word in connection with some aspect of your life.

Direct Explanations

Volatility refers to the ease with which a liquid vaporizes, becoming a gas. The lumber industry hires *bushers*—persons who trim the limbs and large knots from felled trees.

Appositive

The *swizzle*, a drink made with crushed ice, rum, and bitters, is popular in the tropics.
  The *sycamore*, a shade tree with an edible fruit, is mentioned often in the Scriptures.

Contrast

The value of most furniture decreases as soon as it is sold, but antique furniture *appreciates* with age.
  It was never seen at the apex; on the other hand, its orbit was viewed at *perigee.*
  Select the answer that best defines the italicized word.

1. In contrast to the vigor of Edith, Viola was characterized by her *evanescence.*
     a. enduring quality
     b. fleeting quality
2. Instead of hardening the skin, it was an *emollient.*
     a. softening application
     b. stiffening application
3. He wasn't a miser, but a *prodigal.*
     a. given to extravagance
     b. an extraordinary person
4. Humorously, his nose was a *proboscis*, a long flexible snout.
     a. trunk of an elephant
     b. wings of an insect

  Should you want to remember a new word from this exercise, use it in a statement about something related to your personal life.

  Some possible conclusions are that any instructional method produces better word learning than no instruction, but no method is consistently superior. There are advantages from both a variety of techniques and repeated exposures to the words to be learned.

REFERENCES

Anderson, Richard C., and Freebody, Peter. "Vocabulary Knowledge." In *Comprehension and Teaching: Research Review*, John T. Guthrie, editor. Newark, DE: International Reading Association, 1981.

Frayer, Dorothy A., Frederick, Wayne C., and Klausmeir, Herbert J. *A Schema for Testing the Level of Concept Mastery*. Working Paper No. 16. Madison: Wisconsin Research and Development Center for Cognitive Learning, University of Wisconsin, April 1969.

Gipe, J. P. "Investigating Techniques for Teaching Word Meanings." *Reading Research Quarterly* 14, no. 4 (1978-1979): 624–644.

Hanf, M. Buckley. "Mapping: A Technique for Translating Reading into Thinking." *Journal of Reading* 14 (January 1971): 225–230.

Koeze, Scott. "The Dictionary Game." *The Reading Teacher* 43, no. 8 (April 1990): 613.

Jenkins, Joseph R., Matlock, Barbara, and Slocum, Timothy A. "Two Approaches to Vocabulary Instruction: The Teaching of Individual Word Meanings and Practice in Deriving Word Meaning from Context." *Reading Research Quarterly* 24, no. 21 (Spring 1989): 215–235.

Johnson, Dale D., Toms-Bronowski, Susan, and Pittleman, Susan D. *An Investigation of the Trends in Vocabulary Research and the Effects of Prior Knowledge on Instructional Strategies for Vocabulary Acquisition*. Madison: Wisconsin Center for Educational Research, University of Wisconsin, November 1981.

McKeown, Margaret G., Beck, Isabel, Omanson, Richard, and Perfetti, Charles. "The Effects of Long Term Instruction on Reading Comprehension." *Journal of Reading Behavior* 15 (1983): 3–17.

Mervis, Carolyn B. "Category Structure and the Development of Categorization." In *Theoretical Issues in Reading Comprehension*. R. J. Spiro, B. C. Bruce, and W. F. Brewer, editors. Hillsdale, NJ: Erlbaum, 1980, 279–307.

Miller, G., and Gildea, T. "How Children Learn Words." *Scientific American* 257, no. 3 (1987): 94–99.

Nagy, William E. *Teaching Vocabulary to Improve Reading Comprehension*. Urbana, IL: National Council of Teachers of English, 1988.

Nagy, William E., Herman, Patricia, and Anderson, Richard. "Learning Words from Context." *Reading Research Quarterly* 20, no. 2 (Winter 1985): 233–253.

Nagy, W. E., Herman, P., and Anderson, R. "Learning Word Meanings from Context During Normal Reading." *American Educational Research Journal* 24 (1987): 237–270.

Peters, Charles. *A Comparison Between the Frayer Model of Concept Attainment and the Textbook Approach to Concept Attainment*. Madison: Wisconsin Research and Development Center for Cognitive Learning, University of Wisconsin, February 1974.

Schatz, E. R., and Baldwin, R. S. "Context Clues and Unreliable Predictors of Word Meanings." *Reading Research Quarterly* 21 (1986): 439–453.
Stieglitz, E. L., and Stieglitz, V. S. "Savor the Word to Reinforce Vocabulary in the Content Areas." *Journal of Reading* 25 (October 1981): 46–51.
Van Daalen-Kapteijns, M., and Elshout-Mohr, M. "The Acquisition of Word Meaning as a Cognitive Learning Process." *Journal of Verbal Learning and Verbal Behavior* 20 (1981): 386–399.

Useful Readings

Beck, Isabel, McKeown, M. G., and Omanson, R. C. "The Effects and Uses of Diverse Vocabulary Instructional Techniques." In *The Nature of Vocabulary Acquisition*, M. G. McKeown and M. E. Curtis, editors. Hillsdale, NJ: Erlbaum, 1990, pp. 462–481.
Irvin, Judith. *Vocabulary Knowledge: Guidlines for Instruction*. Washington, DC: National Education Association, 1990.
Nagy, William E. *Teaching Vocabulary to Improve Reading Comprehension*. Urbana, IL: National Council of Teachers of English, 1988.

Improving Comprehension of Sentences

OVERVIEW

Experienced teachers know what sentences are difficult for students to understand. They know, for example, that students have more problems with the passive patterns (*It was seen by Bill*) than the more common noun-verb-object pattern (*Bill saw it*). Other troublesome patterns are appositives with commas (*Betty, my sister, came*) and clauses as subjects (*What you think is your business.*)

It is not only the pattern that signals ease or difficulty in interpreting sentences; difficulty is often associated with pronouns and sentences that require a referent (anaphora), particular connectives, punctuation, and figurative language. It is important that sentences are not conceived as isolated, because they can only be understood in light of the sentences that precede them and, in some cases, the subsequent sentences and the wider context of the reader's knowledge of the subject and situation.

133

This chapter will illustrate the types of reading problems that frequently arise with sentences, give reasons for the difficulties, and describe strategies for helping students overcome them. The explicit teaching of writing conventions is especially relevant for students whose social backgrounds rely on the school to teach the organization patterns of written language.

SENTENCE PATTERNS THAT REQUIRE TRANSFORMING

You might recall from Chapter 2 that good readers differ from poor readers in their ability to transform or reformulate sentences into more meaningful patterns. The importance of transformation was recognized by Noam Chomsky, who drew attention to the difference between surface syntactic structure, one of the innumerable forms in which an idea may appear in print, and deep syntactic structure, which reflects in a simpler form the basic idea itself (Chomsky 1957). (For example, *I wrote a letter to the president* and *I wrote to the president a letter* both say *I wrote the president a letter.*)

Consequently, we now believe that sentence comprehension involves translation from surface to deep syntactic structure. In some sentences, however, there is a close match between surface and deep structure; little transformation is required. A simple sentence such as *The boy hit the ball* has the same pattern at both levels of structure. Other sentences require that readers carry out special operations in order to make the transformation from surface to deep structure. Consider the example *We elected Mary president*. The reader must insert the idea *Mary is president* into the basic sentence *We elected Mary*. Although the hypothesis that the difficulty is in understanding a sentence is related to its transformational history is not fully confirmed, the importance for comprehension of separating the assertions in a sentence is clear (Caplan 1972).

The following types of sentences appear frequently and present difficulties because their surface structures differ from their deep structures. Each of these types of sentences requires a transformation:

1. *Passive voice.* Comprehension of sentences written in the passive voice can be difficult, because passive voice frequently disrupts the correlation between the succession of words and the succession of events. Passive voice is made up of a form of *be* (children often use *got* as the passive form) and the past participle of the principal verb (*The game is played by Tim*). It is produced by inverting basic word order (noun-verb-object), and introducing a form of *be*:

> Tabby was given milk by Meg.
> Milk was given Tabby by Meg.
> Her cat was called Tabby.

These passive forms can be transformed into the simple active form by the addition of an actor and an action:

> Meg gave Tabby milk.
> Meg calls her cat Tabby.

In transforming passive sentences, the key question is "Who is the recipient of the action?" Students need to know how to remove the inversion. To this end, a teacher may first model the transforming process. A number of transformations may be given and the students may derive from these examples their own rule for making transformations. Later, students may be given simple sentences and asked to produce passive forms from them. Or students may play a game in which they challenge each other in recognizing the passive form for basic sentences:

> Larry hit the ball.
> a. The ball was hit by Larry.
> b. Larry was hit by the ball.

S. L. Sebesta has told me that students who learn to read sentences of varying complexity aloud seem to get better at comprehending them. Also, he suggests having primary children act out passive sentences: *Mickey was told by Mary to stand on the rock.*

Mature readers may want to discuss why writers use the passive voice. They may be led to see how it modifies the topic of a sentence. Instead of known information being presented at the beginning of a sentence and new information at the end, for example, the passive may be used to relegate the known to the object. This shift in order removes attention from the actor and emphasizes the content. Sometimes the author shows an unwillingness to accept responsibility for the idea by using the passive (*It is believed* versus *I believe*).

2. *Sentences with relative clauses.* Comprehension difficulties sometimes occur when the subordinate clause immediately follows the main clause and when the subordinate clause is embedded in the main clause. For example, *The girl saw the boy who caught the fish* must be transformed into two sentences: (1) *The girl saw the boy* and (2) *The boy caught the fish.* *Who* does not refer to *girl* but to *boy*. In helping students be aware of the need for making transformations in sentences with clauses, give students sentences that have relative clauses and ask them to identify the sentences involved.

Relative clauses that make use of the words *which* and *who* may cause confusion. This is true at least when it is not clear which element of the sentence is being referred to by *which* or *who*. For example, consider the sentence: *The painting, which Otterson drew and which attracted so much negative comment, received a prize at the exhibition.* In comprehending this sentence, one must inhibit a quick decision about the meaning and join together widely separated components into a single sense: *The painting won a prize. Otterson drew the painting.*

Clauses may make it easier to comprehend passages. This is true at least if the clause makes the text more coherent so that the parts hang together in the same way that they would in normal speech. It is easier for a child to comprehend: *I have a black cat that loves liver and sleeps all day* than to confront separate units: *I have a cat. It is black. It sleeps all day.*

3. *Reverse ordering of events.* Sometimes the succession of words in a sentence is not the same as the natural succession of events. *I played after I did my homework* means that I did my homework earlier and played afterward. The reversal in temporal order requires that the reader make a mental transformation. Consider how a child might transform the following question to conform with temporal order: *How many marbles did Susan end up with if she found two marbles and she started out with three?*

4. *Conflict in semantic structure.*

The Russian psychologist Alexander Luria refers to a class of comprehension difficulties that arise because of discrepancy between surfaces and deep *semantic* (not *syntactical*) structure of sentences. (Luria 1981) Semantic inversions are not easy to understand directly. They often involve mixing something negative with something positive—*She was the last of the group* (negative) *with regard to independence* (positive). The statement means that she was first with regard to dependence. Thus, in order to understand a semantic inversion, we really must transfer the sentence into its opposite. Sentences requiring replacing a negative with an affirmative are *Which of these is less empty?* (*less empty* means *more full*) and *It's not likely that I won't go.* Try asking students to create semantically inverted sentences for their companions to transform. Here are some examples:

> I'm not unhappy.
> There is no one who can't go.
> Don't call me if he doesn't come.

COMPREHENDING ANAPHORIC RELATIONSHIPS

Anaphora refers to the use of expressions that link sentences, such as a pronoun linked to a noun. The resulting relationship is called an anaphoric relationship. By way of example: *The dog barked. It was trying to get attention. It* is related to *dog* in the previous sentence.

Although pronouns are frequently used as substitutes for nouns or groups of nouns, a pro-verb (not proverb) can be linked to a verb: *Tom washed the windows. He did it very quickly. It* is linked to the verb *washed.*

Prosentences are words that substitute for previous sentences: *The highest learning rates were achieved in a program that used poor assessment techniques and had a large number of drop-outs. This makes it impossible to determine the impact of instruction itself. This* is a prosentence referring to the previous sentence in its entirety. Sometimes the anaphoric term does not appear in an adjacent sentence but five or six sentences later. Also, it may appear before the word it will replace: *Now that you've burned this, we don't have enough mix to make another cake*. In this example, the referent *this* precedes its reference *cake*. Such backward-leading relationships are called *cataphoric*. Cataphoric relations become clear as more of the text appears.

"Invisible" anaphora involved elliptical sentences:

"Is Bill going to enter the contest?" asked Joe.
"I don't know," answered Mike.

In this example, the reader must supply the invisible anaphoric terms:

"I don't know if Bill is going to enter the contest."

Other examples of invisible anaphora are:

If Rex told Joe he would ride, he will. (He will *ride*.)
If you want him to sell the tickets, he will. (He will *sell the ticket*.)

Invisible anaphora require that the reader infer the words that will complete the relationship.

One final kind of anaphora involves substitution of a superordinate word for a word lower in a hierarchical relationship or the reverse:

Will you feed *Oscar and Harriet?*
Reptiles have to eat, you know.

"Do you want to see the biggest *mammals?* asked Kay.
"I love *whales,* replied Sandy.

Anaphora and Inferencing

As with other aspects of comprehending text, the most important factor in recognizing antecedents is the ability to make inferences about the content. For example, in the sentences *A Scot loaned me money. They are really thrifty people,* one must infer that *they* refers to the class *Scots* on the basis of the lexical term *Scot* and a schema for loaning money and thrift. That is, the meaning of an anaphoric relationship is determined as much by the background experience of the reader as by linguistic conventions indicating antecedents, such as the way number and gender provide clues to the meaning of pronouns.

Teaching Strategies for Comprehending Anaphoric Relationships

Typically students are only 60 to 80 percent accurate in recognizing antecedents. Improvement can occur through instruction, but the improvement will only be noted when the readers are interpreting word relations within familiar contexts. Peggy Moberly and Dianne Monson, for example, have had success in teaching fifth-graders four kinds of anaphoric ties in immediate, mediated, and remote positions (Moberly and Monson 1981).

Strategies for helping students interpret anaphora include metacognitive awareness, question probing, antecedent matching exercises, and rule generation.

1. *Metacognitive awareness.* Many students have never thought about anaphoric relations and their ability to interpret them. One suggestion for increasing students' consciousness of their ability to interpret anaphora is to take a selection with which students are familiar and ask them to identify all words that substitute for other words. Once the replacement words have been identified, students should name the antecedent of each. The relations identified can then be classified by students into such categories as pronouns, pro-verbs, prosentences, and superordinate terms.

The reverse of this activity is also recommended: Here, the teacher first defines the categories of anaphora and then asks students to find instances of these categories in the selection.

2. *Question Probing* Exhibit 8.1 illustrates questions for helping readers interpret different kinds of anaphora in sentences of varying complexity.

3. *Antecedent Matching* One way to carry out antecedent matching is to place numbers over linked terms found in a familiar passage. Students write the same number over the words that are linked in an anaphoric relationship.

             (1)   (1)   (2)
Did you know that a beaver looks something like a big rat? His front teeth are

    (2)   (1)   (3)   (3)
so big they can cut down small trees. His back feet are big and look like they

              (1) (4)   (4)
might be a duck's feet. His coat is brown and from it we make coats and hats.

4. *Rule generation* An excellent activity is to engage students in formulating rules or strategies for interpreting the anaphoric relations they know. The rules may not be stated exactly as you or I would state them, but the idea may be the same. The following are examples of rules or strategies for determining particular anaphoric relations:

   a. *The number-and-gender strategy* Sue and Ann went to the beach. *They* like to swim. Lois saw Steve. *She* saw him on the corner. (In finding the referent for a pronoun, look for an antecedent that has the same number or gender.)

   b. *The using-your-own-experience strategy* He went from home to school. *It* was closed. (*It* must be the school because you know that schools are more likely to be closed than homes.)

   c. *The same-subject strategy* Frank opened the door for Fred. *He* was then on *his* way. (*Frank* is the subject in the first sentence, so the subject in the subsequent sentence is likely to be the same—Frank.)

   d. *The receiving strategy* The principal spoke to the nurse and then asked for Mary. *She* wasn't in her room. (The last-mentioned person

Exhibit 8.1   Example of Anaphora in Sentences

Category	Example	Probe
Pronoun (easy)	Terry looked up. "I will try," he said. "Good!" said Grandpa. "We will both try."	Name the person or persons who will try.
(difficult)	"T'was at the royal feast, one Persia won By Philip's warlike son Aloft in awful state The God-like hero sat On his imperial throne.	Who sat on the throne? What is his name? (Answer: Alexander)
Pro-verb (easy)	Joe made a space helmet. So did Mike.	What did Mike do?
(difficult)	They claim that Beverly Hills is the wealthiest city in the world. She turned to the big man. "What do you think?" "I wouldn't know," said the big man. "It may be so."	What may be so?
Pro-sentence (easy)	No matter where the brothers went, they always went together. That's why it was so strange to see him there alone.	Why was it strange to see him alone?
(difficult)	The guilty soul of a murderer cannot keep its own secret. It is false to itself or rather it feels an irresistible impulse to be true to itself. The honest heart was not made for the residence of such an inhabitant. That is why it must be confessed.	What must be confessed? Why?
Subordinate Term (easy)	At the beginning of our story about the finch, the little bird was still gray.	What color was the finch?
(difficult)	Are fleets and armies necessary to a work of love and reconciliation? We have shown ourselves to be so unwilling to be called in to win back our lives? Let us not deceive ourselves, sir. These are the implements of war and subjugation—the last arguments to which kings resort.	Name the implements of subjugation.

or thing in the previous sentence is likely to be the antecedent for the anaphoric term in the second sentence—not the nurse, but Mary.)

AIDS TO UNDERSTANDING SENTENCE RELATIONS

Relationships among sentences are both explicit and implicit. The latter can only be understood by making inferences, which in turn depend on background knowledge of the context. Explicitly encoded relationships are signaled by a number of conventional aids—typographical cues, relational terms, and guide words. Teaching students how to use these aids is beneficial—especially for the poorer readers, who do not have well-established schemata for interpreting related sentences.

Typographical Aids

A great variety of type styles and punctuation is used in reading selections. Comic strips use drawings of balloons to indicate direct quotes; technical writers may use quotation marks to indicate the ironic use of a word. Whatever materials your students are reading should be previewed for type style and punctuation. Students should discuss how the author signals upcoming ideas of importance, shows how ideas are related, and clarifies meaning through the use of typographical aids. Children enjoy clarifying meanings of sentences that are the same except for punctuation: *Every cat knows it's master,* versus *Every cat knows its master.* Among the more common punctuation devices are the colon, semicolon, and comma.

The colon indicates a two-part idea. The first part is an introduction to get attention, and the second part is either a summation or an elaboration. The semicolon tells the reader that two closely related ideas are in the same sentence. The second idea may be a detail that clarifies or adds emphasis. Although the comma has many uses, its use in signaling a series of items or events is especially important, letting readers know they should slow down in their reading in order to grasp each of the separate concepts.

Frequently in children's literature, ellipses (. . .) signify a pause or interruption; dashes (—) and parentheses indicate an aside comment or a less essential addition to the sentence. The multiple meanings of these and other punctuation marks can be taught in the contexts of reading and writing. For example, have students write messages to each other in which they use different punctuation and type style.

Connectives as Guide Words

Guide words not only link ideas together, they show how the ideas are related. They are signs that let the reader know what's coming up. To see how they work, consider these sentences: *They were fed, clothed, observed for days, and then sent to their new home in apparently fine shape. Each was back in the juvenile hall within the month.*

As you can see, the last sentence just doesn't go with the previous sentence. The transition is too abrupt. In order to warn that the second sentence will call for a change in thought, add the guide word *yet* between *shape* and *each*. Now reread the passage. You will note how much easier it is to relate the final opposing idea to the previous thought.

A technique for sensitizing students to the significance of guide words is to discuss how changing the guide word changes the meaning of sentences such as the following:

Joe stopped	when	Meg kept on running.
	and	
	yet	
I will stay	but	you will go.
	or	
	so	
She eats	where	he cleans the dishes.
	if	
	while	

The guide word most frequently used to signal cause-and-effect relations is *because*. In the sentence *I bought an umbrella because it is going to rain,* the effect precedes the cause. Other connectives link a preceding casual idea to a subsequent effort (*It was snowing, so I put on snow tires.*) Words such as *since, if, as* and *for* often signal causal relations: *If you can't count on the family* (cause) *you may want to get additional resources* (effect). Conclusions or summaries related to previously mentioned causes are signaled by the guide words *consequently, therefore, thus, hence,* and *accordingly.*

Ideas are linked to time by guide words like *when, until, meanwhile, before, always, following, finally, during,* and *initially.* For example, note how *after* and *immediate* relate time in this sentence: *If problems surface in the weeks after the treatment, you have to take immediate action.* As indicated earlier, when the order of time cues does not correspond to the actual order of events, a transformation is required.

One technique for teaching guide words for time is to ask students to write directions for doing something they know how to do (making fudge or tying shoes) using a list of guide words you have supplied. Another technique is to use exercises in which students select the appropriate cue word: *Steve studied (after, before, until) he awakened.*

I want to reiterate that the teaching of guide words is not *the* answer to the problem of comprehending relationships among ideas in sentences. Guide words are aids, especially for poorer readers; however, identification of cause and effect, understanding of sequential relations, and drawing of conclusions rest more upon one's having appropriate schemata for the content of the material than upon one's ability to interpret surface clues.

ANALOGIES, METAPHORS, SIMILES, AND OTHER COIKS*

The idea of using the known to comprehend the unknown takes many forms. An author of a naturalistic selection may introduce an unfamiliar topic by showing its similarity to a familiar idea. Perhaps you recall being introduced to the flow of electrical current by an analogy to waterflow. In the aesthetic area, it is common to put two known elements, which are only remotely related, together in order to create a fresh meaning or image: "All the world's a stage, and all the men and women merely players."

Using Analogy as a Bridge

What do you think of doing when your students lack knowledge of the topic they are to read about? Your answer probably is that it is necessary to increase the experiential background of the students with respect to the unfamiliar topic. That answer is acceptable. However, a less direct approach may also be of value. It may be that the pupils already know something that will help them in learning the topic. Making an analogy between what they already know and the new topic may be an effective teaching and learning strategy.

David Hayes and Robert Tierney have presented evidence in support of analogy as a device for activating schemata and increasing reading comprehension of unfamiliar material. (Hayes and Tierney 1982). They had three groups of students read newspaper articles about an unfamiliar topic—the game of cricket. Students in one group read a baseball passage (familiar material to activate relevant information) and then read about cricket in a selection in which analogies such as the following had been embedded:

> *Unlike baseball,* cricket always has two batsmen in play at the same time. The center of activity is an area in the middle of the field called a pitch, *which corresponds to the infield in baseball.*

Students in another group read the unfamiliar material with analogies but without the preliminary reading of the article about baseball. A third group read the baseball articles and then the material about cricket without the embedded analogies.

Those students given the knowledge-evoking information (the baseball article) as well as the embedded analogies showed the highest comprehension of the new material. Those who were given the knowledge-evoking article but not the embedded analogies comprehended the new material better than those who did not have the background text.

The use of a semantic map as described in Chapters 2 and 7 offers a practical approach to generating analogies. The map can easily be adapted

---

*COIK stands for "clear only if known."

to making an analogy between a known and an unknown topic by selecting a familiar coordinate term in the map to use for comparison with the new term.

Teachers also may create their own introduction to unfamiliar material by suggesting relevant personal analogies ("Before you read this chapter, imagine yourself as a light beam whose reflection is being measured.") and by making direct analogies ("Photosynthesis in plants [new content] is like eating in people. What does eating do for people?"). The important points are that (a) the pupil must have the knowledge structure for the element to which the new information is to be related, and (b) this structure must be activated.

New findings about the use of analogy in the reading of scientific topics show the importance of *distant domain analogies* in comprehending text (Halpern, Hansen, and Riefer 1990). A distant analogy is where the two items compared do not share surface similarities but do have similar underlying concepts (schemata). A near-domain analogy relates a base and a target domain by common topic or other surface links. Baseball and cricket are near-knowledge domains because as team sports, they are played with a ball that has high surface similarity. Baseball and mathematics are conceptually "far" knowledge domains because the links between our knowledge of these topics are not apparent, although they may have common underlying structures. Students are unlikely to use an analogous solution to a structurally similar problem without an explicit hint. Once the analogy is recognized, it is the structural, not the surface, similarity that is important. The surface features of a near analogy may help in giving the context clues needed for recognizing the analogy, but students may preclude the deeper level of processing afforded by an analogy. Near analogies are better for spontaneous use in problem solving and far analogies are better for comprehending text because, in reading text with far analysis, students must seek underlying relationships to render its meaning. Students reading scientific passages with far analogies understand the text better than when reading text without analogies or with only a near analogy.

Comprehending Figures of Speech

The interpretation of metaphors, similes, and hyperbole involves connotation:

- You're so disagreeable, your own shadow won't keep you company. (hyperbole)
- She's busy as a bee. (simile)
- She's a bee in her activity as well as in her sting. (metaphor)

Central to the comprehension of figures of speech is the understanding that the literal interpretation of words won't always work. There is more meaning than what the words actually say. Exercises to introduce students to this prerequisite may take these forms:

1. Matching a literal meaning with a figurative expression
   Roberta is fragile.   Roberta is like:
   fine china.
   rough diamonds.
   bubble gum.
2. Rewriting literal statements.
   Students may, for example, rewrite the sentence *He loses his temper quickly* as *He's a firecracker* or *He's got a hair trigger.*
3. Interpreting figurative language

It's easier to interpret similes than metaphors. Unlike metaphors, similes make an explicit reference and signal that a comparison is being made with such words as *like* and *as.* Indeed, one way to interpret a metaphor is to first transform it into a simile:

This revolving door policy won't work.
The policy is like a revolving door.
The policy permits a problem to reappear.

According to schema theory, people interpret figurative language when they have a schema for each of the items compared. To understand the sentence *Fred is an encyclopedia,* one must have a schema for *Fred* (male person and other associations) and a schema for *encyclopedia* (something that is filled with facts, has knowledge separated into compartments, is heavy, has many pages, and other connotations).

In comparing the two schemata, readers will find that not all parts match. They must ask,"What aspects of both schemata are the same?" Both Fred and the encyclopedia are sources of a fund of information, but number of pages is not a common element.

Schemata or comparisons that don't match are called *tensions.* Usually, the literal element being discussed (called the *topic*) is compared with a figurative item (called the *vehicle,* or the thing to which the topic is compared). The commonality between the literal topic and the figurative vehicle is the *ground.*

In teaching, it is important to give students opportunities to identify the topic and the vehicle, to figure out the ground, and to recognize tension. Comprehension depends on the students' having schemata for both topic and vehicle. Consider a remark attributed to Boswell: "Well," said Dr. Johnson, "we had a good talk." "Yes, sir," said Boswell, "you tossed and gored several persons." Only someone with schemata for bulls and matadors could appreciate the comment.

It may be necessary to help some students recognize that writers sometimes represent inanimate objects or ideas as persons or as having the qualities of persons. Students should be asked to identify words that are actually only associated with living things but that in figurative expression may be attributed to the inanimate. (*The* patient *stone* nestled *against the tree.*) Children learn to interpret figurative language by constructing sentences that transfer human qualities—dreaming, smiling, laughing—to objects in nature. (*The sun* stuck his tongue out *before* hiding *in the night.*)

The problem of when to take a statement figuratively rather than literally is resolved through context. The expression *He put his sights on the wrong star* should be read literally in a story about a navigator. In the context of a tale of a wayward son, the reader would properly regard it as metaphorical.

As an instructional activity, you may wish to have students describe the contexts in which statements such as the following would be literal and then describe the contexts in which they should be comprehended as metaphorical:

> Let sleeping dogs lie.
> You've got egg on your face.
> Voters sent a message to Congress.
> She put all her eggs in one basket.

Many of the reading strategies introduced in Chapter 3 are useful in helping students deal successfully with noncohesive text (where links within and between sentences are broken or unclear.) Reciprocal teaching—with its emphasis on teaching students to monitor their comprehension and to do something about statements that need clarifying, for instance—is especially effective. In addressing the need for cohesive inferencing, teachers can concentrate on questions such as *What makes us believe* X (character) *did* Y (specific action from the text)? *Why did* Y *occur and what evidence do we have?*

Sentence-combining Exercises   The technique of sentence-combining can be used with many of the problems identified in this chapter—transformations, anaphora, guide words, figurative language. Basically, the sentence anagram task is an organizational activity that calls for applying a grouping strategy. This teaching has been successful in improving the sentence comprehension of students of widely different backgrounds and age. Phyllis Weaver, in particular, has demonstrated the value of this activity (Weaver 1979). The Weaver procedure for solving sentence anagrams resulted in dramatic increases in reading comprehension. The program itself took 15 minutes a day, 3 days a week, for 5 weeks.

Weaver taught children to solve sentence anagrams of increasing length in relatively less time by "chunking" words into higher-order units. Students were taught to use a word-grouping strategy by which they arranged words systematically into phrases and then arranged the phrases into sentences. The strategy called for first identifying the action word or verb and then asking a series of questions to group the remaining words and to relate the groups to the verb. Exhibit 8.2 shows the general structure of the word-grouping

Exhibit 8.2   Model of Sentence Anagram Word-grouping Strategy for Declarative Sentences in the Active Voice

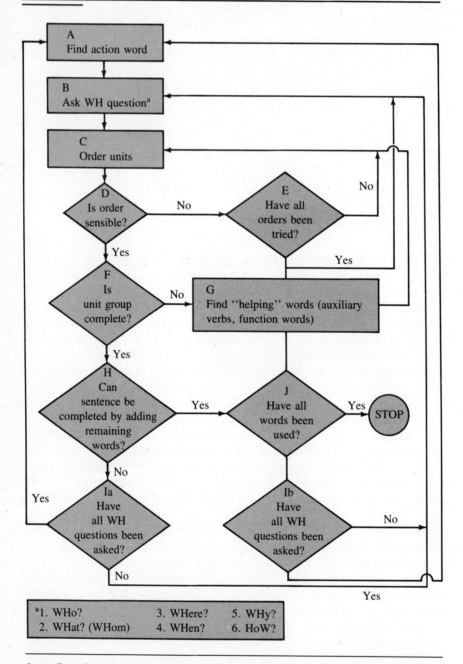

Source From "Improving Reading Comprehension: Effects of Sentence Organization Instruction" by Phyllis A. Weaver, *Reading Research Quarterly*, Vol. 15, 1979. Copyright ©1979 International Reading Association. Reprinted with permission of Phyllis A. Weaver and the International Reading Association.

strategy for constructing an array of words into declarative sentences. The actions are shown in rectangles and the decisions in diamonds.

Students were taught to perform the actions shown in the rectangles and to monitor their actions by asking and answering the questions shown in the diamonds. The strategy assumes knowledge of several concepts: *action words, wh* questions (who? what? where?), and *sensibleness* (does the grouping make sense, both semantically and syntactically?).

Once a student had solved a sentence anagram using the word-grouping strategy, a time element was introduced. Time was recorded and students were encouraged to decrease the time needed to solve sentence anagrams. When students could solve anagrams of a given length within 60 to 90 seconds, longer sentence anagrams were introduced.

In Weaver's study, vocabulary was no higher than second-grade level, and punctuation was omitted. Also, Weaver worked with individual students. Activity 8.1 offers you an opportunity to use the sentence anagram task for developing vocabulary.

Activity 8.1 Using Sentence Anagrams for Improving Reader Comprehension

General Plan for the Activity

Try teaching a modified form of the word-grouping strategy. You may wish to teach an entire group of class or individual pupils.

Jumble the sentences provided in Exhibit 8.3 or make up your own anagrams, using a vocabulary with which your students are familiar.

The activity is conducted over a period of several days.

Procedure

1. Model the word-grouping strategy.
   a. A sample anagram, such as *see weak helps the that people he,* can be used. Say aloud: "I first find an action word—*helps.* Then I ask a *wh* question: *Who* helps? *He* helps."
   b. "I find another action word—*see*—and ask the *wh* question: Who see? *People see.*"
   c. "I order the units *people see* and *he helps.*"
   d. "I check the words for meaning. People *see the weak* doesn't make sense. *He helps the weak.* makes sense."
   e. "Can I add other words to complete the sentence? *People see that he helps the weak.*"
2. Ask students to imitate the above procedure in applying the strategy. Start with the jumbled sentence *owner ran him the after.* Perform all steps in this order:
   a. Find the action word
   b. Ask *wh* questions.
   c. Order units.
   d. Ask, is the order sensible? If not try other orders.
   e. Complete the sentence by adding the remaining words.

3. Let students organize sentence anagrams derived from the sentences in Exhibit 8.3 or anagrams of your own construction. Start with sentences five to six words in length. Record time and encourage pupils to better their time. Move to anagrams of greater length when there are no errors.

Exhibit 8.3   Sentences to Jumble as Anagrams

Number of Words	Sentences
5–6	the happy boy found him
	your dog won't growl at friends
	let's eat in a little while
	the lion cut his paw
7–8	you can learn to earn money now
	the clock fell down from the wall
	she didn't want to kill the duck
	the fast ball was thrown by Andy
	the bird builds her nest in the water
9–10	the little cub ran home but the others didn't
	a bright light filled the room bringing cheer and hope
	you must scrub the wall before asking for any money
11–12	she saw that the dark cake baked giving off a sweet smell
	the tree came from a seed that had been brought from Spain
	does it help to plan before going on a long trip
13–15	the black and blue colors showed that something had
	happened before the circus left town
	dogs bark lions growl but
	only people brag and without a very good reason

You will note that the sentences in the panel call for comprehending passive voice, anaphora, and connectives.

SUMMARY

Comprehension as translation depends on recovering the meaning that underlies different kinds of sentences. The meaning of some sentences are more difficult to recover: those in passive form, with relative clauses, with reverse temporal ordering, or with a semantic conflict. Strategies are presented for helping students unravel these difficult sentence structures.

Obviously the comprehension of a simple sentence depends on both the existing schemata that readers bring to the text and the use of a wider context—successive sentences in the paragraph, successive paragraphs, and the discourse of the text. A key factor in relating sentences within the paragraph is the ability to interpret anaphoric relationships. This chapter introduces some of the most commonly encountered anaphoric relationships and suggests strategies for helping readers recognize them. The point is made that deriving antecedents for particular expressions depends not only on form as it appears in the sentence but on context as well. A young reader may be able to interpret pronouns or prosentences in beginning materials but not in advanced materials.

Strategies are given for teaching other aids to comprehending and relating sentences—typographical devices, analogies, and figures of speech. The practical activity of solving sentence anagrams is presented in detail as an illustration of a way to help learners integrate a number of sentence-processing abilities.

REFERENCES

Caplan, D. "Clause Boundaries and Recognition Latencies for Words in Sentences." *Perception* 8, no.11 (1972): 73–76.

Chomsky, Noam. *Syntactic Structures*. The Hague: Mouton, 1957.

Halpern, Diane, Hansen, Carol, and Riefer, David. "Analogies as an Aid to Understanding and Memory." *Journal of Educational Psychology* 82, no.2 (1990): 298–305.

Hayes, David A. and Tierney, Robert J. "Developing Readers' Knowledge Through Analogy." *Reading Research Quarterly* 17, no. 2 (1982): 256–280.

Luria, Alexander, R. *Language and Cognition*. James V. Wertsch, editor. (New York: John Wiley & Sons, 1981).

Moberly, Peggy, and Monson, Dianne L. *Effects of Instruction on Fifth Graders' Comprehension of Anaphoric Structures*. Unpublished paper, University of Washington, Seattle, 1981.

Weaver, Phyllis A. "Improving Reading Comprehension: Effect on Sentence Organization Instruction." *Reading Research Quarterly* 1, no. 15 (1979): 129–145.

Useful Readings

Halliday, M.A.K., and Hasan, R. *Cohesion in English*. London: Longman, 1976.

Halliday, M.A.K. *Spoken and Written Language*. Geelong, Victoria (Australia): Deakin University Press, 1985.

Irwin, Judith W. *Understanding and Teaching Cohesion Comprehension*. Newark, DE: International Reading Association, 1986.

9

Comprehending Different Types of Discourse

Types of Discourse
Comprehending Narrative Text
    Metalevel Schemata for Stories: Story Grammar
    Questions That Integrate Text
A Strategy for Appreciating Literature
    Rhetorical Devices for Identifying the Author
    Strategies for Finding the Inner Sense of Narrative
Comprehending Expository Text
    Identifying Top-Level Structures
    Using Pattern Guides
    Restructuring Text
    Summarizing
Reading to Perform a Task: Documents
    Simple Lists
    Combined Lists
    Intersecting Lists
    Nested Lists
    Graphs and Charts
    Forms
Summary

OVERVIEW

Previous chapters have featured the active processes by which the learner ties informational content to prior knowledge and uses general strategies in comprehending text. This chapter focuses on the ways the learner can examine the text itself for the logical structure of the material—its form as well as its content. Although meaning does not reside in the text alone, it is important for the reader to know how authors cue meaning and flag important statements. Indeed, a powerful tool is to know how to take the author's organization plan and restructure it into a form that will give greater understanding.

Children are more successful in acquiring information from stories than from prose organized in other ways. Yet, much of the knowledge of greatest worth comes from interaction with texts having more formal structural properties than simple narrative. Sophisticated literature, exposition, and descriptive writing involve a variety of organizational forms. The purpose of this chapter is to attend to the most important of these and to suggest ways for helping students learn how to apply knowledge of the forms in comprehending.

TYPES OF DISCOURSE

William Brewer has an interesting classification scheme for illuminating the cognitive structures underlying different organizational forms (Brewer 1980). This scheme is based on the prose of the traditional types of writing—narrative, exposition, and description. Each category in the scheme emphasizes a different intent on the part of the author—to inform, to entertain, to persuade, or to present an aesthetic experience.

As seen in Exhibit 9.1, Brewer refers to these purposes as *discourse force*. An underlying cognitive structure is hypothesized for each type. Descriptive discourse attempts to capture a perceptual scene. Since the predominately involved sense in this category is vision, the cognitive structure is thought to be visual-spatial. In the case of narrative, a series of events in time are depicted and related through a causal or thematic chain. Thus, the underlying cognitive structure consists of temporally occurring events having a causal or thematic coherence. Expository discourse sets require abstract logical processes. Therefore, the underlying structure features induction, classification, and comparison.

As you probably noticed, the notion of discourse force involves some problems. Some types of discourse can be designed to inform and entertain at the same time; and, of course, the classification system considers only the point of view of the author, who may not have the same intention as the reader. Nevertheless, by noting surface clues to the underlying structure, the reader may be able to anticipate the author's purpose and to adopt a reading strategy appropriate for the structure. The presence of location words (*near, above, behind*) may indicate spatial structure; words such as *thus* and *because* suggest logical structure; and choice of a particular vocabulary (e.g., colloquial or formal language) may indicate whether the author's purpose is to entertain or inform.

In this chapter, Brewer's classification is adapted to focus on the teaching of strategies and concepts related to the reading of three different types of text: reading for literary experience, reading to be informed, and reading to perform a task.

Exhibit 9.1   A Psychological Classification of Written Discourse Types

Discourse	*Discourse Force*			
(Underlying Structure)	*Inform*	*Entertain*	*Persuade*	*Literary-Aesthetic*
Description (Space)	Technical description Botany Geography	Ordinary description	House advertisement	Poetic description
Narrative (Time-Events)	Newspaper story History Instructions Recipies Biography	Mystery novel Western novel Science fiction novel Fairy tale Short story Biography "Light" drama	"Message novel" Parable Fable advertisement Drama	Literary novel Short story "Serious" drama
Exposition (Logic)	Scientific article Philosophy Abstract definition		Sermon Propaganda Editorial Advertisement Essay	

Source: from "Literary Theory, Rhetoric, and Stylistics: Implications for Psychology" by William F. Brewer. In *Theoretical Issues in Reading Comprehension,* R. Shapiro, B.C. Bruce, and W.F. Brewer, editors. Hillsdale, NJ: Erlbaum, 1980, p. 225.

COMPREHENDING NARRATIVE TEXT

Metalevel Schemata for Stories: Story Grammar

A key to comprehending narrative is a sense of plot, theme, characters, events, and how they relate. Analysis of children's story recall reveals which events in a selection are more memorable to them because of their interpretations. Analysis also indicates how well-developed a child's sense of story structure is. Story structure is the explicit grammar, or pattern, by which stories are constructed. One such grammar, depicting episodic story structure, is that of Stein and Glenn (1979). It has these elements:

1. *Setting:* Introduction of the protagonist and information about the context in which story events will occur.
2. *Episode.*
   a. *Initiating event* (cause for action and setting of goal).
   b. *Internal response* (emotional reaction that causes the protagonist to initiate action).

c. *Attempts* (overt actions carried out in order to attain a goal).

d. *Consequence* (event, action, or end of tale, marking the attainment or nonattainment of the goal).

e. *Reaction* (expression of the protagonist's feelings about the outcome of the action or its broad consequences).

Children's schemata for story structure greatly influence their memory of what they read. Older children are generally more competent in using their sense of story structure to aid factual recall. However, a schema for story structure can be developed. One way to develop the schema is to teach students to use story grammar in generating their own narratives. Story writing is an excellent way to enhance story comprehension. Activity 9.1 will illustrate the technique. Stephanie McConaughy has found that different types of story schemata are used by adults and children (McConaughy 1980). The schemata vary in both the components of information and the way the information is organized. She asked adults and children to read several stories and then to write summaries of them, telling only what they considered to be the most important parts for the meaning of the whole story. The summaries by young children showed a *simple descriptive schema*—beginning and ending components (the setting, initiating events, and resolution) and some details about intervening events and actions. Their schema answered the basic questions: What did X do in the story? What happened in the story? These children comprehended the stories at a literal level. Older children revealed an *information-processing schema;* they made inferences to supply missing information that fit logically into the story and supplied explanations to ac-

Activity 9.1 Using Story Grammar to Develop a Schema for Reading Narrative

---

First ask students to supply answers to the questions listed.
Record their answers and then have them rewrite the answers as in an original story.

1. *Setting:*
   a. Where will our story take place—at the beach, in an airplane, in a classroom? What is the place like?
   b. Who is the heroine or the hero? What is she or he like? Describe.
2. *Episode:*
   a. What will happen?
   b. How will the heroine or hero (protagonist) feel about what happens?
   c. What does the protagonist want now? What does the protagonist plan to do? What does the protagonist do?
3. *Consequences:*
   a. What happens when the protagonist carries out the plan?
   b. Does the protagonist succeed or not?
4 *Reaction:*
   a. What did the protagonist learn from this?
   b. What do we learn from this?

---

count for actions and events. The adult summaries represented a high-level, *social-inference* schema. The social-inference schema not only includes the basic components for actions and events, but also adds components that explain the motivation behind the characters' actions. This type of schema answers the question: Why did X do what he did in the story? Thus, the social-inference schema includes the goal of the character and the internal responses, thoughts, and subgoals that lead the character to action. Social-inference theory incorporates both the psychological and physical causality to explain the sequence of actions and events. The addition of a moral to the story carries comprehension beyond the plane of the simple story schema to an inference about the author's intentions.

The evidence that children even up to the fifth-grade spontaneously focus on more literal aspects suggests that students may need the help of specific problem questioning on order to focus on higher levels of comprehension. In kindergarten and first grade, questions about motivation may be inappropriate for testing comprehension. Children at these early levels are better at answering questions about simple details than they are at answering higher-level questions requiring inferences and justifcations of outcomes. However, the teacher might draw out inferences about motivation *after* the literal aspects have been discussed.

Older children (sixth grade) could be asked to derive the theme themselves. They could also be asked questions that change the focus from actions and events to the goals and internal responses of the characters. Questions about the thoughts, feelings and intentions of the characters, which focus on the motivation behind actions, might be appropriate for those with a social-inference schema.

Asking students to summarize a story has several advantages (see Activity 9.2). The summary serves as a method for organizing the most important

Activity 9.2   Using the Summary of a Story to Reveal the Students
                   Schema for Stories

Ask students in your class to read and summarize a story. Analyze the summaries according to type of story schema:

Simple descriptive schema — the summary has a beginning and ending components, including a setting, an initiating event, and a resolution.

Information-processing schema — the summary includes inferences to supply missing information that logically fits the story; and explanations to account for the causes of actions and events may be given.

Social-inference schema — in addition to the sequence of actions and events, this summary explains the motivation behind the characters' actions.

After completing your analysis, decide what the findings mean to you as a teacher. How might you take the results into consideration when assigning written material to children? How does the particular schema used influence what the pupils are learning from their reading? What follow-up questions might you ask in order to help children fill in the missing story components?

Exhibit 9.2 is an illustration of the results obtained when this activity was undertaken at one primary school. Notice how attempts and major goals are better recalled than minor statements about setting.

Exhibit 9.2 Story Summaries

"The Lion and the Mouse"

A Lion was awakened from sleep by a Mouse running across his face. With a terrible roar, the Lion seized the Mouse with his paw and was about to kill him.

"Oh please," the Mouse begged. "Spare my life! I will be sure to repay your kindness."

The King of the Beasts was so amused at the thought of a Mouse being able to help *him* that he let the frightened creature go.

Shortly afterward the Lion fell into a trap set by some hunters and was hopelessly caught in a net of strong ropes. In his misery the Lion roared so loudly that all the beasts in the forest heard him.

The Mouse recognized the roar of his former captor and ran to the place where the Lion lay trapped. At once, the Mouse began to gnaw the ropes with his teeth. He gnawed rope after rope until at last the Lion was free.

"Thank you," said the grateful Lion. "I know now that *in time of need the weak may help the strong.*"

Source: Aesop's Fables, retold by Ann McGovern. (New York: Scholastic, Inc., 1963), p. 42.

The children listened while the teacher read "The Lion and the Mouse," one of Aesop's fables (reproduced here). Then they wrote the story in their own words. Here are seven accounts, one from each grade level of primary school. Note the different meanings that the children have given in the story. Is it possible to perceive any relationship between individual accounts and the types of story schema, (simple descriptive schema, information-processing schema, and social-inference schema)?

The Lion and the Mouse

A lion got trapped in a net and mighty mouse came and saved him

Prep.

The lion and the mouse

One day a lion was nesting under a tree. Under his paw was a nut. a mose saw the nut and tried to get it but the lion awoke and was Just about to eat it but the mouse Said don't eat me. If your kind I will do something for you but you must let me -go. So the lion let the animal go and the mose Scamped off. After a while the lion got trapped in a trap. The mouse came to rescue the lion the lion said thank you.

Grade 1

The Lion and the Mouse

There once was a Lion awoken by a Mouse. The Lion was just about to reach out his paw when the mouse said Don't Do That I will Do anything to rePay you back and one Day he did. The lion got cought in a trap and he to mouse heard him and the roar and ran to him and nibbled one rope after another and the Lion was free.

Grade 2

The Lion and the Mouse

Once there was a Lion and a mouse. The mouse went walking with his eyes closed and walked right over the Lion. The Lion grabbed him. The mouse said I will help you any time you want me to. The Lion let him go. the next day. the Lion went for a walk. He fell into a net he roared. The mouse woke up and went running to the Lion. The mouse nibbled at the net it woke and the Lion got free.

Grade 3

The Lion and the Mouse
Once upon a time there lived
a lion.
He went for a walk.
A mouse was running along
and banged into the lion
It roared.
The mouse said " Don't eat me.
If you don't eat I will help
you."
All right said the lion
The lion went for a walk.
He landed in a net.
The lion roared.
The mouse came running
and with his teeth he chewed
the net and he let the lion out.
The lion thanked the mouse
and they lived happily ever
after.

Grade 4

The Lion and the mouse

There was a little mouse and a big lion.
First the lion was awaked by the mouse and
the lion grabbed the mouse and the little
mouse said "Please let me go I will pay you
back with a favour." The lion laughed.
ha ha ha you can't help me. So the lion
let him go. Late on the lion got stuck in a
net. The lion roared so loudly the whole
Jungle could hear him. The mouse recogniged
his roar. The little mouse ran to the lion
and saw in the net a started growing on
the net. When he got the lion out of the
net the lion thanked him and said sometimes
little can help big.

Grade 5

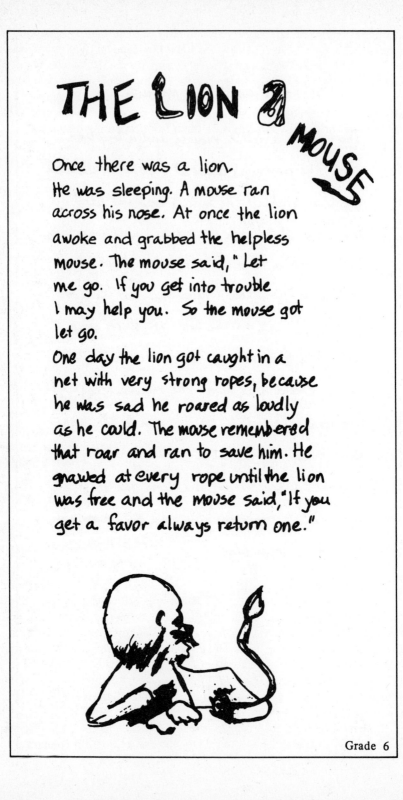

THE LION & MOUSE

Once there was a lion.
He was sleeping. A mouse ran
across his nose. At once the lion
awoke and grabbed the helpless
mouse. The mouse said, " Let
me go. If you get into trouble
I may help you. So the mouse got
let go.
One day the lion got caught in a
net with very strong ropes, because
he was sad he roared as loudly
as he could. The mouse remembered
that roar and ran to save him. He
gnawed at every rope until the lion
was free and the mouse said, "If you
get a favor always return one."

Grade 6

information. It gives the teacher a good firsthand picture of the nature of students' schema for a story, focusing on what the students think is important, rather than on what the teacher thinks is important. The teacher can then proceed, on the basis of the students' schema, to fill in missing components through questioning. The summary provides the schema for organizing basic information in memory from which elaborating details can be reconstructed. The schema, or framework, keeps children from becoming distracted by minor points as they retell a story. Encouraging children to develop and use their schemata should help them learn what to expect in a story and how to decide what is important to remember.

Similarly, with schema theory, assessment of reading comprehension moves away from the practice of giving students unnatural tasks–paragraphs taken out of context and questions that fragmentize rather than integrate text. Instead, teachers have students engage in free recall and the writing of summaries for their reading. Interpretation of these ecologically valid activities offers clues to what readers are comprehending and how they are processing text.

Do you know about "Story Maker" and "Textman"? They are language arts activities represented in microcomputer courseware created so children could gain a sense of what makes a story (Newman 1981).

These programs teach the structure of genres and the use of themes and rhetorical devices. In using "Story Maker" the child constructs a story by selecting a series of episodes. Children read the initial episode, then choose the next episode from several options. Children quickly learn that early choices have definite consequences. Children can work toward their own goals or a goal generated by the computer. The computer generated goal serves to focus attention on the sequence of the story and to guide the user in making choices about events, characters, and final outcome. Examples of high-level constraints are:

> "Try to construct a story in which the main character gets his enemies to like him."
> "Try to construct a story that uses suspense."
> "Try to construct a story that illustrates the theme that it is important to take risks in order to succeed."

Similarly, in "Textman" the child must keep in mind the audience and purpose of the selection as well as attend to paragraphs that precede and follow a missing paragraph. Choosing correct sentences depends on comprehending the context. The player draws meaning from context, which in turn helps develop an understanding of the structural relations of sentences to paragraphs and paragraphs to the complete text.

"Story Maker" and "Textman" are interesting in their own right and because they illustrate how instruction in reading comprehension is being influenced by research on the overall structure of narrative.

Students who have schemata for stories (a knowledge of story grammar) comprehend and recall stories better than students without the schemata. Instruction in the schematic aspects of narrative helps comprehension. Jill Whaley and Dixie Spiegel, for instance, directly taught story structure to a group of fourth-graders, who thereafter outscored a control group in comprehending stories (Whaley and Spiegel 1982). Lessons typically consisted of (1) conducting an overview and review (2) telling about and illustrating one story element (protagonist—reaction and goal, attempts to achieve the goal, outcome), (3) giving other examples of the element, (4) eliciting examples of the element from the children, and (5) having students participate in activities that reinforce the element taught. A reviewer of this text points out that a sense of story comes about through comparing many stories to see how they are alike and different.

The issue of nonstandard narrative is important in the light of multicultural education. The story in an "oral" as opposed to a "literate" style is characterized by technical devices such as repetition, parallelisms, sound play, juxtaposition, foregrounding, and showing rather than telling.

Through a structural analysis of a child's story, J. P. Gee was able to reveal an underlying theme and the use of oral technical devices (Gee 1985). Although the teacher thought that the second-grade child lacked language skills, Gee revealed that the child was using an oral story grammar in a sophisticated fashion. Parenthetically, children's reading ability is evaluated on their narrative style and use of prosody; children whose sense of style and prosody match the teacher's implicit model of reading are evaluated as more competent readers.

The following excerpts illustrate Gee's structural analysis:

Part 1:   *Introduction*
      Part 1A: Setting
          1.   Last yesterday in the morning
          2.   there was a hook on the top of the stairway
          3.   an' my father was pickin me up
          4.   an I got stuck on the hook up there
          5.   an' I hadn't had breakfast
          6.   he wouldn't take me down =
          7.   until I finished all my breakfast =
          8.   cause I didn't like oatmeal either //
    Part 1B
          9.   an' then my puppy came
        10.   he was asleep
        11.   he tried to get up
        12.   an' he ripped my pants
        13.   an' he dropped the oatmeal all over
Part 3:   *Resolution*
      Part 3A: Concluding Episodes
       ·
       ·
       ·
         36.   an' last yesterday, an' now they put him asleep

37. an' he's still in the hospital
38. (an' the doctor said ...) he got a shot because
39. he was nervous about my home that I had

Part 3B: *Coda*

41. an' he could still stay but
42. he thought he wasn't gonna be able to let him go //

Gee's analysis of this story describes groups of ideas that have parallel structure and match each other in content or topic. These groups are called "stanzas." Stanzas comprise episodes. The first part of the story takes place in the child's home; the second part involves going to school and complicating actions; and the last part is in a hospital with "resolutions" told in two four-line stanzas and a concluding two-line coda. The underlying theme is the child's sense of being counterpoised between the world of the puppy and the adult world where she must deny her own longings and those of the puppy in turn, so he will not disrupt the discipline of the world.

Questions That Integrate Text

Isabel Beck and Margaret McKeown have found that many sets of questions in instructional materials appear to disrupt comprehension of the story. That is, the questions suggested in the teachers' manuals are not likely to help students organize and integrate text content (Beck and McKeown 1981). On the contrary, the frequently recommended practice of asking questions at different taxomonic levels (literal, inferential, critical) is suspect. Instead, teachers should ask questions based on the logical organization of events and ideas of central importance to the story and their interrelationships—story grammar. Thus, the teacher has the students first decide on the starting point of the story and then list in summary form the major events and ideas that constitute the plot and the links between events, or the gist of the story. Implied ideas, which are part of the story but are not directly stated, should be included. Asking questions that will elicit information matching the progression of ideas and events is the last step.

Singer and Donlan's schema-general questions for use in summarizing narrative appear to conform to Beck and McKeown's recommendations (Singer and Donlan 1982). These questions follow the organization of a story and suggest a way to synthesize story information and reconstruct it as a unit:

1. *The Leading Character*
   a. Who is the leading character?
   b. What action does the character initiate?
   c. What did you learn about the character from this action?
2. *The Goal*
   a. For what does the leading character appear to be striving?
   b. What did you learn about the character from the nature of the goal?

   c. What courses of action does the character take to reach the goal?
   d. What did you learn about the character from the courses of action taken?
3. *The Obstacle*
   a. What is the first (last) obstacle the character encounters?
   b. How does the character deal with it?
   c. How does the character alter the goal because of this obstacle?
   d. What does this tell you about the character?
4. *The Outcome*
   a. Does the character reach the original goal or a revised goal?
   b. If successful, what helped most?
      ––Forces within the character's control.
      ––Forces outside the character's control.
   c. If unsuccessful, what helped most?
      ––Forces within the character's control.
      ––Forces outside the character's control.
   d. Name them.
5. *The Theme*
   What does the story basically show? A struggle with self, nature, other people?

Of course, questions don't do it all. Reading, activities, and discussions precede questions and diagrams.

A STRATEGY FOR APPRECIATING LITERATURE

There is evidence that children comprehend stories better when teachers help them establish and link together the events that make up the plot (Omanson, Beck, Voss, and McKeown 1984). Richard Omanson and others found greater comprehension when they revised a commercially directed reading lesson to introduce information related to the story and to help the children form a "map" of the central story content. Questions in the revised lesson were developed from the central events to help the children grasp the plot. In contrast, the questions in the commercial material often tapped information that was unrelated to the story. Unlike the commercial material, the revised lesson tied the child's personal experience to the story.

A successful strategy for advanced readers to use in reading narrative has been documented by Alan Purves in his study of high-achieving readers in New Zealand (Purves 1979). With this strategy, the reader gives detailed attention first to the form of the text and then to its content and affect:

Questions of Form.   Is the story well written? Is it like any other story I know? How does the story build up? How is it organized? How is the way of telling the story related to what it is about? What metaphors, image, or references to things outside the story are used? Has the writer used words or sentences differently from the way people usually write?

Questions of Content.   Is the story about important things? Is it a trivial or a serious work? Is there a lesson to be learned? Does the story tell one anything about people or ideas in general? How can we explain the way people behave in the story? Is there a hidden meaning? Is there one part that explains the whole? When was the story written? What is the historical background of the story and the writer? What happens? Is this a proper subject for a story?

Questions of Affect.   Does the story succeed in getting me involved? What does it tell me about people I know? What is the writer's opinion or attitude toward the people in the story? Are any of the characters like people I know? What emotions does the story arouse in me?

Rhetorical Devices for Identifying the Author

In keeping with the view that reading first of all is an act of communication between reader and author, Bertram Bruce recommends teaching rhetorical devices by which pupils can identify the author in the narrative. He calls these devices "stories within stories" (Bruce 1981). Bruce refers to explicit *embedding,* such as in Washington Irving's *Rip Van Winkle,* in which an implied author introduces the text, supposedly written by a historian. Other forms of explicit embedding are drama, letters, and parts of books within a text.

A second device that creates a story within a story is *commentary* by the author: "I cannot draw you a picture of Peter and Benjamin because it was quite dark." When readers recognize commentary, they sense the implied author as a character.

Other rhetorical devices by which the author expresses himself or herself include *irony,* when an author says something naive or ridiculous and the putative author's position is satirized; the *unrecognized narrator,* where a character who narrates is not a participant in the story; and the *engaged author,* where the narration is in the first person and the defined storyteller is separate from the implied author. *Immersion* is a device by which the author puts the reader into the story, as happens in "you are the hero" type books. And there is the *in-effect narration,* in which we as readers see the world so much through the mind of one character that we feel that the character is telling the story.

Strategies for Finding the Inner Sense of Narrative

Comprehension of literary text—biographies, plays, short stories, novels—requires that the reader get away from the direct meaning of statements and move to an analysis of their inner sense. This is true not only for the interpretation of figurative expressions but in the reading of what appears to be a straightforward statement. Even a sentence like *The cab is here* may involve a deeper meaning, such as *How difficult it is to part from a friend.* It is possible to read a work superficially, identifying the progression of events, or to read it deeply, making inferences about the motives of characters and author. By way of example, Flora Lewis, foreign affairs correspondent for the *New York Times,* in reading Zbigniew Brzezinski's memoirs as national security adviser to President Carter, was sensitive to how Brzezinski revealed more than he intended (Lewis 1983). Lewis believed Brzezinski's Polish background permeated his outlook and cited statements from the memoirs that revealed how this heritage colored the security adviser's thinking on every issue:

1. In recounting his exhilaration at the signing of the treaty turning over the Panama Canal to Panama, he compared U. S. relations with Central America to Soviet domination of Eastern Europe.
2. He said that he, an immigrant, felt a (typically Polish) sense of outraged national honor during the Iranian hostage crisis that was not shared by others.
3. He displayed a deep dislike for Russia, although he was not particularly anticommunist (China's ideology or even Cuba's didn't bother him unduly.

Deeper meaning is dependent on the schemata with which the reader interprets the text; hence the meanings derived are more varied than those grasped by logical relationships alone. Equally good readers viewing the same set of complex facts will be sensitive to different facets and will strike different emphases in their comments. The ability to read deeply is a reflection of the reader's emotional sensitivity, reading accuracy, and ability to make logical inferences.

The teaching of reading for inner meaning has been inadequately studied. Some direction can be found, however, to the process of literary analysis and the techniques used by actors to convey the inner sense of a play. For example, students can be introduced to the variety of meanings in a given selection by reading the selection orally using different intonations and pauses. They will immediately note how the meaning of text changes even though not a single word is changed. Likewise, just as method actors never begin by studying the text of their role but by getting familiar with the images and motives of the characters they are to portray (deciding what the characters would do in specific situations), so students can be asked to first master the motives and images of the characters they will read about. Later, when reading the text, students will not be limited to the superficially conveyed meanings but will instead be more open to the deeper meanings that lurk within a text.

A common link between text and the reading experience is "feelings," perhaps an empathy with a character. Students may describe a similar emotional experience without reflecting on its meaning for them or the character. However, students may reflect on the differences between their perspectives and that of the character. In distancing themselves from the character's perspective, students clarify their own perspectives. In recognizing limitations in the character's perspective, students are better prepared to interpret the text.

COMPREHENDING EXPOSITORY TEXT

In expository writing there are predominant metalevel or top-level structures that organize the presentation of information and ideas. The structure in most textbooks is likely to be either cause and effect (showing how something occurs because of other factors), comparison and contrast (pointing out likenesses and differences among ideas and events), time order (putting facts and events into a sequence), problem and solution (stating a question and its answer), or simple listing (enumerating facts, events, and ideas).

Activity 2.2 (page 26) introduced the idea of patterns in text. In that activity, patterns were considered in light of how best to read a given text. The emphasis in this section is on recognizing the author's organizational structure (top level) as a means to comprehend exposition—to see the logical connections in text. Attention is also given to other organizational techniques: pattern guides, restructuring text, and summarizing. The aim of these techniques is to relate the concepts in the text to each other and to draw out generalizations rather than specifics.

Identifying Top-Level Structures

Identifying and using the author's organizational framework are important in comprehending expository text. Students with this knowledge can relate the structure of the text to their own schemata, thereby learning what to expect from the text and how to process it. Bonnie Meyer, a specialist in the organization of text, has a classification system for identifying top-level structures in expository writing. She and her associates have found that use of this system benefits recall and comprehension (Meyer 1982). In fact, one associate, B. J. Bartlett, taught ninth-graders the top-level structure and thereby enabled them to recall nearly twice as much information from their reading as students without instruction in the system (Bartlett 1978). Activity 9.3 provides practice in the recognition of these structures (Bartlett 1978).

Using Pattern Guides

A pattern guide is a device to help readers see relationships and distinguish important from less important ideas. Steps in preparing and using guides are:

1. Identify the key idea or generalization to be gained from reading the material.
2. Identify the predominant pattern used by the author in the material—cause and effect, comparison and contrast, or other.

Activity 9.3   Identifying Top-Level Structures

Four top-level structures are featured in this activity: covariance, adversative, attribution, and response. In using the covariance structure, the author compares two equally weighted arguments regarding the cause of something: "Most wrecks result from a lack of power and a lack of steering equipment to handle emergency situations." An *adversative* structure compares a favored view with a less desirable opposing view: "In contrast to the ineffective remedy of offering more phonics for the poor reader, specialists recommended building background knowledge." The *attribution* structure describes the qualities associated with a person, event, or idea: "Trustworthy, kind, and reverent, Spike earned his merit badge." The *response* structure is found in question-answer and problem-solution formats: "How can we conserve energy in this house? We can insulate and look at the use of solar power."

In her teaching of these structures, Meyer uses entertaining advertisements for practice. Can you find adversative, attribution, and response structures in these advertising captions?*

1. Most wraps just wrap. Reynolds Wrap wraps, molds, and seals tightly.
2. Cover Girl Oil-Control Makeup: no shining, no streaking, no yellowing, no fading, no blotching, no caking.
3. Want a tough stain out? SHOUT it out!

Directions

Read each of the following passages—"Miracle Rice," "Anthrax," "Chicken-Hawks," and "How Historians View History." Identify the top-level structure in each passage. Check your responses with the answers at the end of the activity.

Miracle Rice*

There is a miracle rice that grows well in places in the Phillipines. And in West Africa, too. It is a miracle rice because it grows well where it is hard to grow anything at all. It grows fast. It produces big crops. It has the right color and taste. It contains large quantities of vitamins, particularly of the vitamin B family. These vitamins help people fight disease so that the rice is a good food. It is an easy crop to harvest and store. The rice is larger than other varieties and is bulkier. It can produce food for many, many, people. So, it is a miracle rice.

Anthrax*

Scientists had puzzled for a long time about how animals got a disease called anthrax. It was a disease that was killing many cattle and other farm animals. It was also killing many wild animals, but it was the loss of stock that worried farmers, scientists, and the general public most of all. Sick animals had rod-like organisms in their blood. The animals gradually lost weight and strength and finally died. No one could understand why or how it happened. Finally, Robert Koch discovered the cause of anthrax. The disease was caused by bacteria. Koch's discovery led to a treatment for anthrax.

Chicken-Hawks*

In one district, farmers began to kill the chicken-hawks. Large parties of men would go on bird-shoots. They not only shot adult birds, but also destroyed nests and breeding areas used by the hawks. Any young found in the nests were killed immediately. As a result of these hunts the farmers' chickens were not eaten. But, the farmers found something else wrong. Their store of grain was eaten by rats. Soon the rats were overrunning the farms. There was nothing to stop the spread of the rats. The farmers had removed a natural enemy of the rats—the chicken-hawk.

How Historians View History **

Different views exist among historians on how history might be studied. These differences may be grouped into the view of history as a game, and the view of history as a stream. Some historians view history as a game with players, rules, and clever plans. The players are people of all civilizations. The rules are the many sciences: such as biology, geology, archaeology, and geography. By studying people of the past and their planned "moves," we discover which moves lead to success or bring destruction. However, each person must first decide whether to be an active player in the game of history or a "pawn." As players, we try to improve the world in which we live. As pawns, we ignore the moves and decisions that others make which affect our lives.

Other historians see history as a stream. On the surface it appears to flow steadily onward, moving at will. Actually, however, it is slowed down, changed, and forced onward by strong undercurrents. This view is not as prominent as the other, but no matter what their viewpoint, historians agree that history does repeat itself. Human nature and life today are not much different from the way they were in the days of Noah, Caesar, or Kennedy. Decisions facing us today are much the same as ones that had to made in the past. History is the study of things that are past. It also helps us to understand what is happening in the world today, and it is a guide to what might be happening tomorrow.

Answers

"Miracle Rice," Most of the text is attribution, giving a collection of descriptions about the rice.

"Anthrax." This text is organized with a response problem-solution structure.

"Chicken-Hawks." This passage is organized with a covariance structure. Two conflicting ideas are presented. (If you noted that an antecedent-and-consequence structure is also used, you are correct.)

"How Historians View History." This passage contains an element of adversative structure: "This view is not as prominent as the other."

---

*Answers:(1) adversative, (2) attribution, (3) response, (4) response.

*The passages above were created from E. Marholdt, P. F. Brandwein, and L. S. Ward, *Biology: Patterns in the Environment* (New York: Harcourt Brace Jovanovich, 1972).

**This passage was created from A. Hyma and M. Stanton, *Streams of Civilization* (San Diego: Creation Life Publishers, 1976).

3. Illustrate the pattern and tell the class how you identified it.

4. Make clear to the students that their task is to place relevant information from the text within the pattern. If, for example, you have identified a comparison and contrast pattern, students should know what is to be compared and contrasted (the central idea) and then look for information that can be used in making the comparison.

5. Provide the pattern guide, consisting of key concept or generalization, pattern to be used, and directions. The directions should indicate
the kind of information to be placed within the pattern.

Exhibit 9.3 illustrates pattern guides. Notice how the pattern guides
alert the reader to the appropriate relationship in the textbook. Numbers of
pages where relevant information is to be found may also be given. Partially
completed answers serve to model the responses desired. Modeling may be
necessary when pattern guides are first introduced.

Exhibit 9.3   Pattern Guides

"Organizing the Forces of Labor—Chapter 20[a]
Cause/Effect

In this section, look for cause-effect relationships in the situations mentioned below. Add the cause or effect in the proper column.

Cause	*Effect*
1.	1. Saving money was difficult or impossible for unskilled labor (p. 400).
2. Owners felt it was necessary to keep labor costs as low as possible (p. 400).	2.
3.	3. Only the boldest workers dared to defy management and join a labor organization (p. 400).
4. By the 1800's wages of unskilled workers exceeded skilled artisans (p. 401).	4.
5.	5. The workingmen's parties supported Jackson after 1828 (pp. 402-03).

---

[a]Pattern guide created from Henry Craft and John Krout, *The Adventures of the American People* (Chicago, Rand, McNally, 1970).

"The United States Divided—Chapter 14[b]
Contrast/Compare

Using pages 264-265, you will contrast and compare the repercussions in the
South and the North to the Supreme Court's Decision in the Dred Scott case.

the South	**the North**
1. (Hint: newspapers)	1.
2. (Hint: Democratic Party)	2.
3.	3.
4.	4.

---

[b]Pattern guide created from Craft and Krout, 1970.

Exhibit 9.3 (Continued)

Listing

"Sleep, Fatigue, and Rest—Chapter 4[c]

This section of your textbook *lists* many causes of fatigue (pp. 96–97). Some of the causes are physical and some are mental. Fill in the causes under the appropriate heading.

I. Physical causes of fatigue
    A. short burst of intense effort
    B. rapid growth
    C. lack of important food
    D. pg. 96, par. 3
    E.
    F.
    G.
II. Mental causes of fatigue
    A. pg. 96, par. 1
    B.

[c]Pattern guide created from Benjamin F. Miller, et al., *Investigating Your Health* (Boston: Houghton Mifflin, 1971).

"Religious Change in Western Europe"—Unit 4, Chapter 3[d]
Time Order

A time line is an excellent way to see the sequence of events. As you read about the religious leaders (pp. 229–236), fill in the events on the time line below. Write what happened under the date.

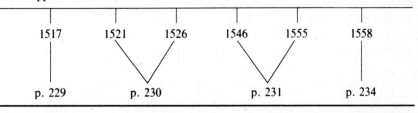

[d] Pattern guide created from Allan O. Kownstar, *People and Our World*, (New York: Holt, Rinehart and Winston, 1977).
    Source: From "Pattern Guides: A Workable Alternative for Content Teachers" by Mary W. Olson and Bonnie Longnion, *Journal of Reading*, May 1982. Copyright©1982 International Reading Association. Reprinted with permission of Mary W. Olson and Bonnie Longnion and the International Reading Association.

    After students complete their reading and respond to the pattern guide, the class should discuss the concept and the organizational pattern. Students may suggest other patterns that would have been appropriate. As with other aspects of reading comprehension, there are surface clues to aid readers in recognizing organizational patterns. Some words signal a comparison-contrast pattern (*on the other hand, but, in contrast*); others, a cause-and-effect-pattern (*consequently, since, therefore, as a result, hence*).

Pattern guides do more than help students comprehend particular selections. Continued use of the guides will develop learners' perception of organizational patterns, as well as the habit of looking for structure in text and connecting information in the text to important generalizations.

Restructuring Text

The most common textbook organization is simple listing; the author makes a general statement and then supports it with a number of statements listed in no particular order. Words such as *also, moreover, and,* and *another* are surface indicators of a listing pattern. This pattern does not help the reader discern the more significant from the less significant ideas. It does not stress the relationships among key ideas.

A useful strategy for overcoming the disadvantages of listing is *restructuring*. Restructuring calls for taking a simple list and reorganizing it into a comparison-contrast pattern, a cause-and-effect pattern, or another pattern suggested by the context.

Donna Alvermann has found that using the restructuring strategy results in better comprehension of major point than merely following the author's listing (Alvermann 1982). In teaching a reconstruction strategy, Alvermann uses text material that contains randomly listed facts about a topic. This allows for a decision about a more useful pattern, such as cause and effect. A key term or organizer for the material is identified. A form is drawn that corresponds to the pattern selected. This form consists of empty boxes arranged to represent the slots into which information can be mentally or physically inserted by readers as they process the material in their search for missing information.

After the teacher has modeled the restructuring technique, students are given an opportunity to construct their own organizers to reconstruct passages from their textbooks, using whatever patterns appear appropriate.

Activity 9.4 "Restructuring a Passage" is an opportunity to practice restructuring by changing a listing pattern to a comparison-contrast pattern.

Summarizing

Making a summary is an important tool for understanding. It involves the basic operations for comprehending and remembering prose. In 1978 Kintsch and Van Dijk published a model for comprehending text. This model specified the basic rules for processing text.

Subsequently, after studying examples of children's and experts' successes in summarizing, Brown and Day (1980), identified six rules essential to summarization. These rules are similar to the processing rules given by Kintsch and Van Dijk:

1. Delete unnecessary material—information that is trivial.
2. Delete material that is important but redundant.

Activity 9.4   Restructuring a Passage

Instructions

See if you can restructure the following passage on the topic of outlining, which is written in a listing pattern, by processing the passage as a comparison-contrast pattern. The key term in the passage is *forms for outlining*. This term suggests what is to be compared and contrasted. A response sheet, which includes the key term and empty boxes that represent slots for the contrasting ideas, has been provided in Exhibit 9.4. Read the passage and then fill in the empty slots. After your own effort at reconstructing the passage, look at the sample restructuring appearing in Exhibit 9.7 (page 175).

Exhibit 9.4   Response Sheet for Restructuring a Passage on Outlining

Key term—*Forms for outlining*
Pattern—comparision and contrast

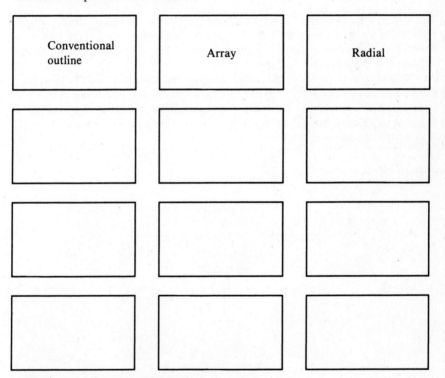

Passage to Restructure: Outlining

Outlining is used to help students clarify relationships. The conventional form for outlining is the familiar linear, hierarchical ordering of ideas at different levels of subordination, with Roman numerals signaling the superordinate concepts; upper-case letters, the supporting or coordinate concepts; Arabic numbers, the subordinate details; and lower-case letters, the sub-subordinate details.

    Another form is the *array,* a popular free-form outlining procedure whereby the student uses words, lines, and arrows as symbols to show the nature of the relationships. As indicated in Exhibit 9.5, an array reveals the reader's interpretation of text relationships.

Exhibit 9.5   An Array

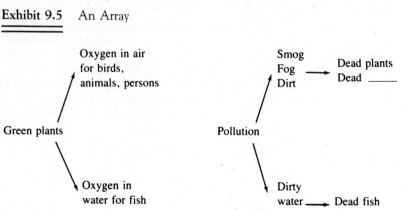

The correctness of an array depends upon the justification offered by the designer, with the information presented in the text and the inferences drawn taken into account. An array shows a spatial arrangement among key words and phrases. As indicated, it may also show sequence.

    A third type of outline is the *radial,* another free form. The radial is used to distinguish superordinate from supporting or coordinate ideas, as shown in Exhibit 9.6. A disadvantage of the radial is that subordinate details are difficult to organize as a visual display. An example of how the passage on outlining can be restructured appears in Exhibit 9.7.

Exhibit 9.6   A Radial

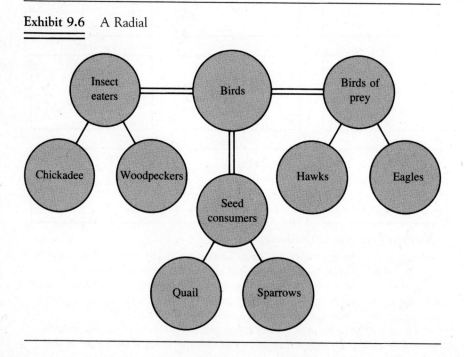

Exhibit 9.7   Sample Response for Restructuring a Passage on Outlining

Key term—*Forms for outlining*
Pattern—Comparison and contrast

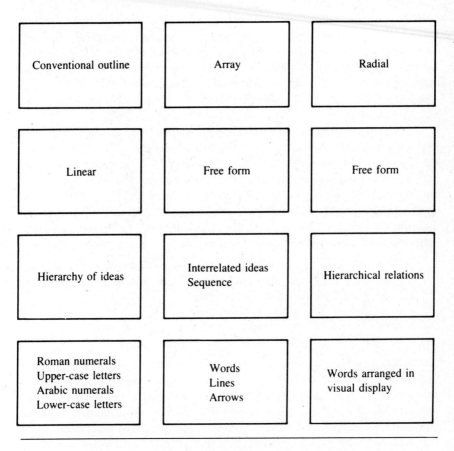

---

3. Substitute a superordinate term for a list of items. If a text contains a list such as *chair, table, desk*, substitute the word *furniture*.

4. Substitute an encompassing action for a list of subcomponents of that action. For example, *John went to London* may be substituted for *John left the house. He went to the train station. He bought a ticket . . .*

5. Select a topic sentence. The topic sentence, if there is one, usually is the author's summary of the paragraph. Fewer than one third of all paragraphs in exposition have topic sentences. Fictional best-selling writers seldom use topic sentences because narrative moves in time—they feel that it is a mistake to clog it up with topic sentences.

6. If there is no topic sentence, invent your own (Brown and Day 1980).

Day trained junior-college students to apply the basic rules and to check to see that they were using the rules appropriately (Day 1980). Prior to training, students deleted most of the unnecessary and redundant material but had difficulty selecting topic sentences (only 25 percent did so accurately) and in inventing topic sentences (only 15 percent had success). Training in rule use—explicit instruction and modeling in the use of rules—was effective in general. Poorer students needed instruction in the control of the rules in order to maximize their performance. That is, they needed to be shown how to check that they had a topic sentence for each paragraph, that all redundancies were deleted, and the like. Application of the invention rule was difficult for most students and required the most explicit instruction and monitoring. The invention rule requires that students add information, producing something of their own, rather than merely deleting, selecting, and manipulating.

Note that the rules of summarization are general reading comprehension strategies involving operations essential in comprehending a wide range of texts. Lisbeth Donant taught fifth-graders to apply the summarization strategy in reading unfamiliar passages. The reading comprehension of those so taught exceeded that of a comparable group of students (McNeil and Donant 1982). In teaching the rules, Donant used materials two grade levels lower than the reading level of the students. The following paragraph illustrates materials used in helping students learn to find the topic sentence:

> The midnight rain stopped, leaving the house quiet with only the echo of the dripping water. It was cold in the dark, empty building and the inspector shivered as he kept watch for the mysterious trespasser.
> a. A detective is staking out a house at night.
> b. Empty houses are scary at night.
> c. Someone is trespassing in the rain.

In teaching them to invent topic sentences, Donant had students listen to passages from selections in science, social studies, and literature. As the passages were read, students offered their own ideas about what the topic sentence should be, and these responses were discussed. Later, students invented topic sentences for paragraphs they read. Isolated practice of a rule was replaced with exercises demanding that all rules be applied in writing summaries for passages. The strategy training enabled students to excel both in summary writing and in the comprehension of fresh paragraphs. These results are consistent with those reported by Wittrock and others (Chapter 5), who found that elaboration by composition of summaries and headings greatly improved comprehension.

One caveat is in order. The rules for summary writing call for determining the relative importance of different parts of a text. What the reader thinks is important may not be what the author intended to be important. Someone reading for a particular purpose may judge relevancy differently from someone reading for another purpose. To the extent that students have shared goals, they should agree upon the parts of the text that form its gist.

Activity 9.5 has two purposes: (1) to give you the opportunity to validate the summarization strategy for yourself and (2) to help you think through

Activity 9.5   Applying the Summarization Strategy in the Study of
Reading Comprehension

Instructions

First, read the following essay; then, write a summary sentence for each paragraph, applying as many summary-writing rules as are applicable. Finally, combine your summary statements into a summary of summaries (use format at end of essay). You should find that the procedure has a positive effect on your understanding of central ideas in text.

Essay to Be Read and Summarized

What is meant by *finding the main idea*? How should we teach students to do it? Let's start by looking at how comprehension tests define *finding the main idea*. Some require that the student choose the best title for a passage. Others ask that students identify the most general statement of three—for example: *The husky pulls the sled. Dogs work. The sheep dog watches the herd.* In some tests a brief story is presented along with several moral pronouncements, one of which might be inferred from the story. Other tests present a paragraph from which the student must select the factual generalization most consistent with the information in the paragraph. Occasionally, the student must identify or propose a theme that subsumes the ideas expressed in a number of paragraphs. Obviously, these tests are not measuring the same things. Identifying a topic sentence is much easier than inferring an unstated theme or generalization for a work.

Similar differences regarding the meaning of main ideas are found in writings on the subject. One writer says that any text can be divided into two, often unequal, parts. The first is the *theme*, or topic, of the text—the part that deals with what is already known. The second part, the *rheme*, is composed of new information about this subject. By this definition, topics are not main ideas, for they simply prepare the reader for what is to come. On the other hand, drawing conclusions from the new information is a main idea.

In contrast, another writer defines a theme as the main idea of a book, article, or a chapter in a text. The theme may be implied or directly stated. If implied, the reader has to infer what the content of the text suggests about an aspect of the human condition or world knowledge. Still other writers say that the main idea of any piece is related to its location in the hierarchy of superordinate, coordinate, and subordinate terms. In a passage giving an example, a concept, and a generalization, the generalization must be the main idea.

Importance has something to do with main ideas. In fact, one author has proposed (facetiously) a test to rate the importance of main ideas. He calls it the *aha!—so what!* test.* If the main idea elicits an *aha!* reaction, it is probably a meaningful conclusion. If it elicits a *so what!* reaction, it is probably a relatively vacuous summary label. The problem is, there is not always general agreement among readers of all ages and places as to what is important. When readers are asked to read from given perspectives, they show greater agreement as to which ideas are important than when they read from their own perspectives.

---

* P. David Peasron and Dale D. Johnson, *Teaching Reading Comprehension* (New York: Holt, Rinehart, and Winston, 1978).

Identifying main ideas in expository pieces is more difficult than in narrative. In narratives, importance means centrality to the story; character, goals, and setting are high in the hierarchy, and particular events are low. In expository texts, importance usually means how superordinate the idea is in a hierarchy leading from specific to general statements.

What does all this have to do with helping students recognize main ideas? For one thing, it means you have to be clear about what you mean by main ideas before preparing your lesson. Teaching strategies should match whatever variety of main idea is the target of instruction. If the goal is to recognize what part of a text is essential to the meaning, then the student must be taught the elements that, if changed or omitted, would result in a different meaning. If the goal is to determine the important idea, students must be taught to ask, "Important to what?" Importance of ideas depends upon context and perspective.

When recognition and invention of topic sentences are the aims, students should be taught to differentiate among sentences that (a) tell what is to follow, (b) give brief definitions, (c) make statements to be explained, and (d) sum up the details of a passage. Also, it is helpful for students to know that sometimes they must infer the topic sentence from other sentences, as indicated in Exhibit 9.8.

The inferring of a topic sentence, a low-level definition of main idea, requires a general ability to reason. Exhibit 9.8, one might have reasoned that an appropriate topic sentence would include the idea of food chain, cycle of events, or another generalization that relates the three sentences.

When the goal is to remember central ideas of textbooks, teach pupils to study textbook summaries rather than merely reread the original prose. When the goal is to recognize a hierarchy of ideas, then semantic mapping, outlining, and categorizing, whereby propositions are placed in logical relation to each other, are appropriate. Keep in mind, however, that there is no such thing as *the* main idea of any work. Readers with different backgrounds and purposes for reading will generate different main ideas from the same text.

Write your summary, using this format for checking your work:

Rules Applied		**Summary Sentences for Paragraphs**
1. Deleted unnecessary material	— —	1.
2. Deleted redundancies	— —	2.
3. Substituted superordinate term for list	— —	3.
4. Substituted superordinate term for a number of actions	— —	4.
5. Selected a topic sentence	— —	5.
6. Invented a topic sentence	— —	6.
		Summary of Summaries

Exhibit 9.8   Inferring the Topic Sentence

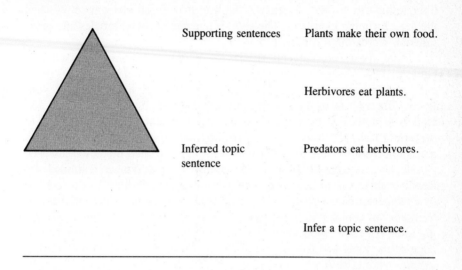

Supporting sentences   Plants make their own food.

Herbivores eat plants.

Inferred topic   Predators eat herbivores.
sentence

Infer a topic sentence.

a concern of many teachers of reading comprehension—how best to teach students to derive the main idea in text.

READING TO PERFORM A TASK: DOCUMENTS

The reading of documents is commonly associated with functional literacy—reading to do, as opposed to reading for pleasure (as in reading narratives), and reading to learn (as in using exposition). Documents include subfeatures such as diagrams, forms, schematics, schedules, and charts. The reading of documents occurs in workplaces and in reading instruction related to personal and societal functions.

Studies of document-reading tasks in occupational settings show that reading in these situations is mostly problem solving: setting a goal, categorizing, inferencing, and integrating (Guthrie 1988). Most job-related reading is undertaken for purposes that arise within the context of the job at hand—getting a parts number or tolerance level from a "manical," synthesizing information from several documents, and conveying information through conversation with others.

Five categories summarize the content of most job material (Sticht 1978):

1. Tables of content and indexes.
2. Standards and specifications.
3. Identification and physical descriptions.
4. Procedural directions.
5. Functional descriptions.

A technical-writing style predominates in most workplace documents. Sentence and paragraph structures emphasize following of directions and interpreting graphs and diagrams. The use of pictorial elements eliminates the need for more modifiers. The style is telegraphic, with articles and other function words often omitted.

There have been several studies of workplace literacy (Kirsch and Guthrie 1984; Mikulecky and Drew 1991; Sticht 1987). These studies point out several important facts: (1) The reading that is done in the world of work is very different from the way reading is viewed and taught in school. Job readers seldom read for the gist or main idea of text; instead, they read to perform a task; (2) Students who perform well on school literacy activities are not necessarily able to perform as well on job-related literacy tasks. The transfer of reading skills from the classroom to the workplace is limited; (3) Reading ability as measured by standardized tests has little to do with either job performance or ability to successfully engage in on-the-job reading. Workers can competently read work-related material that is from two to six grade levels above their school-defined literacy level. Background knowledge of the topic and format of job-related material is more important than general reading ability.

Among the instructional implications of these findings are those that call for combining literacy training with requirements for the job. For maximum transfer from the classroom to "real life," teachers should use the contexts, tasks, and the reading materials of the workplace.

Comprehension for functional reading can best be improved by improving knowledge of what is to be read and the nature of the work task. Indeed, programs that most effectively improve comprehension of technical material integrate technical training, task simulations, and literacy applications while using the exact reading material that is found on the job.

With respect to functional reading of documents in daily life, Peter Mosenthal and Irwin Kirst have concentrated on developing a scheme for teaching documents so that readers can process the documents differently depending on their purposes (Mosenthal and Kirst 1990).

Simple Lists

To get started teaching documents, Mosenthal suggests, begin with the concept of simple lists—eliciting the general response that simple lists consist of one label and a related set of items. Characteristics of simple lists, such as vertical and horizontal organization, numeral and alphabetical ordering, and the like, are identified as students bring in and examine as many simple lists as they can find.

Combined Lists

Next, combined lists and their characteristics are introduced. The combined list is structured as a table to organize information in a matrix format—rows and columns. After becoming familiar with the characteristics of combined lists (e.g., labels in combined lists are telegraphic topics that require the reader to infer or seek additional information from footnotes or accompanying text), students engage in such activities as forming combined lists from simple lists. In the process, students learn that not all simple lists can be combined and that a semantic relationship is necessary.

Intersecting Lists

Intersecting lists that provide a structure for representing different types of information are taught through example, such as a TV show list and telephone rate schedules. Students bring in additional examples of intersecting lists and learn that such lists are limited to only three simple lists.

Nested Lists

Nested lists are a type of document structure in which row or column information is placed in a hierarchy. Nesting involves adding a second list of modifying information. Examples of nested lists from the *World Almanac* and *Book of Facts* are used to illustrate the characteristics of such lists.

Graphs and Charts

Pie charts are introduced as a type of combined list structure useful in presenting percentage data. Bar charts are treated as another way to present information in tables and include one or more lists of modifying information and highlight comparisons. Line graphs are a third way to represent tabular information pictorially. Students can be presented different graphs and asked to identify the respective lists that make up the graphs. Students discuss the advantages of the different formats.

Forms

Forms are considered by Mosenthal and Kirst from the viewpoint of their use, information source, response mode, and structure. Their use ranges along a continuum from personal to societal. Examples of personal use are memory aids, requests for information, and directions to others. Societal use includes income tax reports and other monitoring forms used to register or verify something. Information source refers to the extent to which (a) the user supplies requested information from prior knowledge, (b) the requested information is on the form itself, or (c) the user has to refer to a secondary source to complete the form. A useful activity for the classroom is to collect forms, determine their uses, and identify the information source required.

The response modes for forms ranges from placing a check in a designated area, to entering a word or phrase on a line, to generating an open response. The structure of forms may be (a) a single-item list, such as a person's name followed by a listing: address, account number, phone number, signature, date; (b) categorical listing by which sets of single-item lists are grouped; and (c) combined and intersecting lists such as check ledgers, where one list of information is added to other lists.

Most documents can be understood in the contexts of one or more of these lists. In addition to activities suggested for learning about these lists, students should be given the opportunity to read sets of instructions and perform accompanying tasks—getting money from an automatic teller, assembling toys, completing job applications, ordering information, and the like. In view of plans by those at the National Assessment of Educational Progress to assess the functional literacy of students at grades 8 and 12, we expect more emphasis on document literacy and reading to do. Dolores Janick and Timothy Shanahan have designed practical classroom activities at the first-grade level that involve students using a variety of materials for accomplishing specific purposes (Janick and Shanahan 1988). Their activities focus on instrumental, regulatory, personal, and interactive uses of literacy. The instrumental function is introduced through written directions on how to make crafts and snacks. Directions are read with the children and step-by-step instruction is given to help them accomplish the tasks. Finished products, such as butterflies, boats, houses, and flowers made out of paper, are displayed with the instructions for students to reread again and again. Snack-making activities using recipes and written directions for preparing treats are popular. One student remarked that they "must be learning to read because they could make a snack all by themselves and didn't need a teacher to help them."

The regulatory function of print is illustrated through the use of signs in the classroom, school, and home. Students make their own signs to regulate the behavior of others: "Walk down the stairs." "Turn out the lights." Personal uses of written language include reading and writing and sharing stories about the lives of the first-grade students. Language-experience techniques are used in generating and recoding the stories. The interactional functions of print develop through the use of notes written between students and teacher. Students write to peers, parents, and others who respond by writing to them.

SUMMARY

This chapter introduces *three* types of discourse—narrative, exposition, and documents and presents teaching strategies for helping readers comprehend them. With respect to comprehending narrative, emphasis is given to understanding story grammar, identifying the author in the text, and asking questions that will integrate the events and ideas of central importance. In considering exposition, primary attention is given to the organizational patterns that structure the presentation of information and ideas. Strategies for teaching these patterns are recognition of top-level structures, pattern guides, summarization, and restructuring techniques.

Documents are treated in relation to reading to do, paying attention to the importance of synthesizing information from several documents, and conveying information through conversations. Emphasis is on teaching documents in the context of carrying out a specific job or task.

The teaching strategies associated with both narrative and exposition can contribute to a greater goal than enhanced comprehension of particular passages. They can become learning strategies that transfer to a wide range of material. At least this is true when the strategies are successfully modeled and practiced, as well as when there is a conscious recognition by readers of how the strategies can help them derive meaning from text. On the other hand, there is little transfer of reading skills from the classroom to the worksite, and we don't know how much use of documents in one job transfers to other occupational areas.

REFERENCES

Alvermann, Donna E. "Restructuring Text Facilitates Written Recall of Main Ideas." *Journal of Reading* 25 (May 1982): 754–758.

Bartlett, B. J. *Top-Level Structure as an Organizational Strategy for Recall of Classroom Text*. Doctoral dissertation, Arizona State University, 1978.

Beck, Isabel L. and McKeown, Margaret B. "Developing Questions That Promote Comprehension of the Story Map." *Language Arts* 58 (November/December 1981): 913–917.

Brewer, William F. "Literacy Theory, Rhetoric, and Stylistics: Implications for Psychology." In *Theoretical Issues in Reading Comprehension,* R. Spiro, B. C. Bruce, and W. F. Brewer, editors. Hillsdale, NJ: Erlbaum, 1980, 221–239.

Brown, A. L., and Day, J. D. "The Development of Rules for Summarizing Texts." Unpublished manuscript, University of Illinois, 1980.

Bruce, Bertram. "Stories Within Stories." *Language Arts* 58 (November/December 1981): 931–935.

Day, J. D. *Training Summarization Skills: A Comparison of Teaching Methods*. Doctoral Dissertation, University of Illinois, 1980.

Gee, J. P. "Units in the Production of Narrative Discourse."*Discourse Processes,* 9, (1985) 391–422.

Guthrie, J. T. "Locating Information in Documents: Examination of a Cognitive Model." *Reading Research Quarterly* 23 (1988): 178–199.

Janick, Dolores M., and Shanahan, Timothy. "Applying Adult Literacy Practices in Primary Grade Instruction." *The Reading Teacher* (May 1988): 880–886.

Kintsch, W., and Van Dijk, A. "Toward a Model of Text Comprehension and Production." *Psychological Review* 85, no. 5 (1978): 363–394.

Kirsch, I. S., and Guthrie, J. Z. "Prose Comprehension and Text Search as a Function of Reading Volume." *Reading Research Quarterly* 19 (1984): 332–342.

Lewis, Flora. "The Adviser's Advice." *New York Times Book Review* (April 17, 1983): 3, 29.

McConaughy, S. "Using Story Structure in the Classroom." *Language Arts* 57 (February 1980): 157–165.

McNeil, J. D., and Donant, L. "Summarization Strategy for Improving Reading Comprehension." *New Inquiries in Reading Research Instruction,* 31st Yearbook at the National Reading Conference, J. Niles and L. Miller, editors. Rochester, NY: The National Reading Conference, 1982.

Meyer, Bonnie. *Prose Analysis: Purposes, Procedures, and Problems,* Research report no. 1. Tempe: Department of Educational Psychology, College of Education, Arizona State University, June 1982.

Mikulecky, Larry, and Drew, Rod. "Basic Literacy, Skills in the Workplace." In *Handbook of Reading Research,* Vol. 2, Rebecca Barr, et al., editors. New York: Longman, 1991.

Mosenthal, Peter, and Kirst, Irwin. "Understanding Documents." A yearlong *Journal of Reading* series, 1989–91. Reading and Language Arts Center, Syracuse University, 170 Huntington Hall, Syracuse, NY 13244.

Newman, Andree, "Story Maker" and "Textman." Boston: Bolt, Beranack, and Newman, Inc., 1981.

Olson, Mary W., and Longnion, Bonnie. "Pattern Guides: A Workable Alternative for Content Teachers." *Journal of Reading* (May 1982).

Omanson, Richard, Beck, Isabel, Voss, James, and McKeown, Margaret. "The Effect of Reading Lessons on Comprehension." *Cognition and Instruction* 1, no. 1 (Winter 1984): 44–67.

Pearson, P. David, and Johnson, Dale D. *Teaching Reading Comprehension.* New York: Holt, Rinehart, and Winston, 1978, pp. 157–164.

Purves, Alan C. *Achievement in Reading and Literature.* Wellington, New Zealand: Council for Educational Research, 1979.

Singer, Harry, and Donlan, Dan. "Active Comprehension: Problem-Solving Schema with Question Generation for Comprehension of Complex Short Stories." *Reading Research Quarterly* 17 (1982): 166–187.

Stein, N. L. and Glenn, C. G. "An Analysis of Story Comprehension in Elementary School Children." In *New Directions in Discourse Processing,* R. O. Freedle, editor. Hillsdale, NJ: Erlbaum, 1979.

Stich, T. G. *Reading for Working.* Alexandria, VA: 1 Human Resources Research Association, 1975.

Sticht, T. G., Armstrong, W. B., Hickey, D. T., Caylor, J. P. *Cast-Off Youth: Policy and Training Methods from the Military Experience.* New York: Praeger, 1987.

Whaley, Jill F., and Spiegel, D. L. "Improving Children's Reading Comprehension Through Instruction in Schematic Aspects of Narratives." Paper presented at the annual meeting of the American Educational Research Association, New York, March 1982.

Useful Readings

Beach, R., and Appleman, D. "Reading Strategies for Expository and Literary Text Types." In *Becoming Readers in a Complex Society.* 83rd Yearbook NSSE, Alan Purves and Olive Niles, editors. Chicago: University of Chicago Press, 1984, 115–144.

Hegarty, M., Carpenter, P. A., and Just, M. A. "Diagrams in the Comprehension of Scientific Texts." In *Handbook of Reading Research,* vol. 2, Rebecca Barr, Michael L. Kamil, Peter B. Mosenthal, and P. David Pearson, editors. New York: Longman, 1990, pp. 641–669.

Hernadi, P., editor. *The Rhetoric of Interpretation and the Interpretation of Rhetoric.* Durham, NC: Duke University Press, 1989.

Hynds, S., and Rubin, D., editors. *Perspective on Talk and Learning.* Urbana, IL: National Council of Teachers of English, 1990.

Muth, K. D., editor. *Children's Comprehension of Text: Research Into Practice.* Newark, DE: International Reading Association, 1989.

Writing to Comprehend

OVERVIEW

In this chapter, writing is considered as a schema-building process. As a prereading activity, writing helps students (a) relate the new knowledge embedded in a writing task to prior experience, thereby creating a framework for instantiating information in forthcoming texts, and (b) activate prior knowledge that is relevant to subsequent reading. As a postreading activity, writing is an effective form of elaboration, contributing to both understanding and retention of text.

Finally, writing is a vehicle for revealing aspects of reading comprehension that might not be apparent without binary considerations. A composing model offers the hypothesis that one becomes an active reader by reading as a writer.

WRITING TO DEVELOP AND ACTIVATE SCHEMATA FOR READING

One function of writing is to clarify thought. George Herbert Palmer used to say that when confused he wrote himself clearheaded. Similarly, there is the anecdote of an old lady on a train who, upon being accused of illogicality and wandering inconsistency in her conversation, protested "How can I tell what I think 'til I see what I say?"

In brief, writing is a mode of learning.

Writing helps the reader acquire a base knowledge of specialized styles, vocabulary, and cohesive devices with which to interpret text. As students themselves learn to write about setting and people, developing and resolving conflict, using dialect, giving directions, describing phenomena, and so forth, they become better able to understand and interact with writers who are writing about the same things.

Writing can be a powerful form of elaborating, useful for both comprehension and retaining important ideas. Colleen Harrison's experiment in asking high school students to rewrite passages from science texts that they found confusing or incomplete is a case in point. Harrison gave different students either the original or student-edited versions of the text to read and found that the student-written versions were better comprehended and remembered than the originals. (Harrison 1982).

Writing is the active process of creating meaning, a tool for representing, interpreting, and shaping one's experience. Thus, in seeking to develop active as opposed to passive readers, teachers might teach students to read like an author, using a composing model of reading to develop thoughtful readers.

Underlying the writing-to-comprehend approach are the assumptions that by writing, students become more sensitive to the characteristics of written language, better prepared to deal with the subject matter concepts that will appear in text (prereading), and better able to relate their reading to their own lives, thereby contributing to both comprehension and memory of text (postreading).

Chapter 1 introduced the concept of parallel texts introduced by which readers rewrite texts in terms of other texts and their own backgrounds and knowledge. Concrete dealing with a text yields understanding only when what is said in the text begins to find expression in the interpreter's own language (Gadamer 1976). Although mentally constructing a parallel text is important, writing that text physically prompts the reader to engage in more thoughtful exploration.

As indicated previously, one study addressed the question of whether thoughtful engagement is attributable to writing alone, reading alone, or the effects of both reading and writing together. Students who wrote prior to reading read more critically than students who were given an introduction to the story. Students in the latter group tended to read in order to remember ideas, not to reflect on their writing. Writing together with reading resulted in more thoughtful consideration of ideas than writing alone or reading alone (Tierney, Soter, O' Flahavan, & Mc Ginley, 1989).

WRITING TO PREPARE FOR READING

Language Experience

Beginning readers have long profited from the language-experience approach in learning to read. Roach Van Allen (1973) and Paulo Freire (1985) are associated prominently with this approach. Proponents of language experience aim at helping learners recognize that what they think about, they can talk about; what they say, they can write; and what they can write, they can read.

Accordingly, learners are encouraged to express themselves orally about matters of personal concern or interest. The teacher then assists in writing the expressions and in helping the learners see the correspondence between what is written and what is spoken. Students often collectively compose while the teacher writes and then together they focus on particular linguistic representations—punctuations, spelling, vocabulary, letter-sound relations. In reading their own thoughts and language, learners see that print can be meaningful. Later, as they write and discuss their writings with others, they recognize that print is an opportunity for writers and readers to communicate. Students learn that written language is more than speech written down—that writing has many features and forms that are different from oral expression.

Homemade Books

The writing of classroom books is a good activity for acquiring schemata for features of text. In this activity, children write about what they know, and their writings are "published" for peers or for younger children. In preparing their books, students consider how to vary their copy in light of their intended audience—keeping in mind the intentions and background experience of those who will read the book.

In writing, children become more familiar with written language and with various purposes for writing and reading—to persuade, to inform, to entertain. As they compose so that readers are likely to respond in given ways, the young writers become readers who are better at exploring the world through the eyes of a writer.

Functional Tasks

Kenneth and Yetta Goodman stress that writing by beginners should meet personal and functional needs (Goodman and Goodman 1983). They recommend starting with tasks where there is only one intended reader, who is often the writer. Examples of such tasks include making a variety of lists (shopping, Christmas, invitations, names and phone numbers), notes, diaries, logs, and journals.

More complete forms of personal writing for a limited audience follow as children write conversations and letters in which they tell about their feelings, events in their lives, and make requests—all of which contribute to a sense of author-reader transaction. Still later, children extend their audience by writing to less familiar people than classmates, teachers, and family. The writing of poems, stories, news reports, or essays to be read by others requires attention to how the intended readers will be able to draw appropriate inferences.

Teaching Composition

Functional writing should not be merely to satisfy external demands, but to meet personal needs. However, the teaching of composition is more likely to be successful if it allows students to interact with each other about some particular aspect of writing. For example, in learning to write about a personal experience, the teacher might structure, for special attention, topics such as setting and people, developing and resolving conflict, and using dialogue. Students might be asked to write as specifically as possible about faces in photographs, and then meet in small groups to share their pictures and what they have written, applying some criteria before revising. Or students might pantomime a situation and the audience write several sentences capturing the details of bodily movements, expressions, and other characteristics of the pantomimers. Students then read what they have written, with peers reinforcing the strongest details. Other activities might consist of writing out dialogues or an extended paper about a personal experience, including brain-storming for ideas, preparing several drafts, trying out each draft, and and revising in the light of feedback. Students might discuss samples of their writing and apply particular criteria to them. Then they might apply the same criteria to other pieces of writing, not just judging a piece but generating ideas about how to improve it. George Hillocks, Jr., has described a promising strategy for learning to write. (Hillocks 1984). Students examine model compositions in small groups with the aid of guide questions before presentation of the findings and whole-class discussions. The models of writing used in teaching the criteria will be useful not only in evaluating texts but in generating items. Successful revision requires that the criteria be brought to bear on the product to be revised. In all instances, standard usage and typographical conventions are taught in the context of real writing problems.

WRITING TO READ IN THE CONTENT FIELDS

In writing about science, children learn the vocabulary, thought processes, and genres necessary for reading difficult science texts. Consider this example by James Squire (1983) where a daily log in a fifth-grade class is used to record observations as a child watches a polywog growing to a frog.

> Such activities are almost routine science. So is writing up a science experiment—a laboratory report—in eighth grade physical science. But as the children write science, they process the ideas of science. They use the language of science. They learn to think in science. They prepare themselves to understand their reading of science. By the time they are enrolled in tenth grade biology, they are reading to comprehend with reasonable understanding textbooks far more difficult in science than in any other field. (Squire 1983)

Similarily, in her math classroom, Christine Sabray Evans uses writing to help fifth-grade students learn and read. (Evans 1989). During a unit on computation and one on geometry, students completed three types of writing for an uninformed third party. Exhibit 10.1 (page 191) illustrates three types of writing for helping students learn and read geometry.

Writing tasks are not equally effective. In a study of the effect of writing on students' understanding of literary text, James Marshall considered student responses to literature at three levels of understanding—descriptive, interpretive, generalization—as a consequence of writing activities. (Marshall 1984). During a five-week period in an instructional unit on the work of J.D. Salinger, students completed one of the following classroom writing tasks:

- *Restricted Writing:* responses to short-answer questions calling for description, interpretation, and generalization.
- *Personal Writing:* explanations and elaborations on their individual responses, drawing upon their own values and previous experiences.
- *Formal Writing:* interpretations of a story in an extended fashion, drawing inferences from the text alone.

The tasks of extended writing—both personal and formal—were associated with more positive effects that increased over time. Students writing about stories in either personal or formal modes understood literary text at all levels better than when they wrote in a restricted mode.

In a similar study, George Newell demonstrated how writing tasks such as notetaking, study questions, and essay writing enact with recall, concept application, and gain in knowledge of science and social studies. (Newell 1984). Eleventh-grade students read prose passages, completed writing tasks, and responded to three measures of learning. Essay writing contributed more to the learning of concepts than short-answer exercises and notetaking. It seems that writing requiring the composing of coherent text for another's reading results in more extensive thought and consideration of prose passages. Planning for study questions leads to concern for correct answers rather than to engagement of text in anticipation of reading. Answering study questions generates much information that never gets integrated in a coherent text or into the students' own thinking. Notetaking

Exhibit 10.1   Writing to Learn Mathematics

First, students write explanations that describe "How to Do Something."

Here Carrie tells President Washington, whose picture is posted in the room, how to mutiply with a zero in the multiplier:

$$\begin{array}{r} 5\overset{4}{7}\overset{2}{6}4 \\ 3764 \\ \times 70 \\ \hline 363480 \end{array}$$

Mr. Washington

I would like to tell you how to do the math problem above. First, you dont mulliply the zero, you just write it under the problem in the one's place. You do multiply the next number witch in this case is a seven (7). You multiply seven (7) and four (4) witch is twenty-eight (28). You carry the two (2) and put the eight (8) under the line in the ten's place. Next, you multiply

In the unit of geometry, Yvonne taught Libby, the class hamster, how to draw a 60° angle.

Dear Libby
This is how to do it
You will need
a pincel
a piece of paper
and a protractor 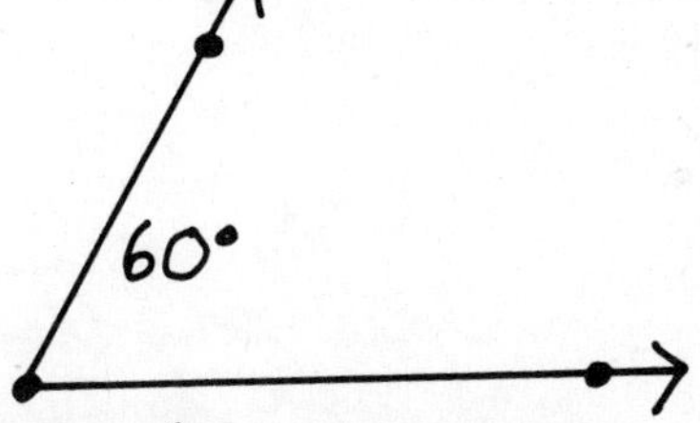
first you make a line and line it up with the bulls eye and you make a dot where the 60 is and you conect the dot to the dot you made with the bulls eye and thers your answer 60°. You can do it any number below 90° is acute and above 90° is obtuse

60°

The second type of writing involves students writing their own definitions, describing something new in their own familiar words.

Assignment: *What is a ray?*

a ray is a line that goes for
ever from one side of its endpoint.

—*Emmanuel*

a ray is a line that go's one way
forever and the other side stays
in place

—*Jeff*

ray = Path that goes on far
ever in an way.

—*Eric*

A ray is a ~~line~~ *path* that starts at
one point go's through the other
+ go's on forever.

M •————————————————————————• Y →

—*Marty*

The third type of writing is "trouble shooting" in which students explain their errors on homework or quizzes.

This problem because ^I missed
I put forty-two
down on seven times
seven instead of
forty-nine.

—*Angela*

#4 I multiplied 8x5 wrong
#2 I multiplied and added wrong also no decimal or dollar

—Mike

① I misset it because I used my caculater and it was rong

—Yvonne

I made my mastake by multiplyling instead adding

—Tiffany

3. put a 4 instead of a three witth made the whole thing wrong

—Janet

Source: From "Writing to Learn Math" by Christine Sabray Evans, *Language Arts 61* no.8 (December 1984): 828–833. Reprinted by permission of the National Council of Teachers of English.

also has its disadvantages. When students take notes, they focus more on the process of transforming thought into written language than on the reordering of information that results in learning.

Preparation for critical reading may occur by encouraging students to find errors in their textbooks and to write letters requesting rectification. A general science teacher in Rhode Island pointed out an error in a textbook and then asked his students to see if they could find more. One student found so many mistakes running the gamut from grammatical to incorrect theories that he decided to write the publisher. For example, "the books says that atoms are basic particles–'*basic* meaning they can't be broken down' — and later the book says atoms are broken down into protons, neutrons, and electrons."

WRITING TO UNDERSTAND AND REMEMBER

Writing is a form of elaboration that aids comprehension and retention of content. The books we remember and the parts we best recall are likely to be those we have written about. Expressive or spontaneous reactions to text in which language is personal and loosely structured following the reader's preoccupation go beyond superficialities and move into reflection and knowledge.

James Britton has hypothesized that expressive writing is important in the initial stage of grappling with new concepts and that the transition to more informative forms occurs as students mature and gain familiarity with the concepts. (Britton 1982).

Writing for genuine purpose and a real audience is better for comprehension than completing worksheets or copying from the book. By way of illustration, Denise S. Levin was disappointed with the results when students were asked to write summaries of their reading and when the teacher was to be the audience and evaluator. The summaries showed little understanding and ownership of the concepts. No links were made to personal experience and learning—students "limped around" in the technical vocabulary.

In contrast when students were encouraged to write expressively and to share work with classmates, their writings became more specific and included examples. (Levin 1985):

> Today I learned about solids, liquids, and gas and how much room molecules have to move. And we have different kinds of solids, liquid and gas. And thats what I learned today.
>
> Aissatou, Grade 8
> (*Summarizing a Class Lesson*)
>
> The way you might be able to tell if an element is metallic, you might use a dry cell and see if the object conducts electricity. If the element conducts electricity you know it's a metal. Metals usually have luster too. Most metals are malleable which means they can be hammered into different shapes. Also, some are ductile which means they can be drawn out into thin wire. *Copper* is a good example of a ductile metal ... Electrical wires are made of copper therefore it should be a good conductor of electricity.
>
> Andrea, Grade 7

One advantage of classroom research is that you learn what you intuitively think is true—that writing can help students comprehend. Activity 10.1 (page 195) suggests inquiries about the value of writing for secondary and elementary classrooms.

READING AS A WRITER

A Composing Model of Reading

In "Madness and Cure," Robert Langs tells how he interviewed 20 patients and found that most had been manipulated by their therapists for

Activity 10.1   Writing to Learn and Remember

Secondary School Teachers

Select two classes in the same subject and compare the progress students of the same ability (high-low) in the two classes make *after* you introduce in one of the two classes personal and formal writing tasks with each reading assignment. In personal writing, students should give their opinions on what they have read, explaining and elaborating. In formal writing, students should prepare essays in which they draw inferences from the text. Relative progress can be assessed by scoring performance on a common test covering the subject matter for a fresh selection. Quality of the summaries made by students in the two classes should be compared with respect to the presence of generalizations (integration of text), accuracy of interpretation, and supplying of examples.

Elementary School Teachers

Replicate Christine Evans' research (page 191). Have selected children write in a given content areas — math, science, social studies. Children should write to an uninformed third party about what they are learning. The writing opportunities should be of three types:

(a) "How to": Children write explanations describing how to do something.

(b) "Writing definitions" : Children are given new key concepts from the text and are asked to describe what the new term means in familiar words.

(c) "Troubleshooting": Children write a specific explanation of why they had difficulty with an assignment (home or quiz).

Indicators of the effect of these writing assignments are found in performance or end-of-unit tests and in ability to recall a sample of the assigned reading. The performance of children selected for the writing tasks should be compared with those who were not selected. In making your selection of students, first match students of the same ability and then flip a coin to decide which member of the pair will be given the writing opportunities.

---

reasons related to the therapist's personality rather than their own. Some patients reacted by trying to cure the therapist or seeking a therapist with a madness comfortably suited to their own needs (Langs 1985). The late Anatol Broyard saw something like that going on between novelists and their readers.

> While novelists used to analyze, criticize, and rectify social behavior with consequent benefits to the reader, many authors today are "madder" than their audience. And it is the reader now who offers the therapy, rather than the other way around.
>
> "I do what I can," one reader said. "The average novel is full of unfinished business, and I try to pull it together for the author. Like I fill out the characters, supply the plot and push it toward some kind of resolution. You know, close the Gestalt."
>
> Another reader said, "I'm willing to be manipulated. I'd like nothing better—it's almost as relaxing as a good massage. But it takes two to manipulate—the author's got to work a little, use a bit of art." (Broyard 1985)

Although Broyard may have exaggerated the active role of the reader, there is strong support for the idea that reading is more than getting the author's ideas off the page. The reader must prepare a text for himself or herself in order to be a thoughtful reader.

The composing model of reading is premised on the belief that text is a framework to guide readers in constructing their own view of what the text means. David Pearson and Robert Tierney have written extensively on the model indicating that no one can be a thoughtful reader unless one reads as a writer. (Pearson and Tierney 1984). That is, there is an analogous relation between reading and writing. The following outlines illustrates the parallels as they appear in four reading-writing roles:

Planning Role

The Writer	*The Reader*
Sets goals and purposes	Sets purposes
Brings to bear right background	Calls up exsisting knowledge about topic
Decides how to approach the topic	Aligns self with author or character
Considers audience	

Composing Role

The Writer	*The Reader*
Prepares draft	Looks over a few lines to see what the writing is about
Finds right first line	Fills in gaps
Chooses schema	Strives to make things fit
Decides what to include/exclude	Makes text fit dynamic needs Revises purpose

Editing Role

The Writer	*The Reader*
Changes words to have more impact	Annotates the text reactions
Reacts to what is written	Evaluates meanings constructed
Rewrites	Revises meanings
	Rereads
	Reads from different perspective

Monitoring Role

Both writer and reader decide when to plan, compose, and edit.

Obviously writing and reading are not independent acts. The writer produces text with readers in mind, considering what will enable readers to construct particular kinds of interpretations; readers try to determine the author's plans and purpose as well as what is expressed. The composing model of reading, however, emphasizes that reading and writing are both acts of composing; good readers "write" as they read.

Robert Tierney sees that reading as a writing concept influences the teaching of reading by focusing on composing behaviors—self-questioning, brainstorming, visualizing, rethinking—and he holds that the practice of sharing written interpretations from reading has given reading a collaborative thrust (Tierney 1990).

There is some empirical support for the composing model. Scholars at the Center for the Study of Reading have found that successful readers concern themselves with both what the author is trying to get them to think and what they themselves must do. (Tierney 1983). Investigators found that modifying an essay—adapting the setting and stance (position) of the writer—made a big difference in the reader's perception of the intimacy of the writing, attitude toward the writer, and recall of the text.

Also, topic familiarity and the presence of the dialogue influence how readers perceive text and how they "make sense" of it. When encountering inconsistencies, readers exposed to unfamiliar and nondialogue conditions are likely to search the text for a solution to the problem or to blame themselves. In contrast, readers exposed to familiar and dialogue conditions often resolve inconsistencies by suggesting that the author add specific information.

An excellent illustration of how readers align themselves with author and character and how readers make text fit dynamic needs is Janice Radway's classic study of the functions of romance reading. (Radway 1984). This study provides further evidence that interpretation of text depends as much on who the reader is, how the reader understands the process of reading and the cultural context as on the text itself. Radway's "Smithton" women—romance readers—plan and edit their novels in surprising ways. For example, many of the women readers observe that their favorite writers always write about intelligent and independent heroines. In fact, while the authors declare at the outset that their heroines are special, bright, and self-reliant, they later portray them as victims of circumstances. Smithton readers do not see the contradiction because they do not use subsequent narrative action to revise a character portrait established by description at the beginning. Unlike Smithton readers, those reading the novels from a literary perspective apply the rule of unity, producing a unified characterization that takes details of action into account. Hence, the sophisticated readers' final assessment of the romantic heroine shows the heroine as only a superficially independent woman, who is, in reality, deeply dependent and incapable of action herself. Radway suggests that the romance reader's failure to unify action and description may be a product of a particular attitude toward language. The women believe that words have meanings that are fixed and definite. Thus, they believe that romance authors intend words to describe correctly the characters in question. As a result, they do not judge verbal assertions by comparing them with the characters' actions. Smithton women believe they are reading a story about an extraordinary woman who is overcome by unforeseen circumstances, but who manages to teach the hero how to care for her and to appreciate her as she wishes to be appreciated.

Teaching Implications of the Composing Model

The composing model of reading pulls together many of the reading strategies featured previously. It is consistent with strategies for different phases of reading: (a) the prereading strategies of activating background knowledge (semantic mapping), predicting, and setting purposes; (b) the reading strategies of confirming initial schema selection, schema instantiation—making inferences, filling in the slots or the spaces among words in making sense of the text, and metacognitive self-monitoring by which readers evaluate how well they are reading and decide how to revise their reading when it doesn't make sense; and (c) strategies for processing text during and after reading—elaborating (imaging, dramatizing, restructuring, and summarizing text) and responding to text through essays and other

Activity 10.2   Annotating Text: The Reader as Writer

Instructions

1. Read the following passage in Exhibit 10.2 on the teaching of reading. As you read or reread the passage, express your thoughts and concerns on the margin. Try to interact with the author.
2. Make your annotations.
3. Annotations tell you about yourself as a reader. What do the annotations reveal about your background and purposes? Did you suggest how the author could have improved the text, making it more considerate? Did you concern yourself with style, practical application, or criticism? Did you try to unify or to fragmentize the passage? You may wish to compare your annotations with those of your peers or with the annotations in Exhibit 10.3. Consider adapting the activity for your own students.

Exhibit 10.2   Teacher Questioning (with Annotations)

There are two ways teacher questions can be effective in improving children's comprehension. First, teacher questions can direct the child's attention to what is important. By emphasizing certain information, teacher questions help students focus upon the information they must learn and recall.

Second, teacher questions can serve as models of the comprehension progress, showing the children the qualities of fruitful questions.

The effective teacher uses questions to activate children's relevant background knowledge, to elicit comparisons of personal experiences with what the text says, and to help children integrate the new information of the text with what they already know.

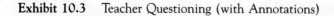

Exhibit 10.3 Teacher Questioning (with Annotations)

First in sequential order, priority, or merely first in the sense of enumeration?

There are two ways teacher questions can be

What are the two ways?

effective in improving children's comprehension.

Effective in what way: motivating, mastering a concept, creating cognitive dissonance?

First, teacher questions can direct the child's

Important to whom?

attention to what is important. By emphasizing

certain information, teacher questions help students

Does this procedure develop active readers who generate their own questions and sense of what is important?

focus upon the information they must learn

and recall. — *How long will they recall if it is not related to their own lives?*

Second, teacher questions can serve as

models of the comprehension process, showing

the children the qualities of fruitful questions.

How do different kinds of questions relate to the process of comprehension?

Does the child always have the relevant background to be activated?

The effective teacher uses questions

to activate children's relevant background

knowledge, to elicit comparisons of personal experi-

ences with what the text says, and to help

The procedure seems similar to Au's ETR method.

children integrate the new information of the

text with what they already know.

Although this procedure helps children create meaning from a particular text, will it develop independent readers?

forms of expressive writing. The model's emphasis on the reader aligning self with author is similar to the strategy of adopting a given perspective or reading from several perspectives and attitudes (sympathetic, critical, neutral).

Finally, the composing model's emphasis on reading and writing as transactional reminds us of the essentials of communications and the need to restructure schemata. Three essentials dominate: (1) The reader perceives that the author has truthful intentions in writing and is not deceptive. (One possible reason for the failure to read is the fear of being manipulated by writers.) If there is some initial doubt about truthfulness, the reader should see if the writers follows through on promises. (2) The validity of the writer's ideas is shown. Ideally, one reads with two eyes—with candor as well as prejudice. Logic, evidence, force, and argument are the bases for determining validity. (3) When the reader recognizes validity in the text but finds if difficult to accept the author's message because it conflicts with exsisting situationtal views and practices, the message must not be rejected as necessarily inapplicable. Instead, the familiar regularities should be regarded as hypothetical rather than certain. The reader then should appeal to the values that exsisting practices purport to serve and decide whether the new is more likely than the old to advance these values.

One procedure for understanding and developing the processes that constitute "reading as a writer" is to have students think aloud while reading. Annotating text is a close approximation of this technique. In annotating text, students write their reactions to what they are reading, relating the text to other authors and to their own experiences. Activity 10.2 (page 198) requires that you express your thoughts as a writer while reading a passage.

SUMMARY

Three aspects of writing to comprehend were featured in this chapter.

The first was the idea of writing as a way to become more sensitive to the characterisitcs of different kinds of text. Such a sensitivity contributes to understanding what other writers are trying to say.

Next, there was a focus upon writing as an elaboration of text—especially essays—for the purpose of encouraging deep processing and retention of meaning.

Finally, there was the idea that reading itself involves writing as the author and reader interact in the creation of meaning.

REFERENCES

Britton, James. "Notes on a Working Hypothesis About Writing." In *Prospect and Retrospect*, G. Pradl, editor. Montclair, NJ: Boynton/Cook, 1982: 1 105–113.

Broyard, Anatol. "Weird Stuff in the Circumambient Numerosity." *About Books: The New York Times*. Section 7, (November 1985): 1.

Evans, Christine S. "Writing to Learn Math." *Language Arts* 61, no. 8 (December 1984): 828–833.

Freire, Paulo. *The Politics of Education*. South Hadley, MA: Bergin & Garvey, 1985.

Gadamer, H. G. *Philosophical Hermeneutics*. Berkeley: University of California Press, 1976.

Goodman, Kenneth, and Goodman, Yetta. "Reading and Writing Relationships: Pragmatic Functions." *Language Arts* 60, no. 5 (May 1983): 590–599.

Harrison, Colleen. "The Nature and Effect of Children's Rewriting School Textbook Prose." Paper, presented at the Ninth World Congress on Reading, Dublin, 1982.

Hillocks, George, Jr. "What Works in Teaching Composition: A Metaanalysis of Experimental Treatment Studies." *American Journal of Education* 93, no. 11 (November 1984): 133–170.

Langs, Robert. "Madness and Cure," *About Books: The New York Times* (November 1985): section 7, 1.

Levin, Denise S. "The Biggest Thing I Learned But It Didn't Have to Do with Science." Language Arts 62, no. 2 (January 1985): 43–47.

Marshall, James D. *The Effect of Writing on Students' Understanding of Literary Text* (ERIC 252842). Palo Alto, CA: Stanford University, 1984.

Newell, George E. "Learning from Writing in Two Content Areas: A Case Study of Protocol Analysis." *Research in the Teaching of English* 18, no. 3 (1984): 265–287.

Pearson, P. David, and Tierney, Robert J. "On Becoming a Thoughtful Reader: Learning to Read Like a Writer." *Becoming Readers in a Complex Society*, 83rd Yearbook NSSSE. Alan Purves and Olive Niles, editors. Chicago: University of Chicago Press, 1984, 144–173.

Radway, Janice. "Interpretive Communities and Variable Literacies: The Function of Romance Reading." *Daedalus* 13, no. 3 (Summer 1984): 49–73.

Squire, James R. "Composing and Comprehending: Two Sides of the Same Basic Process." *Language Arts* 60, no. 5 (May 1983): 584.

Tierney, Robert J. "Redefining Reading Comprehension." *Educational Leadership* 47, no. 6 (March 1990): 37–41.

Tierney, Robert J. *Author's Intentions and Readers' Interpretations*. Technical Report No. 276. Urbana, IL: Center for the Study of Reading, University of Illinois, 1983.

Tierney, Robert J., Sofer, A., O'Flahavan, J. F., & McGinley, W. "The Effects of Reading and Writing upon Thinking Critically." *Reading Research Quarterly* 24 (2), (1989): 134–173.

Van Allen, R. "The Language Experience Approach." In *Perspectives on Elementary Reading*. Robert Karlin, editor. New York: Harcourt Brace Jovanovich, 1973, 158.

Useful Readings

Peterson, B. editor. *Conveyences: Transactions in Reading and Writing*. Urbana, IL: National Council of Teachers of English, 1986.

Shanahan, T. "The Reading-Writing Relationship: Seven Instructional Principles." *The Reading Teacher* 41 (1988): 636–647.

Tierney, Robert J. and Shanahan, Timothy. "Research on the Reading Writing Relationship: Interactions, Transactions and Outcomes." In *Handbook of Reading Research*, volume 2, Barr, Rebecca, Kamil, M.C., Mosenthal, P. B., & Pearson, P. D., editors. New York: Longman, 1990: 246–280.

Evaluating Reading Comprehension

OVERVIEW

Because evaluation of reading comprehension has been driven externally by testing mandated from national and state policy makers and internally by assessments teachers carry out to guide their instructional decisions, the conflict between new and old definitions of literacy affects assessment at both the policy level and the classroom level. New definitions of reading comprehension and the goal of literacy require new ways to evaluate progress and achievement in comprehending text. Older assessments emphasized the memorization and recall of passages, and included questions whose answers were usually stated explicitly in the text (although some require an inference) and test items purporting to assess subskills comprehension, such as identifying the main idea, interpreting sequence, and recognizing cause-and-effect relations. Newer assessments are based on (1) the interactive view that readers construct meaning from a text in accordance with their prior knowledge as well as from clues left in the text by the author and (2) the transactional and socialized views whereby the reader or groups of readers generate meanings to suit their own intentions and achieve self-actualization. This chapter reviews current changes in assessment at the policy and classroom levels that reflect newer views of reading comprehension. Attention is given to three principal features of assessment—observations, a variety of methods and measures, and integration and interpretation of information—with additional focus on the teacher's role in the new evaluation.

CHANGES IN COMPREHENSION EVALUATION AT NATIONAL AND STATE POLICY LEVELS

Chief among the instruments used in externally mandated assessment are the commercial standardized tests in reading, the National Assessment of Educational Progress Test in Reading, and instruments constructed by various state departments of education for monitoring the reading achievement of their students and for maintaining accountability.

Standardized Tests

The 1980s saw much criticism of standardized tests of reading comprehension, including the charge that tests purporting to measure comprehension often measure something else. Standardized tests, for example, are often developed according to a procedure whereby the items that everybody gets right are discarded, although these items might represent important aspects of reading comprehension; conversely, items retained might not be valid measures of comprehension.

Students may score differently on tests of reading comprehension depending on whether the tests assess the amount of knowledge gained, the ability to answer questions that one couldn't answer before, or the strategies used in answering questions. It may also make a difference whether immediate or deferred recall is required, or whether a test is an open or closed book.

Publishers of standardized tests are attempting to overcome some of the weaknesses. Publishers of the California Achievement Test, for instance, are trying to develop multiple-choice items so that incorrect responses are more diagnostic—one incorrect response might indicate a lack of background information, while another might suggest a failure to recognize the antecedent of a pronoun (Valencia and Pearson 1986). Also, publishers are responding to the criticism that standardized tests are too short for readers to develop a coherent view of the text and that they are unlike the materials that students usually read. As testmakers present more lengthy passages to which readers must respond, they will likely abandon the notion of a single right answer because closer approximations to real-life reading situations can be interpreted in different ways.

National Assessment of Educational Progress (NAEP)

The NAEP Test of Reading is a national assessment of student achievement that has been administered every four years since 1971. Beginning in 1984, NAEP began defining reading as an "interactive-constructive process" and the nineties format of the test reflects that emphasis. All reading passages consist of typical classroom reading selections up to 1500 words. There is no subskill assessment of comprehension. Instead, items are classified into three categories: constructing meaning, extending meaning, and examining meaning. The test aims at assessing the students' ability to form an initial understanding, develop interpretation, respond personally, and take a critical stance. The 1992 NAEP in reading will also assess the students' ability to read different types of text: reading for literary experience, reading to be informed, and reading to perform a task. Forty percent of student response time will be allocated for open-ended items. The student's ability to effectively use strategies for reading will be assessed. An oral reading with a comprehension component and a portfolio component to link the assessment to classroom practice will be piloted.

The International Reading Association opposes the NAEP model partly because, as a large-scale assessment scheme, it cannot improve instruction in any reasonable fashion—"to perpetuate the belief that assessment data taken from a large pool are sufficiently sensitive to the fine-tuning of instruction is indeed 'regressive'" (Braun 1990).

State Assessment of Reading

At the state level and in some large city school districts, tests are used to control the level of reading that is taught (Turlington 1985). Many states have developed reading competency testing programs that purport to measure a critical list of reading skills. Typically, these tests focus on what is easy to quantify, and they have all the faults of standardized tests: short passages followed by multiple-choice questions, fragmentations, arbitrary standards for performance, and questionable validity of the skills selected for measurement. Two states, however, are pioneers in their attempts to develop tests that reflect the interactive view of reading comprehension. The Illinois Goal Assessment Program (IGAP) measures three areas: (a) *comprehension,* including answering textually explicit as well as textually implicit questions and solving a novel problem using the information read; (b) *reading strategies,* such as clarifying misunderstandings and making choices in retelling a passage; and (c) *literacy experiences,* including in-school and out-of-school reading, functional uses of reading, and strategies used while reading and writing. An important part of the assessment involves determining the student's *topic familiarity* as a basis for interpretation of the responses. Accordingly, the examinee rates a series of ideas as to the likelihood that they will appear in a selection on a given topic (Illinois State Board of Education 1988).

The Michigan Educational Assessment Program (MEAP), a pilot-testing system, consists of four areas: construction of meaning, knowledge about reading, attitudes and self-perception, and topic familiarity. The reading selections are complete stories and informational passages taken from classroom materials. The meaning-construction section tests inferencing, determining central themes, and locating details. In addition to deriving information from the entire text as well as parts of the text, students must use prior knowledge in constructing meaning beyond the text. The knowledge-about-reading section assesses knowledge of text structure, literary devices, and comprehension strategies. The student's awareness of how a reader's purpose affects comprehension strategy, for example, is measured. The attitude section determines the student's interest in the text and self-perceived ability and effort (Michigan Educational Assessment Program 1987).

In brief, as indicated in Exhibit 11.1, assessment at policy levels is changing in that it is now using authentic passages, that is, ecological validity (the reading passages presented in the test are taken from real life or the tasks and materials are equivalent to what the students are experiencing in their classrooms) allowing for many right answers to questions, attending to metacognitive strategies, and interpreting responses in light of the reader's prior knowledge.

CHANGES IN COMPREHENSION EVALUATION AT THE CLASSROOM LEVEL

Assessment at the classroom level is chiefly for helping teachers make instructional decisions. However, the data collected is useful for students, teachers, and school accountability purposes. New procedures in the classroom attempt to overcome the narrow and artificial measurement associated with formal and published testing. Assessment is becoming less test centered

Exhibit 11.1   Changes in Assessment of Comprehension at Policy Levels

Old Tests	*New Tests*
single right answer	many acceptable answers
short passage out of context	authentic selections
discrete subskills of comprehension	metacognitive strategies
literal and limited-inferential questions	text-implicit and application questions
no allowance for prior knowledge or purpose for reading	prior knowledge and purpose for reading are considered in reader's response
assess recall of text	assess learning from text and reading to perform a task

and more student centered with emphasis upon observation, use of portfolios, self-assessment, retelling, and free responses. Older diagnostic tools, such as cloze tests and reading inventories, are being modified to reflect interactive views of reading.

Observations

In the traditional classroom, passive students don't do enough in reading to provide the teachers with something to see. But if the students are constantly producing and receiving discourse, and if the teacher is free to circulate and observe lesson invitations and responses to reading, observational evaluation is possible. Small group discussions, writing responses to literature, and teacher conferencing give opportunity to observe student progress in reading. Exhibit 11.2 illustrates an evaluation based on selected dimensions of reading.

Observation of literacy for self-actualization is found in the use of checklists comprising items such as enjoys reading, shares books, has a reading preference, reads outside school, reads for own purposes, recommends books, learns from books, seeks books outside of class, expresses what

Exhibit 11.2   Reading Evaluation of Nancy Holt, September

1. *Valuing* Aspects prized; how student uses text.	Attends mostly to characters, not themes. Uses books chiefly for recreational purposes or escape.
2. *Critical Thinking* Questions assumptions, logical inconsistencies, and suggests alternative strategies to those presented.	Never questions author's statements.
3. *Sharing* Recommends material to others; relates favorite parts; seeks clarification of the text.	Initiates conversation with friends about the book.
4. *Taking Action* Seeks other readings on same topic or by same author; writes author; prepares a review for the library or newspaper.	No action taken; not interested in dramatizing scene from the book

has astonished, purged, exhilarated, or dismayed. Of course, discussions, dramatizations, and writing extensions of the original work also provide opportunity for the teacher to observe reading comprehension.

Portfolios

The portfolio in which teachers collect student work, the "artifacts" of their literacy, is increasingly regarded as a valid method for evaluation. In this approach, there is an actual collection of items such as writing samples, observational notes, comprehension checks, the student's self-evaluations, and progress notes collaboratively prepared by the student and teacher.

The range of items is extensive, including written responses to reading, reading logs, writing at various stages of completion, and audiotapes or videotapes. Sheila Valencia has suggested that one be selective about what to look for when evaluating the items: Will they be used to assess progress in critical reading, development of interest and desire to read, improvement in summarization strategies, ability to learn from expository material, or skill in using texts to carry out a task (Valencia 1990). She also suggests organizing the content of the portfolio into two layers: (a) the actual evidence, and (b) a summary sheet to help synthesize the information so it will facilitate instructional decisions and communication with students and others.

Evidence may be collected independently or collaboratively by the student and teacher (e.g., a student may choose to submit a letter to an author of a favorite book, a semantic map completed before and after reading, a reading log). Of course, the portfolio is easily accessible to student and teacher.

The teacher and student periodically discuss what the items collected reveal about the student's progress in reading comprehension and the next steps to take. At the end of the year, they decide together which pieces will remain in the portfolio for next year and which pieces are ready to take home.

Self-Reporting

Self-reporting is useful in determining both processes and products of comprehension. Students are better comprehenders when they are able to describe what goes on in their heads when they read. When asked, they can tell where they are in the sequence of reading a book. They can state their purposes for reading, describe the information needed, and their plans for getting it. Procedures for helping readers acquire this self-knowledge (metacognition) are found in Chapter 7. Assessment of metacognition doesn't focus on how many correct answers students have but on how they behave when they don't know. It also includes noting if the student is using the strategies of making predictions, seeking clarification, self-questioning, and summarizing in one's own words.

When assessing depth of comprehension as a product, it is better to ask questions that require linking text relationships that are not explicitly stated rather than to ask questions that demand only recall. The difference in the kinds of questions is great: *What did you read that you should remember for a test?* and *What did you learn that is so important you want to remember it always?* The first question gets at what students think the teacher expects; the second taps meanings that students have created for themselves. Junior high students in 60 classrooms were asked these questions after reading assignments in social studies. Responses to the first question usually consisted of specific factual information—trivial pursuit answers such as, "Jefferson purchased Louisiana." Further, most children in the same classroom identified the same information. Responses to the second question were usually major generalizations such as "Countries should not find war as an answer to their problems," and they were unique to the learner. It is important to note that the different kinds of responses indicate that young adolescents who repeatedly face questions of a detailed factual value nevertheless concurrently generate significant personal meanings from their reading assignments. Current emphasis on achievement tests, however, has minimized teacher assessment of the meanings that students generate from their reading. Activity 11.1 helps overcome this dysfunctional consequence of testing and provides valid data about students' ability to comprehend.

Retelling and Responding

Chapter 9 emphasized that student summaries are a good way to gain a picture of what students think is important in their reading. The use of summaries to reveal the student's schemata for stories was illustrated.

In addition to retelling and summarizing text, other forms for eliciting reader response are used to reveal aspects of reader comprehension: level of engagement, conception of literary characters, integration of text with personal experience, problem solving, interpretation, and explanations of text. Open-ended responses, interviews, and "think alouds" may reveal whether students are comprehending in any of these ways. Indeed, students may begin with engagement or conception responses, which in turn lead to integration, interpretation, and judgment responses (Langer 1989).

Numerous categories are used to interpret the reader's responses: inhibition, stock responses, critique; information driven, story driven; normalizing, generalizing; text invoked, reader involved; engagement, disengagement; event oriented, theme oriented; unreflective, reflective on the significance of events and behaviors; and reviewing the text as the author's creation, as well as defining both one's own ideology and the author's (Beach and Hynds 1990). A response to a literature checklist might be used to note whether the student's response focuses on characters, setting, problem, events, solution, theme, application, or personal response. The teacher's goal is not to deny the integrity of each student's response but to broaden the range of reader response.

In order to learn more about how readers process and comprehend tests, it's a good idea to ask them to recall what they have read and then interpret

Activity 11.1   Studying Comprehension of Ecologically Valid Material

Many students are labeled poor comprehenders on the basis of their performance on standardized tests of reading comprehension. Although these tests show a high reliability, this reliability comes through dubious practice. To gain sufficient samples of test structure, content, and difficulty; the test makers offer short selections. Information tested for short selections is usually trivial. Also, to hold context constant across examinees, test makers unfairly discriminate among students on the kinds of background knowledge required for making sense out of the selections.

Directions
Preparation

1. Consider a student known to you who has been categorized on the basis of a standardized test as a poor reading comprehender. Ask that student to bring a favorite text (book, magazine, almanac) that he or she finds interesting or useful.
2. Read the text, characterize the material as high, middle, or low difficulty and design an assessment procedure. I recommend having the student read parts or all of the material and then without using the text (a) either orally (if student doesn't write well) or in writing, retell what was read (if material is narrative). If the material is expository, ask the student to prepare a summary (without referring back to the text). Specify how you will evaluate the retelling or the summary. (If narrative, does the reader include key elements—characters, goals, setting? If expository, what main ideas are present/absent? Are supporting details related to main ideas?) What distractions or omissions are present?

Administration

Administer the task to your learner and evaluate the responses.

Interpretation

Interpret the results by asking these questions: Does the learner comprehend better than the test scores would predict? Why? Was it motivation, match with personal background, familiarity with material? Other reason? What do you now believe about the learner's ability to comprehend? What do the results suggest about what to teach this learner?

---

the recall protocols in light of both text and what is recalled. Patterns of distortion and omissions may indicate the influence of reader background knowledge. Instead of relying on formal tests of comprehension, you will learn more about the comprehension of your learners by examining what they do, what they experience when reading, and how this experience is affected by the particular reading assignment. Find out what kinds of meaning different readers construct from reading, and observe what they do with a diversity of materials in many different situations—while reading, prior to reading, and subsequent to reading.

The following is a list of questions to use in assessing whether students have the prerequisites for successful reading comprehension:

- *Do students understand that they must attempt to make sense of text instead of focusing on reading as a decoding process?* Good readers know that reading should be meaningful.
- *Do students modify their reading strategies for different purposes?* For example, good readers know when to read for general impressions (*skimming*) and when to read for specific information (*scanning*).
- *Can students identify information in the text that is important to a particular theme, problem, or personal goal?* The ability to group propositions that belong to the gist of the text or to a given purpose requires a schema.
- *Can students tell when the descriptions of characters match the behavior of characters?* If they can do this, they have knowledge of logical structure.
- *Do students notice statements that are incongruous with daily living and their own prior experience?* Recognizing alternative frameworks and experiencing conceptual conflict are prerequisites to change and accommodation to new ideas.
- *Do students know when they understand the text and when they do not?* Good readers ask themselves, "Do I understand this?" "Could I repeat this?" "Where is all this leading?"
- *Do students know what to do when they know they do not understand?* Rereading, continued reading for clarification, asking for help, and self-questioning are among the relevant strategies to be assessed.

Modifying Cloze Tests

The cloze test has been used to assess comprehension and to determine the readability of a text. Usually the teacher removes every fifth word and studies what the reader puts in the blanks. A useful modification to get more information about how the teacher processes text is to delete specific categories of words rather than every fifth word. If, for instance, one wants to know if the student is using information from prior or subsequent passages, and tying the information together in a meaningful unit, the deleted word is one that can only be supplied by attending to a separate paragraph. The sample in Exhibit 11.3 from "Assessing Comprehension in a School Setting" (Dieterich, Freeman, and Griffin 1977) illustrates a modified cloze test. Supplying the omitted words requires attention to subordinate and conjoined statements in the context of both a single and adjacent paragraph. As with other variants of cloze, the test is an evaluation of syntactic knowledge rather than general comprehension.

Changing Informal Reading Inventories

The Informal Reading Inventory (IRI) has long been used to assess the student's instructional, independent, and frustrational reading level. A

Exhibit 11.3   Sample of Modified Cloze Test

The New House
Mrs. Alexander was trying to fix dinner. First, though, she had to find where
the boxes marked for the kitchen had _____. The boys had unloaded the station
                                    (1)
wagon in a hurry and _____ back to the old house to get the final load of boxes.
                        (2)

  "What's the use," she said aloud. "Put the food in the bedroom. Put the pots
and pans in the bathroom. Put the underwear in the refrigerator." Her voice rose
along with her _____
                 (3)
  "Mom, I don't have the _____ ." Little Mark looked around at the open
                          (4)
boxes. "How come we have to put it in the 'frigerator? Why do we have to do
everything different?" Mark started to cry while he talked and peeled _____ off
                                                                       (5)
boxes. "Can't we have drawers in our bedroom in this house, I don't like new
houses. I like old apartments. I can't have my friends, can't ride elevators, can't
even have drawers for my stuff. And I'm hungry, too. No milk or apples in the
'frigerator in new houses.

Answer List

1.a. passed	2.a. wrote	3.a. esteem
b. burned	b. spread	b. prestige
*c. gone	c. jumped	*c. frustration
d. left	d. paddled	d. appropriation
e. held	*e. rushed	e. technique
(subordinate sentence)	(conjoined sentence)	(same paragraph)
4.a. bucket	5.*a. tape	
*b. underwear	b. heat	
c. newspaper	c. coffee	
d. flashlight	d. thunder	
e. soap	e. bread	
(separate paragraph)	(local)	

        *indicates correct answer

series of short selections graded by readability formulas are presented to the
student. Questions are posed that require understanding of the selection—
vocabulary, main idea, and the making of inferences. From the perspective
of schema theory, the IRI is defective.

  Children's success in understanding a passage depends more on what
they already know about the topic than on a grade level determined by
a readability formula. Indeed, the most important factor in a readability
formula is vocabulary difficulty due to unfamiliar words and words of low
frequency. The key to determining readability is not so much in the text but
in the reader. A text is readable when the reader can match the concepts of
the text and has a schema for processing it.

In her proposal for improving the Informal Reading Inventory, Joanne Caldwell recommends that teachers control for the effect of prior knowledge (Caldwell 1985). Instead of choosing a passage only by designated grade level, teachers should take content familiarity into account by selecting passages that match the child's interests and by asking the child to predict the content of the selection: "What information do you think will be in the selection?"

Old informal inventories have problems because they offer short selections rather than a whole context and because of the kinds of questions used. This removal of text segments makes comprehension more difficult. Selections that have an explanatory context are preferable. There is a growing tendency to use longer passages and to assess reading of both narrative and exposition.

The type of questions asked should be considered in light of what instruction can be given in the event answers reveal a failure to comprehend. The taxonomy of questions—text explicit, text implicit, and schema (see Chapter 4)—is especially useful as a guide to questioning because we have a teaching procedure to accompany it. The teaching procedure helps readers improve their ability to answer each type of comprehension question by teaching them the relationship between the questions and how the answers can be found.

Other types of diagnostic questions are, of course, in order. The teacher might ask questions that will reveal whether the reader has (a) sufficient background knowledge for reading the passage, (b) selected an appropriate schema for the text, (c) used the schema while reading, (d) modified the schema in response to the information in the text, (e) related what was read to his or her own life, and (f) had feeling about the reading.

Authentic Assessment

In view of the limited transfer from any school-related instructional task to situations outside school, there is an indication that future assessment will call for applications of reading comprehension to real-world reading. Authenticity has several dimensions (Newman 1988). First, it assesses the performance of students on tasks that approximate those that experts perform—social reading, for instance, where several readers interact with each other and with one or several texts in many work sites. The clarification and defense of an alternative interpretation of a literary selection is another instance.

Second, students are required to join the pieces of a project into an integrated whole. An authentic task might ask the student to relate a character's motive to others' motives in the same text, to other narratives, to famous people in society, or to friends. Third, authentic assessment might range from civic tasks, such as voicing an opinion in a letter to the editor, to vocational tasks in which one is expected to read in order to do.

SUMMARY

Changing definitions of reading comprehension require different ways to evaluate reading progress. In this chapter, we reported on changes in the instruments used at national, state, and district levels to assess reading comprehension. It is clear that at these levels there is increasing support for the interactive view of reading and greater consideration of readers' prior background experience when interpreting their comprehension.

At the classroom level, where evaluation is undertaken to guide instruction, the pattern of assessment is growing out of a concern for students' responses to text and their analyses of their reading. Increasingly, teachers and students are focusing on their reading experiences and discussing their opinions, feelings, and thoughts about texts. Observations, portfolios, self-assessment, story retelling, and other assessment devices are also being modified to reflect the interactive and self-actualizing views of reading comprehension.

The teacher's role in assessing reading comprehension is shifting away from asking questions for fixed answers, and moving toward the student's perspective—providing and impelling responses to text, but not controlling them.

REFERENCES

Beach, Richard, and Hynds, Susan. "Research on Response to Literature." *Handbook of Reading Research*. vol. II, Barr, Rebecca, Kamil, M. L., Masenthal, P. B., and Pearson, P. D., editors. New York: Longman, 1990, pp. 453–489.

Braun, Carl. As cited in *Reading Today* (August/September 1990): 6.

Caldwell, Joanne. "A New Look at the Old Informal Inventory." *The Reading Teacher* 39, no. 2 (November 1985): 168–173.

Dieterich, Thomas, Freeman, Cecilia, and Griffin, Peg. "Assessing Comprehension in a School Setting." In *Linguistics and Reading Series*: 3, Peg Griffin, editor. Arlington, VA: Center for Applied Linguistics, 1977, 99–100.

Illinois State Board of Education. *Assessing Reading in Illinois*. Springfield, IL: Illinois State Board of Education, 1988.

Langer, J. A. *The Process of Understanding Literature*. Albany, NY: Center for the Study and Teaching of Literature, 1989.

Michigan Educational Assessment Program. *Blueprint for New MEAP Reading Test*. Lansing, MI: Michigan State Department of Education, 1987.

Newman, Archibald. *For Beyond Standardized Testing*. Reston, VA: National Association of Secondary School Principals, 1988.

Turlington, R.D. "How Testing Is Changing Education in Florida." *Educational Measurement Issues and Practices* 4 (August 1985): 9–11.

Valencia, Sheila. "A Portfolio Approach to Classroom Reading Assessment: The Whys, Whats, and Hows." *The Reading Teacher* 43, no. 4 (Jan. 1990): 338–340.

Valencia, Sheila, and Pearson, P. D. *New Strategies for Reading Comprehension—Illinois Initiative.* Urbana, IL: University of Illinois, Center for the Study of Reading, 1986.

Useful Reading

Afflerbach, P., editor. *Issues in Statewide Reading Assessment.* Washington, DC: American Institute for Research, 1991.

Goodman, Kenneth S., Goodman, Yetta M., and Hood, Wendy J., editors. *The Whole Language Evaluation Book.* Portsmouth, NH: Heinemann, 1989.

National Assessment of Educational Progress. *American Education at the Crossroads.* Princeton, NJ: Educative Testing Service, 1989.

Paris, S. G., editor. *Current Issues in Reading Comprehension* (special issue). *Educational Psychologist* 22, nos. 3–4 (1987).

Index

I

J

K

L

M

N